THIS IS
SURVIVOR RESEARCH

EDITED BY

ANGELA SWEENEY

PETER BERESFORD

ALISON FAULKNER

MARY NETTLE

AND

DIANA ROSE

PCCS BOOKS
Ross-on-Wye

First published in 2009

PCCS BOOKS Ltd
2 Cropper Row
Alton Road
Ross-on-Wye
Herefordshire
HR9 5LA
UK
Tel +44 (0)1989 763 900
www.pccs-books.co.uk

This is Survivor Research

A CIP catalogue record for this book is available from the British Library

ISBN 978 1 906254 14 8

Cover design in the UK by Old Dog Graphics
Cover artwork *Colour in a Dark Place* by Amanda Hickling, www.artinminds.org.uk
Cover artwork photographed by Andrew J. Kelsall, www.akelsall.co.uk
Typeset in AGaramond in the UK by The Old Dog's Missus
Printed in the UK by Athenaeum Press, Gateshead

CONTENTS

List of abbreviations

BME	Black and minority ethnic
ECT	Electroconvulsive therapy
MHF	Mental Health Foundation
MHT	(NHS) Mental Health Trust
NHS	National Health Service (England)
NICE	National Institute for Health and Clinical Excellence (England and Wales)
NIMHE	National Institute for Mental Health in England
PCT	(NHS) Primary Care Trust
R&D	Research and development
RCT	Randomised controlled trial
REC	Research ethics committee
SCIE	Social Care Institute for Excellence (United Kingdom)
SDO	(NHS) Standards Development Organization
SPSS	A computer package to analyse data quantitatively (originally, Statistical Package for the Social Sciences)
SUR	Service user representative
SURE	Service User Research Enterprise, Institute of Psychiatry, King's College London
UFM	User-Focused Monitoring

About the cover artwork

Colour in a Dark Place came about from a visual art exhibition where artists from Art in Minds (AIMS) interpreted their experience of the unique spirit and space of Worcester Cathedral, England. Each member of AIMS has personally experienced mental ill-health although this does not necessarily drive their creativity. AIMS came into being as a project to celebrate World Mental Health Day by showcasing the existing wealth of untapped artistic talent and hopes to put mental health art in the public eye. AIMS is largely run by current and ex-mental health service users, a Health Trust funded artist and an occupational therapist. To survive and develop we need your support. Visit the AIMS website and virtual gallery at www.artinminds.org.uk

Amanda Hickling

FOREWORD

MARY O'HAGAN[1]

This is Survivor Research is a timely, unique and important book.

This book is the most sophisticated and varied account of survivor research I have ever read. It covers much ground, from the epistemological basis for survivor research to a practical guide for novice researchers. It blends intellectual reasoning with personal experience. It delivers a coherent challenge to the research hegemony in mental health, which stubbornly perpetuates a foundation of knowledge and power that many users and survivors find irrelevant, unhelpful or even oppressive.

Survivor research is developing a new foundation, just as users and survivors are in other areas, such as mental health policy, practice, education and anti-discrimination. This foundation is planting itself deep and cracking the bedrock of the most fundamental beliefs traditional mental health systems rest upon. One of these beliefs is the view that madness is all wrong or all bad, that it is not a full human experience. Survivor research, as this book demonstrates so well, challenges this belief in a myriad of ways – by its very existence, its curiosity and respect for subjectivity, its reluctance to distance the researcher from the researched, its critiques of knowledge, power, value-free research and the standard hierarchy of evidence, and its empowering methodologies. All these challenges, implicitly or explicitly, rest on the revolutionary idea that madness is a full human experience.

It's disappointing, though not surprising, that survivor research is still marginalised and underfunded after nearly a generation. It's a further example of the reluctance of the status quo to accommodate another worldview and to share power and resources with the people it has marginalised. This book however, does not dwell on the inequity of survivor research; instead it celebrates the progress users and survivors have made in their thinking and practice, in Britain and elsewhere, since the 1980s.

Most of all perhaps, *This is Survivor Research* shows that survivor research has a hopeful future.

Everyone interested in mental health research, or research involving other marginalised groups, should read it.

---

1. Mary O'Hagan was the Mental Health Commissioner for New Zealand, and the first chair of the World Network of Users and Survivors of Psychiatry.

INTRODUCTION

DIANA ROSE

AND

PETER BERESFORD

Service user/survivor* research has grown enormously over the last 20 years. It has gained in visibility, credibility and reach. It has developed its own significant body of work, its own ethical values and its own knowledge, as well as generating a growing number of experienced and emerging service user researchers. Early efforts to carry out survivor research had minimal funding and were generally under-resourced. They frequently relied on the enthusiasm and commitment of these early pioneers. User/survivor research was closely aligned with the service user movement. People active in that movement who had research skills wanted to use those skills to contribute to the aims of the survivor movement. They took their research agenda from the priorities for the movement, and developed methodologies appropriate to the questions that arose for them. They wished also to involve other service users because they did not see research as an elite endeavour.

Yet while survivor research since then has greatly increased in scale and influence, it is still often marginalised. It receives a tiny proportion of government and other mental health research funding. This is still mainly directed towards traditional, medically focused research, particularly research employing traditional systematic review and randomised controlled trial methods.

However, survivor research has already achieved in a comparatively short time much more than could ever have been hoped for it. It has created new knowledge, provided a knowledge base for change by mental health service users/survivors, challenged the assumptions of traditional research and research theory, and developed its own new research methods and approaches. Survivor research can also be seen as part of a broader development of research from a wide range of service user movements, including those of disabled people, older people, and people with learning difficulties. This research can, in turn, be related to feminist, black

---

* Editors' note: It may be helpful to point out that there is no agreement about terminology in 'mental health' or among 'service users/survivors'. We have not tried to impose any standardised system of language on contributors. We have tried to be respectful to different views about terminology, seeking not to give offence. We hope readers will understand this approach and forgive us if it creates any difficulties for them.

and community development research committed to supporting the rights and liberation of people facing discrimination and oppression.

The benefits that survivor research brings, as well as the barriers it still faces, make it all the more necessary to bring together and share experience, knowledge and information about it. In this way, the learning so far gained can be spread and developed, in order to provide a resource for those who may be interested in taking survivor research forward, whether as service users or survivor researchers, or as supportive research organisations and research funders.

It is to share such experience that is the key purpose of this book. It aims to present a comprehensive picture of the current state of user/survivor research in England. Its discussion runs from philosophical issues, through ethics and particular studies, to accounts of small projects, and it ends with individual accounts of how and why interest in survivor research came about. It is important to have this range of perspectives because, as will be seen, we are not trying to 'copy' the dissemination methods of mainstream research. Such research is mainly disseminated in academic journals and books. They have a standard structure, and the scientist does not include in this any personal information. In *This is Survivor Research*, we think it is important to include brief project accounts from small-scale studies, as well as personal information on what attracted us to do research in the first place. We wanted the book to fit the range of survivor research, rather than force it into traditional structures. There are many other ways in which user/survivor research differs from mainstream research and these will be extensively covered in this book.

We use the terms *service user researcher* and *survivor researcher*. All the authors in this book have used or are using mental health services. However, some regard themselves as *survivors*, either of their own distress or of the negative aspects of mental health services that they see themselves as having survived. At the same time, as service users increasingly collaborate with other stakeholders in research, we sometimes use the phrase 'user involvement in research'.

The intended audience for this book is deliberately wide-ranging. We would hope to give a flavour of the contemporary situation in user/survivor research for those contemplating it for the first time. More experienced user researchers might also find it helpful – although no doubt there will be things with which they will disagree! We would like also to address audiences from mainstream research, both social and medical. We hope such an audience will find the book helpful as a way of getting to grips with a relatively new phenomenon in research. However, as indicated above, a more academic audience might be surprised at the structure of some of the chapters. For example, some chapters do not contain references, but rather are narratives describing the authors' experiences in trying to develop user research and user involvement in research. We argue that it is important to include such narratives, as they give an account of the opportunities offered and obstacles encountered in trying to advance user/survivor research.

Now that we have set the scene for survivor research, the second part of this introduction gives a brief overview of the book to help readers to navigate around its contents and pick and choose what they wish to read or where they wish to start reading. This is a book that is intended to be useful, which we hope people will read in the way that they find helpful – perhaps dipping into it, or starting at the beginning.

Section One reflects on the development and nature of service user research in mental health. In Chapter 2, Peter Beresford and Diana Rose give a historical and theoretical context for understanding survivor research. They emphasise that user/survivor research needs to be as systematic and rigorous as mainstream research, but not on the same terms. They go on to critique what is considered the 'gold standard' in psychiatric research: the randomised controlled trial (RCT). This method is said to ensure objectivity by 'neutralising' the position of the researcher. Survivor research does not seek this, on the grounds that all research includes the subjectivity of the researcher.

Initially, as we have said, user/survivor research consisted of small projects that were under-resourced. This is changing, as funders have started to ask for evidence of user involvement in research when researchers bid for money. There are now large programmes of work, although, as we have said, there remain problems of credibility and power. Also, these programmes tend not to be carried out in user-controlled organisations, and this can dilute what they can achieve.

The different stance offered by survivor research often leads to it being treated as inferior by the mainstream. However, there are power relations within user/survivor research itself. Most apparent, are divisions between white researchers and those from black and minority ethnic (BME) communities. Service users from black and minority communities experience the greatest oppression in mental health services, yet they are under-represented amongst user researchers. Karan Essien, in Chapter 7, addresses this issue in detail.

In Chapter 3, Angela Sweeney asks: So what is survivor research? As user/survivor research is in its infancy, it can be difficult to capture what it is. To help explain such research, Angela Sweeney first explores some of the influences that have shaped it, including the user movement, approaches to providing health and social services, moves to develop users' own theories of knowledge production (epistemology), and different ways of exploring the social world (methodology). She goes on to offer a definition of user/survivor research, as well as exploring its principles, priorities and challenges.

Section Two focuses on the methodological and philosophical underpinnings of our research endeavours. In terms of the development of user/survivor research, these explicitly methodological and philosophical reflections are arguably a recent focus of such research. However, they provide a framework for undertaking user/survivor research, and have grown out of the experience of conducting it, as well as familiarising us with ideas from other areas that we consider helpful. This is why they come early on in the book.

In Chapter 4, Diana Rose suggests that we combine the ideas of Foucault and of feminist standpoint epistemology. Foucault has argued that, since the Enlightenment, society and particularly academics have prioritised 'reason', with the effect that those designated 'mad' have been positioned as the opposite of 'reason', that is, as the bearers of 'unreason'. This is one of the divisions that user/survivor research must challenge. For feminist standpoint theorists, women have also, but not to the same degree, been banished from 'science'. These theorists argue that women will produce different knowledges. This position addresses the charge of 'bias', which is often laid at the door of user/survivor research, as it means that all research, including mainstream research, comes from a particular 'standpoint'.

In Chapter 5, Peter Beresford asks what a social model of madness and distress might look like. He argues that the disabled people's movement has brought about a radical change in how disability is perceived. By drawing a distinction between impairment and a physically and attitudinally disabling world, it has put the emphasis squarely on societal barriers to full participation in society. Beresford argues that such a model is difficult to adapt to madness and distress: the reason for this is the dominance of a medical model in conceptualising and treating mental health problems. There is, first of all, a problem of how to describe the 'impairments' that characterise those with a diagnosis of mental illness, and whether they can even be said to exist. In the medical model, this is done through diagnostic categories, but some users/survivors do not see their 'impairments' as a problem at all. One task is to see if it is possible to develop a theory of the social construction of impairments. The rest of the argument would be straightforward to make, as there are certainly economic and ideological barriers, which disable people diagnosed as mentally ill. For these reasons, Beresford argues that user/survivor research and practice cannot move forward until they have clear theoretical and philosophical underpinnings.

Section Three looks at the practice of user/survivor research. It ranges from a consideration of the ethical issues that need to be taken into account, to the particular problems in research and regarding research participants encountered by researchers from BME communities, to an exploration of the ways in which user/survivor research may influence change. It looks also at the issues facing collaborative research, as well as how a prized method in mainstream research – the systematic review – may be made more user-focused. The final chapter offers users/survivors advice on how to get started in research.

In Chapter 6, Alison Faulkner and Debbie Tallis address the question of ethics in research. Traditionally, this has meant that all proposals for research have to be considered and endorsed by formal Research Ethics Committees (RECs). However, the chapter argues that ethical issues extend far more widely than this for survivor research. The chapter is divided into two parts. In the first part, Alison Faulkner describes a piece of research she carried out involving focus groups and interviews with user researchers concerning what they thought the ethical issues were in survivor research. The issues identified by her participants were quite different from, and much broader than, issues addressed by RECs. In the second part, Debbie Tallis describes her own difficult experience with RECs, focusing particularly on the question of harm to participants and the angle that research ethics forms and committees take on this.

In Chapter 7, Karan Essien poses questions for female participants and researchers from BME communities, particularly those who are African and African Caribbean. Her particular focus is on identity because, both for herself and for her participants, multiple identities are at stake. She argues that black women are invisible in mental health research, which is mostly about white people and black men. In her research, she found a variety of ways in which her participants dealt with their diagnosis of mental illness, sometimes seeing themselves as survivors and sometimes denying the existence of a problem. Essien concludes with some questions about her status as a researcher sharing some of the same identities as her participants.

Carey Ostrer and Brigid Morris discuss the question of collaboration with academics and other stakeholders in Chapter 8. Collaboration is becoming more common in user involvement in research. The two authors had very different experiences with this. Although the project in which Carey Ostrer was involved started positively, her academic collaborators undermined her, together with a voluntary organisation that was taking part, as the project progressed. Brigid Morris had a much more positive experience with a study that involved a range of stakeholders. She felt that the service user research team which she was coordinating was always treated respectfully both in the project steering group and in carrying out the research itself. The chapter ends with the authors identifying a number of issues that need to be addressed in collaborative research, including power differentials and academic hierarchies.

Systematic reviews are considered the acme of science in the academic research community. They assess evidence from the existing literature and then combine it. Usually the evidence consists of RCTs, available only in the peer-reviewed literature, and the aim is systematically to examine these trials so that a more precise estimate of a service or treatment can be made. Systematic reviews are becoming more common as the government pursues 'evidence-based policy'. In Chapter 9, Pete Fleischmann considers how reviews could be made more user focused. He argues that the material admitted to a systematic review must be widened to include the 'grey' literature, which is literature not published in peer-reviewed journals. He also wants to see user testimony included in reviews, thereby supplementing academic knowledge with 'insider knowledge'. He concludes with two examples of user-focused reviews, one on ECT and one on change management involving mental health service users.

A hugely important aspect of user/survivor research is its desire to change things for the better for fellow users and survivors. Two chapters in this section therefore address the important issue of influencing change. In Chapter 10, Rosie Davies describes a user-focused monitoring (UFM) project in Bristol that was successful in influencing change locally. Rosie reflects on the process of translating the research findings into action, and considers the factors that enabled this to happen. It is clear that researchers and funders need to allow time and resources for implementing research findings, as well as for the research itself.

We have already seen that some chapters address the issue of collaboration with academics and mental health professionals in research, and that collaboration with professionals was fundamental to enabling the Bristol UFM project to influence change. In Chapter 11, Heather Johnson Straughan takes a firm view on this. She argues that her research included both 'insider knowledge' (that of service users) and 'outsider knowledge' (that of professionals and academics). She wonders whether we should call ourselves 'user researchers' at all, suggesting that plain 'researchers' might avoid the risk that our work will be marginalised. She gives the example of her own doctoral research where she was concerned that professionals would not validate her work. In the event, they did. Heather Johnson Straughan suggests that user researchers make the perfect 'translators' between the knowledge produced and the methods used by user researchers as against professional researchers.

In the concluding chapter of this section, Alison Faulkner provides what she calls 'a rough guide to getting started'. She discusses all the stages of doing research from planning through to dissemination. She also discusses research governance and the importance of other stakeholders in a research project. These may be people from a NHS trust where the research is taking place or may be academic partners. The chapter ends with a list of resources which user/survivor researchers may find useful. If you have been inspired to get involved in research through this book, Chapter 12 will be invaluable.

Section Four is called 'The inside story'. It brings together accounts of how research and activism can be combined, as well as reporting on a series of small projects carried out by people who are at the beginning of doing research. The book ends with narratives from authors in this book as well as some additional researchers.

In Chapter 13, Jan Wallcraft takes on the positive and negative aspects of synthesising research and activism. The chapter is not chronologically ordered but rather interweaves her experience as an activist and a researcher. She describes a long period of activism stretching back to the mid 1970s where, after a breakdown, she felt alone. Gradually she found friends in the fledgling user movement and was finally employed to set up a national network of mental health service users. During this time she also completed both an undergraduate degree and a doctorate concerned, like many authors in this book, with developing theory. She argues that activism and research can be combined, and does this by telling the story of her own development both as an activist and a researcher.

In Chapter 14, David Armes asks whether Foucault and standpoint epistemology may be synthesised to produce a philosophical framework to underpin our research. To do this he weaves his own experience of mental distress and the mental health system into his theoretical arguments. He cautions against relativism, which could pose problems for the ideas he cites, and offers his own solutions to this issue.

Chapter 15 comprises four project accounts written by service users who were involved in them. They are short narratives describing user involvement mostly in monitoring and evaluation. As we have said, user/survivor research began as a series of small, under-funded and isolated projects. These early projects aimed to give service users and survivors a voice by researching specifically from their perspective. This book demonstrates how user/survivor research has developed since then. Yet its roots remain strong; much important work is conducted in small, local user-controlled projects that explore local issues, services or treatments from user perspectives.

Judy Beckett had a very positive experience in evaluating a user-led crisis house. The researchers were given intensive training in order to interview service users of the crisis house, and those running the service found the outcomes helpful. Judy Beckett felt empowered by the process, for the first time seeing her service user status as an asset.

Matt Sands describes an evaluation project of residential care homes where the experience was much more negative. The service user evaluators worked hard to put the user perspective at the heart of the project. However, they were finally completely undermined by professionals who dominated the project steering group.

Stuart Valentine had a positive experience that he describes in his short account. The value for him was working in a team to monitor a mental health service in North East Scotland. This involved interviewing all service users, carers and staff in the service. He found learning new skills invaluable – something shared by several authors – and counsels that research is serious but can be fun!

In the fourth project account, Phil Hill reflects fully and frankly on his time in academia. He spent a number of years researching the factors that help service users/survivors return to and flourish in work. Although he was conducting this research for a doctorate, he was ultimately awarded a Master of Philosophy qualification. Phil reflects on both the highs and lows of this, and provides some sound advice to other user/survivors thinking about entering academia.

Finally, Sue Goddard describes two mental health service user groups which, with the support of a local voluntary organisation, have carried out a number of projects. Members of the groups felt a strong need to 'put something back'. Like some of the other project accounts, she emphasises the importance of training that stresses that members of the group feel that they are still learning. The main aim, she states, is to put the 'user voice' into service development and improvement.

Chapter 16, edited by Jasna Russo and Tina Coldham, concludes the book. Jasna and Tina aimed to let the people who authored the chapters in this book, together with some other researchers, say in their own words what it personally means to work as a user/survivor researcher, or what motivates service users and survivors to do this. We would argue that this is the natural way for a book on survivor research to end. It gives a picture of the 'real' people behind the texts that you will have read. It would be unlikely for a mainstream edited collection to end like this, because mainstream researchers believe that they must keep their subjectivity out of their research. But then, as we have said repeatedly, survivor research acknowledges that it has its own values and standpoints. We are not trying to copy mainstream research and, for us, it is important that readers know where we come from.

BACKGROUND

PETER BERESFORD

AND

DIANA ROSE

WHAT IS RESEARCH?

In human history, research is in some senses a relatively recent idea. What it means, essentially, is finding things out. This seems to be something that human beings have tried to do from the beginnings of time. There have also long been scientists who have sought to make new discoveries about our world and beyond. But the origins of modern research tend to be associated with the period known as the Enlightenment, which had its beginnings in the eighteenth century. This period saw a great expansion of interest in the West in finding things out, and a particular concern to do this in what were seen as systematic, rigorous and 'scientific' ways. This concern with 'scientific research', research based on careful testing and measurement, has continued and greatly influenced our understandings of modern science. By the nineteenth century, medical science had emerged as a key field for research and clinical practice. New areas of research also developed that focused particularly on the workings of human beings, both individually and collectively. In this way, psychiatry and psychology (studies of the mind) and sociology (the study of society) came into being. All of these continue to be important in the field of mental health and mental health research.

Research has now grown from the basic human desire to find out new things to become huge international industries. There is research in many fields. Perhaps the biggest sadly, relates to weapons and war. But medical research, including research about mental health issues, is also a massive area of human activity, and most research about mental health issues is still medically based research.

HOW DOES RESEARCH CONNECT WITH
OTHER FORMS OF KNOWLEDGE?

Research represents only one means of producing knowledge. There are many ways of both finding out and 'knowing' about something. In our daily lives we use many ways of finding things out. We use maps for directions to get to places, guides to know where to go and where to eat, and read books and check websites to find out things that are new to us. We may ask someone who has already done what we are interested in. We may even read novels to find out more about particular experiences. We may explore land, sea and sky, and develop and test out new technology, in order to find out and do new things.

New knowledge may be acquired through first-hand experience, intuition or by learning from other people. What particularly distinguishes 'research' as a form of knowledge production is its stress on systematic and formalised means of finding things out. Whichever methods are employed to undertake research (and the same is as true of survivor as of more conventional research approaches), stress is laid on doing things in a way consistent with agreed understandings for gaining information – or findings – that are as reliable, accurate and replicable as possible. Research is usually based on collecting information or 'data' from a number of people or data sources in a structured way. Thus research has developed its own rules and values. Because of the emphasis on research as a systematic means of producing knowledge, a particularly high value is frequently placed on it, more than is likely to be attached to other, more day-to-day means of discovery. This can create problems for people who are not highly valued, since their accounts may command less respect than those of the researchers who research them. On the other hand, while research is frequently granted authority, it is still generally subject to broader political processes that can significantly influence the nature, focus and effects of research.

DIFFERENCES BETWEEN SURVIVOR AND NON-SURVIVOR RESEARCH

Most mental health research, as has been seen, is medical research. This perhaps explains one of the key differences between survivor and non-survivor research. Mainstream medical mental health research has stressed its scientific basis. It has highlighted 'positivist' values of 'neutrality', 'objectivity' and 'distance'. In so doing, it has sought to emphasise the potential of research to produce neutral 'facts', which are independent of the people that produce them and are much more than a matter of judgement or opinion. This is seen as the basis of their validity and reliability. They are comparable to the findings of experiments, which can be repeated and produce the same results regardless of who carries them out or when or where they are carried out.

Survivor researchers, like many other researchers, have questioned the capacity of research about human beings to be objective in this way. They argue that it is inevitably based on who we are, how we come to each other as researchers and/or the subjects of research, and the essential 'subjectivity' of human relationships, including research relationships. Survivor researchers generally reject traditional hierarchies of research methods, which see quantitative approaches like randomised controlled trials as having more validity than qualitative research approaches. At the same time, they see the contribution that both qualitative and quantitative research methods can make. They are cautious about accepting conventional assumptions about the validity of different sources of knowledge. Thus from their own experience they are unlikely to agree that the knowledge of psychiatrists has greater validity than that of mental health service users/survivors, even though it may be based on 'expert' knowledge from books and research findings (Wallcraft, 1998).

Perhaps the greatest difference between survivor and non-survivor research is the value that survivors, like some other oppressed groups, place on first-hand experience as a source of knowledge. Such experiential knowledge is seen as having key importance in survivor research. The views of service users are not seen merely as a 'data source' or as inherently 'biased', but as having their own value and integrity, both in research and for researchers, as a unique source of understanding. Service user researchers frequently take the view that the fact they have similar experiences to service user research participants makes for better research. It means that research participants will feel the researcher is more likely to understand what they are saying, better able to frame questions appropriately, and treat service users routinely with respect in the research process (Beresford, 2003).

None of this means that survivor research – or indeed any other service user research – is less committed to good quality and reliable research. There is the same concern with carrying out research carefully and 'professionally', and the same recognition of the need for research training and skills to carry it out, but such research rests on a different value base from that of traditional positivist research.

RANDOMISED CONTROLLED TRIALS AND THE COCHRANE HIERARCHY OF EVIDENCE

We need to say a little more about randomised controlled trials (RCTs) because these are considered the 'gold standard' in health research. They are considered the best way of ensuring 'objectivity' and avoiding 'bias' as a method in health research. They were developed in general medicine, and the concept and practice have been taken up enthusiastically in mental health research.

RCTs are at the top of the Cochrane hierarchy of evidence, which is a ladder going from what is seen as the best way of producing knowledge at the top to the weakest way at the bottom (Cochrane, 1972). RCTs are second only to meta-analyses, which simply pool the results of several RCTs on the same topic to produce an estimate of the effects of a treatment that is more precise than one RCT alone.

Why are RCTs considered the gold standard? To understand this, we must first look to the Cochrane hierarchy as a whole. This is shown in Table 1.

Table 1: *The Cochrane Hierarchy of Evidence*

Meta-analyses of RCTs
Randomised controlled trials
Controlled studies without randomisation
Quasi-experimental studies
Non-experimental descriptive studies
Evidence from experts
(adapted from Geddes & Harrison, 1997: 221)

RCTs use randomised samples and allocate 'subjects' to a treatment arm and a control arm. A medication may be tested for efficacy, for example, by comparing two groups. One group will receive the treatment and the control group will receive a placebo (an inactive substance). An important point about RCTs is that both investigators and participants are supposed to be 'blind' to who is receiving the treatment and who is not. This means that when the two groups are compared at the end of the study, the researcher does not know the group to which the person they are assessing belongs.

Another important feature of RCTs is that they use a single, primary 'outcome measure'. With medication studies, for example, the level of symptoms may be compared between the treatment group and the control group. A single, primary outcome measure is required for statistical reasons, and the analysis itself is statistical. Some studies do comparisons on other outcomes as well, but these are not considered as important as the primary outcome and are generally called 'secondary outcomes'. For example, a secondary outcome measure may be quality of life, although this is still measured quantitatively.

It is because of random allocation and the fact of 'blinding' that RCTs come so high up on the Cochrane hierarchy of evidence. The types of study lower down the hierarchy do not use randomisation and do not use blinding. It is argued that the introduction of randomisation and blinding in RCTs minimises the bias present in other research methods.

We can ask whether these claims of objectivity and lack of bias stand up, and whether the Cochrane hierarchy might not be criticised by survivor researchers. First, is blinding really possible? There are two points about blinding. One is that both participant and researcher can often guess who is receiving a treatment and who is not. For instance, in a trial of medication where an active substance is compared with a placebo, the medication will probably have side effects, and these will be obvious to both participant and researcher. The idea that RCTs are unbiased falls with this criticism. Mainstream researchers often criticise user research as being biased, but we can see that RCTs do not escape this criticism.

An interesting point is that people taking a placebo in RCTs usually react as well and this is known as the 'placebo effect'. It is generally thought to be psychological, and this of course introduces another element into what is conceived to be medicine as a biological science.

As we said, RCTs were first developed in general medicine. Can they really be transferred to treatments and services for mental distress? Mental health interventions are typically far more complex than interventions in general health research. In general medicine, it is usually medication and other physical interventions that are being tested. The outcome measure is clear enough: survival rates. But what if you wanted to test the efficacy of a service such as a home treatment team or of self-help initiatives? This is not the same as testing a single substance. For example, if we want to investigate the efficacy of alternative treatments such as self-help, it would not help to have a control group made up of those attending only an outpatient clinic. This is because people who wish to participate in self-help groups are making a conscious decision to do this. In other words, they 'self-select' and so differ in many ways from those who do not wish to pursue self-help. User researchers would use other ways of finding out about self-help, and their value base would influence these.

Finally, user researchers would criticise the use of 'primary outcome' measures in RCTs. One of the commonest outcome measures used in mental health research is 'bed days'. For example, Burns et al. (1999) tested the efficacy of low caseloads for key workers and compared them with usual caseloads. Their outcome measure was the number of days spent in hospital for the two groups. There was no difference, and so they concluded that reducing caseloads was not an important thing to do. They did not consider what a period in hospital might mean to a person. For example, for some it is totally traumatic, while for others it might be a welcome break from a very stressful situation. But conventional medical research is not interested in what things mean to a person or in meaning in general: meaning is regarded as 'subjective' and hence not the business of science. Ultimately, this study was about which form of service was less expensive, and so it was hardly value free.

It is not that survivor researchers are simply opposed to measurement. But they would choose different topics and go about constructing their measures in different ways. There has recently been a move to develop measures of empowerment (Rogers et al., 2001) and recovery. The development of these has taken place in a completely user-focused way.

Turning to the forms of evidence considered 'weaker' by Cochrane, we can see that the hierarchy is not one that user researchers can accept. For example, evidence from descriptive studies is considered weak. But this would include surveys carried out by user researchers aiming to discover what is important to a group of their peers. In such surveys, the interviewer is generally also a service user, and this, it would be claimed, would introduce bias into the investigation.

This brings us to what is seen as the weakest form of evidence in the hierarchy – 'expert opinion'. Although considered weak, expert opinion is still considered evidence. Of what does it consist? To answer that question we have to ask: who counts as an expert? It will come as no surprise that the experts in question are professionals. They are senior clinicians, academics and methodologists.

In user-led research, as well as in other service user circles and activities, the term 'experts by experience' is increasingly heard. Does that mean that evidence from experience should be admitted to the Cochrane hierarchy? It does, but it goes further than that. It means that evidence deriving from the expertise of service users, and the systematisation of this by service user researchers, should be higher up the ladder than 'expert opinion' currently is. At the extreme, we would completely revise the Cochrane hierarchy. But we should perhaps not be too critical of Cochrane's work: he himself was cautious about the usefulness of any medicine.

HOW HAS SURVIVOR RESEARCH DEVELOPED?

Modern survivor research has an amazingly short history. It has been established for at most twenty or so years. Yet it has established itself during this time as a new and legitimate approach to research (even though, as we have said, it continues to come in for adverse criticism from some mainstream researchers), and has led to the production of a large and growing number of survivor research studies. Even ten years ago, there was relatively little survivor research: progress has accelerated rapidly (Mental Health Foundation, 2003).

Initially, survivor research was often unfunded, carried out by survivors on an unpaid voluntary basis (Beresford & Wallcraft, 1997; Lindow, 2001). Now there are large, externally funded projects led by survivor researchers. Such survivor research has been based in at least three settings. These are:

- independent researchers working on their own
- in survivor/service user-controlled organisations
- in non-survivor organisations, including non-survivor-controlled charities/voluntary organisations and university departments

Three major national initiatives have developed to take forward survivor research. These are:

- Strategies for Living
- User-Focused Monitoring (UFM)
- The Service User Research Enterprise (SURE)

The Mental Health Foundation pioneered support for the development of small, local user-led research projects through Strategies for Living. It developed training and learning material to enable a wider range of service users/survivors to become user researchers, developing an important body of experience and knowledge about survivor research (Faulkner, 1997; Faulkner & Nicholls, 1999; Faulkner & Layzell, 2000; Nicholls, 2001; Nicholls, Wright, Waters & Wells, 2003). User-focused monitoring (UFM), which has now been widely developed and which was pioneered at the Sainsbury Centre for Mental Health, provides a way of evaluating mental health (and other) services through the involvement of service users (Rose, 2001; UFM Network, 2003). The Service User Research Enterprise (SURE) at the Institute of Psychiatry, King's College London demonstrates how service users can carry through big projects successfully in traditional institutions. It carries out major qualitative and quantitative research projects, for example developing new approaches to systematic review and to participatory research that involves service users (Rose, 2003).

In addition, a wide range of smaller, independent survivor research projects has developed, funded by local health trusts, charitable funders and others. However, it should be noted that the major research projects and much of the development of survivor research has taken place in non-survivor-controlled organisations and settings (Turner & Beresford, 2005). This is a measure more of the difficulties the latter encounter in securing adequate resources, and the inferior credibility attached to them by mainstream research and research organisations, than to any inherent limitations or shortcomings. They clearly have problems of capacity in taking forward survivor research, but this is much more to do with their difficulty in securing resources, than with any inherent limitations. Thus inequalities of funding, credibility and power continue to make it difficult for mental health service users/ survivors to ensure that their research is primarily located in organisations that they control, and this is likely to be a factor inhibiting both the independence and development of such research.

WHY DO SURVIVOR RESEARCH?

There is a common view that there is little point to much, if not all, research. The claim is that research frequently states the obvious – things that people already know only too well – or it doesn't have any useful purpose, simply creating an additional expensive industry of researchers who produce reports that sit gathering dust in cupboards. But some mental health service users have felt that research often does have an effect: frequently, this effect is very unhelpful – one that reinforces the views and responses of traditionally powerful interests like psychiatry and the pharmaceutical industry, rather than highlights the difficulties facing service users and what *they* see as helpful in dealing with them.

These are important reasons for doing survivor research. It offers service users/survivors a way of challenging the conventional, medicalised, individual focus of much mainstream research. It provides an alternative to the former's emphasis on diagnostic categories and 'treatment' responses.

There are also a number of other important reasons for doing survivor research. First, it enables service users/survivors to develop another view of themselves and their experience, independent of the psychiatric system. It makes it possible for them to offer their own accounts, views and explanations without these being reinterpreted and modified by others.

Second, like emancipatory disability research, the emphasis of survivor research is on personal empowerment and making broader social and political change (Beresford, 2000). Thus, it is an important vehicle for making a difference and is seen by service users as such. It provides a knowledge base for both levels of change. It allows service users a chance to develop their own knowledge, which can offer an additional challenge to dominant understandings of and assumptions about them and their madness and distress. This research-based knowledge can serve to increase the credibility of service users/survivors – a credibility which is frequently called into question – by offering them their own evidence base. Third, it seeks to develop a more ethical and equal approach to research, one that treats participating service users with respect and equality (Faulkner, 2004). Finally, survivor research represents another aspect of survivor action: it complements self and collective advocacy, campaigning, and survivor arts and culture, and is being used and developed in association with them.

QUESTIONS OF POWER AND EMANCIPATORY RESEARCH

Survivor research, as has just been seen, has an emancipatory purpose. That is to say, it is committed to challenging the disempowerment of mental health service users/survivors and supporting them to have a greater say in their lives and influence in the world in which they live. It aims to be part of a process that changes the distribution of power.

Survivor research has drawn on participatory research (Cornwall & Jewkes, 1995) to bring about a reduction in inequalities in power relations between the researcher and his or her participants. When the researcher is him/herself a service user and shares experiences with participants in the research process, this is completely different from the mainstream research relationship in which researchers go in, ensure that 'subjects' take a medicine or do a test, and make it clear that they are the professionals. After that, the participants have no idea what resulted from acts in which they participated. In survivor research, participants are involved as much as possible, and may indeed go on to be researchers themselves.

However, it is also important to remember that survivor research is itself affected by existing inequalities in the distribution of power relating to research. Less value is attached to its research approach and its valuing of subjectivity. Less status is given to it, and therefore generally less priority attached to it, and less value and reliance placed on it and its findings. There is a growing body of evidence confirming this (Turner & Beresford, 2005).

ISSUES OF FUNDING

One of the sharpest expressions of the inequalities of power affecting survivor and other forms of emancipatory research is their unequal access to funding support. While as has been seen there has been a growing interest in survivor research, it is, like other forms of user-controlled research, still the least supported if most developed expression of research with service user involvement. Furthermore, it has secured as yet only a tiny amount of the many millions of pounds currently spent on medicalised mental health research. This money is still largely directed towards RCT-based studies. There have as yet been relatively few large survivor research projects, and these have tended, as has already been seen, to be based in non-survivor-led settings.

Survivor research not only seems to have more difficulty attracting funding. It tends, like other forms of participatory and emancipatory research, to incur additional costs. This can mean that it is seen as a less attractive option to fund, because it is inherently more expensive than traditional research. These additional costs arise because of the need to ensure the full involvement of service users, to meet their travel and support costs, to ensure equal access (for example, through the provision of information in accessible formats), and also because of ethical commitments to pay service users for their involvement and expertise.

These additional processes also tend to require additional time, which itself creates additional cost requirements. Survivor researchers, on the other hand, argue that such costs should be included in budgeting for *all* research and that all research would benefit from being participatory in the same way as survivor research.

ISSUES FOR BLACK AND MINORITY ETHNIC SURVIVORS AND INVOLVEMENT IN RESEARCH

In 2004, the Toronto Group organized a series of seminars concerning research as empowerment (Hanley, 2005). One of these focused specifically on the involvement of black and minority ethnic communities in research. This concluded that while the voices of black and minority ethnic communities were beginning to be heard in research, both as researchers and research participants, a number of key barriers continued to operate. For example, such research is still marginalised and under-resourced. Some black and minority ethnic communities are under-represented in research, while others feel over-researched. The seminar set out a series of recommendations for improved practice (Hanley, 2005: 34–9).

While there has been some user-controlled and survivor research focusing on and involving black and minority ethnic mental health service users/survivors and their experiences, their inclusion in such research seems so far not to have equalled that of white service users/survivors. This is an issue of some significance, given that it is known that many black and minority ethnic service users face particular discrimination and oppression in the psychiatric system. The first review of user-controlled research observed in 2005 that further review of user-controlled research (including survivor research) from the perspectives of black and minority ethnic communities was required, as they are as yet inadequately developed and understood (Turner and Beresford, 2005: 92). This is an important issue that must be addressed in the future development of survivor research to ensure that it is fully inclusive.

REFERENCES

Beresford, P (2000) What have madness and psychiatric system survivors got to do with disability and disability studies? *Disability and Society, 15*(1), 168–72.

Beresford, P (2003) *It's Our Lives: A short theory of knowledge, distance and experience.* London: Citizen Press in association with Shaping Our Lives.

Beresford, P & Wallcraft, J (1997) Psychiatric system survivors and emancipatory research: Issues, overlaps and differences. In C Barnes & G Mercer (eds) *Doing Disability Research* (pp. 67–87). Leeds: The Disability Press, University of Leeds.

Burns, T, Creed, F, Fahy, T, Thompson, S, Tyrer P & White, I (1999) Intensive versus standard case management for severe psychotic illness: A randomised trial. UK700 group. *Lancet, 353*(9171), 2185–9.

Cochrane, AL (1972) *Effectiveness and Efficiency: Random reflections on health services.* London: Nuffield Provincial Hospitals Trust.

Cornwall, A & Jewkes, R (1995) What is participatory research? *Social Science and Medicine, 41*(11), 1667–76.

Faulkner, A (1997) *Knowing Our Own Minds.* London: Mental Health Foundation.

Faulkner, A (2004) *Ethics of Survivor Research: Guidelines for the ethical conduct of research carried out by mental health service users and survivors.* Bristol: Policy Press.

Faulkner, A & Layzell, S (2000) *Strategies for Living: A report of user-led research into people's strategies for living with mental distress.* London: Mental Health Foundation.

Faulkner, A & Nicholls, V (1999) *The DIY Guide to Survivor Research.* London: Mental Health Foundation.

Geddes, J & Harrison, P (1997) Closing the gap between theory and practice. *British Journal of Psychiatry, 171*, 220–5.

Hanley, B (2005) *Research as Empowerment?* Report of a series of seminars organised by the

Toronto Group. York: Toronto Group, Joseph Rowntree Foundation.

Lindow, V (2001) Survivor research. In C Newnes, G Holmes & C Dunn (eds) *This is Madness Too: Critical perspectives on mental health services* (pp. 135–46). Ross-on-Wye: PCCS Books.

Mental Health Foundation (2003) *Mental Health Users/Survivor Research in the UK: A policy briefing*. London: Mental Health Foundation.

Nicholls, V (2001) *Doing Research Ourselves*. London: Strategies For Living, Mental Health Foundation.

Nicholls, V, Wright, S, Waters, R & Wells, S (2003) *Surviving User-Led Research: Reflections on supporting user-led research projects*. London: Strategies for Living, Mental Health Foundation.

Rogers, AE, Pilgrim, D, Thornicroft, G & Szmukler, G (2001) Users and their advocates. In G Thornicroft & G Szmukler (eds) *Textbook of Community Psychiatry* (pp. 465–75). Oxford: Oxford University Press.

Rose, D (2001) *Users' Voices: The perspectives of mental health service users on community and hospital care*. London: Sainsbury Centre for Mental Health.

Rose, D (2003) Having a diagnosis is a qualification for the job. *BMJ, 326*, 1331.

Turner, M & Beresford, P (2005) *User Controlled Research: Its meanings and potential*. Final report, Shaping Our Lives and the Centre for Citizen Participation, Brunel University, Eastleigh, INVOLVE.

UFM Network (2003) *Doing It For Real: A guide to setting up and undertaking a User Focused Monitoring project*. London: Sainsbury Centre for Mental Health. http://www.scmh.org.uk/pdfs/ufm+doing+it+for+real.pdf (Accessed 17 December 2008).

Wallcraft, J (1998) Survivor-led research in human services: Challenging the dominant medical paradigm. In S Baldwin (ed) *Needs Assessment and Community Care: Clinical practice and policy making* (pp. 186–208). Oxford: Butterworth-Heinemann.

CHAPTER 3

SO WHAT IS
SURVIVOR RESEARCH?

ANGELA SWEENEY

> The expression and experience of 'user-led research' in the UK has over
> the last five years grown wings and begun to fly.
> (Nicholls, Wright, Waters & Wells, 2003)

It has been little more than twenty years since service users and survivors of the mental health system began to use their knowledge of research to give voice to their experiences. These early attempts often occurred without funding or support. Today, survivor research is starting to establish itself as an independent and valid form of mental health research. But because the field is still emerging, it can be difficult to grasp what service user research actually is.

This chapter is an attempt to describe and explain service user/survivor research. In the first half of the chapter, the influences that have shaped service user research will be described. The first of these is the user movement, where the strong principles that the user movement has developed have been carried into service user research. The second influence is based in policy, where different approaches to providing welfare services have influenced how those services are researched. The third influence is epistemology, which means theories of how we come to 'know' about the world. Service user researchers are beginning to develop their own epistemological theories to strengthen the research that is conducted. The final influence that will be outlined is methodology, which means how we investigate and explore the social world. Service user researchers have drawn on a variety of methodological approaches in developing their own particular approach.

In the second half of the chapter, service user research will be described. This will include what service user research is, a brief history, the forms service user research can take, and the principles and priorities of service user research. Moves to develop service users' own theories of knowledge production (epistemology) will be described. Finally, some of the challenges that currently face service user research will be explored.

THE USER MOVEMENT IN ENGLAND

As early as 1620, patients were collectively protesting about the conditions to which they were exposed ('Petition of the Poor Distracted Folk of Bedlam', cited in Campbell, 1996). Yet it was not until the mid 1980s that England saw the emergence of the modern mental health user movement through two international conferences, in London and Brighton. At that time, fewer than a dozen user groups existed. The latest estimate is of a minimum of 300 groups, with an approximate membership of 9,000 (Wallcraft, Read & Sweeney, 2003). This demonstrates the massive and rapid growth of local, organised service user/survivor action in England.

Research conducted on the user movement has found that members do share many common concerns. However, members also hold a wide variety of contrasting views on a number of issues (Wallcraft et al., 2003). This means that the user movement does not constitute a single voice that represents all service users/survivors on all issues. This has led to a philosophy for the movement that prizes choice, self-determination and individual and collective empowerment.

THE INFLUENCE OF THE USER MOVEMENT ON SURVIVOR RESEARCH

There is a strong relationship between service user research and the service user movement. For example, the user movement provides a base from which service users can conduct research and to which they can be accountable. In addition, recent research has identified five major values and principles underpinning survivor-controlled research in health and social care (Turner & Beresford, 2005):

- empowerment
- emancipation
- participation
- equality
- anti-discrimination

Whilst they are not mental health specific, the five principles have strong and clear links with mental health service user approaches to research (e.g. Faulkner, 2004). They also describe many of the principles that underpin the user movement, demonstrating the strong relationship between the user movement and survivor research.

CONSUMERIST AND DEMOCRATIC MODELS

In recent years, there have been major, international changes in how welfare is provided. These changes have been fuelled by a market-led approach to providing services, and an emphasis on individual rights and responsibilities. This approach to providing services has become known as 'the consumerist model'. The core principles underpinning this approach revolve around choice, accessibility and information.

It has been argued that this approach fails to challenge inequalities in the distribution of resources, promote citizenship or address collective agendas (Braye, 2000). However, there is an alternative model based on just these ideas: 'the democratic model'. The core principles underpinning this approach are inclusion, autonomy, independence and rights. The focus is not simply on an individual's experience of services but on all areas of their life (Beresford, 2002). The major features of the two models are compared in Table 1.

Table 1: *A comparison of the major features of consumerist and democratic models (adapted from Beresford, 2002)*

	Consumerist model	**Democratic model**
Focus	Policies and systems	People's lives and aspirations
Change	Consumers are asked for their input but managers decide whether to make changes	People are both encouraged and enabled to give their input
Power	'Managerialist': managers retain power	'Liberatory': aims to empower groups and individuals
Services	Services are provider-led	There is an interest in user-led and controlled services
Ideology	*Treated* as unrelated to any overt ideology	Overtly political

THE INFLUENCE OF CONSUMERIST AND DEMOCRATIC MODELS ON SURVIVOR RESEARCH

Both consumerist and democratic models have influenced social research in general, with two major research responses identified. These have been named the 'reactionary' and 'progressive' responses (Beresford & Evans, 1999). The reactionary or mainstream response emphasises evidence-based policy and practice. Ideas regarding what constitutes evidence are led by professionals, and traditional research methods are used. Conversely, the progressive or alternative response is based on a fundamental challenge to traditional ways of doing research. Notions of objectivity and truth are questioned, and experience is seen as a valid form of knowledge. User research is more strongly allied with this alternative response.

EPISTEMOLOGY:
THEORIES OF HOW WE COME TO 'KNOW'

The dominant model of enquiry of our age is known as 'positivism'. Positivism can be traced to Auguste Comte in the early nineteenth century. Comte believed that in both nature and society, objects and people react to external stimuli and environments in fixed ways that can be observed and measured. The goal of science, whether natural or social, is objectively to collect data on directly observable phenomena. This is then used to develop and test theory. Therefore, the methods of the natural sciences are imported into the social sciences in order to explore the social world.

Positivist research takes a linear form, typically hypothesis, experiment, conclusion, write up and dissemination. This research often has little influence on practice – what actually happens in the real world. The researcher is seen as an objective observer who must strive to remove values and subjectivity from the research process. Participants are seen as a source of data that should not be consulted about the research. Their behaviours during the research are treated as isolated variables. Much of what makes us human – our thoughts, feelings, and the meanings we attach to our experiences – are seen as beyond the scope of scientific enquiry, as they cannot be directly observed.

Positivism is not without critics. In particular, numerous schools of thought, such as phenomenology and postmodernism, have rejected the notion that nature and society can be studied using the same methods. This is largely because people do not respond to environments in fixed ways, but instead have conscious thought, creativity, spontaneity, free will, and attach meanings to their behaviour.

Positivism's dismissal of subjective experience as unscientific has particular implications for mental health research. Foucault was the first to propose that people who experience significant mental distress are seen as representing the Enlightenment's realm of 'unreason' (Foucault, 1967). Mental health service users are therefore seen as separate from a rational, reasoned science and incapable of contributing to or producing their own knowledge. Users' views are invalid because irrational, just as their experiences are unobservable and therefore beyond the scope of research. This means that research has traditionally been done *on* service users, rather than *with* or even *by* them.

THE INFLUENCE OF EPISTEMOLOGICAL DEBATES ON SERVICE USER RESEARCH

Many service users have consistently argued that mainstream, positivist research does not represent how they experience or view services. This has led service user researchers to focus their own research on users' experiences. When this is done, a different type of knowledge from that of mainstream research is produced. This service user-produced knowledge often sits uncomfortably with a medical understanding of mental health and its services. This has contributed to many user researchers not just challenging positivism, but also its related medically dominated belief system (Wallcraft, 1998b).

Thus, service user researchers are beginning systematically to challenge their exclusion from knowledge production and the dismissal of their views and experiences. Through this, an epistemology for service user research is emerging, which will be explored later in the chapter.

METHODOLOGICAL DEVELOPMENTS
IN SOCIAL SCIENCES

Critiques of positivism have contributed to the development of new research models. Three examples are *action research, participatory research* and *emancipatory disability research*, and each has influenced the shape of service user research.

Action research aims to solve problems through the knowledge that is created by research. It originated in the 1940s when authority was questioned less than it is today and social science was concerned with resolving practical problems (Brown & Tandon, 1983). Traditional action researchers such as Kurt Lewin aimed to improve effectiveness by solving a problem identified by a client group. This was typically in an organisational or agricultural setting. It is assumed that a solution that benefits everybody is possible, implying that the distribution of authority and resources is legitimate. Original action research approaches prioritised the role of the researcher as assisting the participants in finding solutions. However, newer forms have enhanced the role of participants (Elden & Chisolm, 1993).

Achieving a balance between theory and action is not easy, and action research has been criticised for emphasising action at the expense of theory (e.g. Bartunek, 1993). Furthermore, participatory researchers are critical of the failure of action research to prioritise the needs of marginalised groups.

Participatory research originated in the developing world with work with marginalised groups. It is currently gaining popularity in a wide variety of fields, including health (e.g. Baker, Homan, Schonhoff & Kreuter, 1999; Minkler & Wallerstein, 2003). The aim is to achieve social change through the production of knowledge. One of the key elements is that participants and researchers act together as 'co-researchers' from the beginning of the process to the end. This can therefore be seen to advance an action approach by combining action and research in a model that shares power and control.

There is of course a great deal of overlap between the two forms of research. Contemporary action research now involves a significant degree of participatory practice. Furthermore, participation is sometimes conceived of as degree rather than approach, with participation being variously achieved at different stages but rarely achieved in every aspect of the research process.

However, participatory research goes beyond action research, as it has at its core a commitment to tackling marginalisation. It would be easy to assume, then, that those themselves marginalised would welcome such approaches unreservedly, particularly groups disillusioned with medically dominated conceptions of disability and distress. However, this has not always been the case, emancipatory disability researchers claiming that participatory research approaches 'have tended to reinforce existing power structures rather than challenge or confront let alone change them' (Oliver, 1997: 25).

During the late 1960s and 1970s, disability activists worldwide were moving towards the politicisation of disability (Barnes, 2003). Traditional research at that time medicalised disability, and failed to acknowledge the role of social barriers such as prejudice and inaccessible transport (Barnes & Mercer, 1997). Disability activists and researchers rejected this approach, and towards the end of the 1980s began to research experiences of disability that addressed societal discrimination.

A major milestone was reached in 1992 when Mike Oliver called for research to be emancipatory (Oliver, 1992). *Emancipatory disability research* shifts control of research from the powerful to the marginalised. It is built upon three fundamentals: reciprocity, gain and empowerment (Oliver, 1997). Rather than a single project ever being fully emancipatory, individual projects aim to build a body of knowledge that challenges exclusion at both macro (large-scale) and micro (small-scale) levels (Barnes, 2001).

The commitment to challenging both the macro and micro is a clear step forward from the use of participatory research approaches, which focus almost exclusively on the micro. Shaw has referred to this as the 'rhetoric of participation', meaning that participation is restricted to the individual level, with major policy and planning decisions unchallenged (Shaw, 2000). There are also fears that participation has become a catch-all concept, even used to describe top-down research with minimal participation (Cornwall & Jewkes, 1995). Such dangers are clearly evident in service user-controlled and involved research.

A second shift from participatory methods is that in an emancipatory approach the researcher is typically a community member. For example, Vernon explored the experiences of black disabled women explicitly as a black disabled female researcher (Vernon, 1997). Similarly, of fundamental importance in user research is that both researcher and researched share an experience of either using mental health services or of experiencing mental distress (Faulkner & Layzell, 2000).

A further shift is that emancipatory approaches rarely seek solutions to specific problems, as in action research, or address community development issues, as in participatory research. Instead, the aim is to enable the emancipation and empowerment of marginalised groups both within the research and more widely, and it is here that we find the strongest echoes with service user research.

THE INFLUENCE OF METHODOLOGICAL DEVELOPMENTS ON SERVICE USER RESEARCH

There are clear links, therefore, between emancipatory disability research and user research. Indeed, each of the three methodological developments outlined has enabled service users to move towards their own empowerment through research. First, traditional action researchers have challenged the separation of research from practice. The commitment to effect change is typically a feature of user research, although action is conceptualised in broad terms. For example, in *The Ethics of Survivor Research*, Faulkner (2004) quotes a contributor as stating: 'undertake research not with the certainty that it could lead to the kind of change that survivors might want, but with that goal in mind'. Second, participatory researchers have reconceived the role of participants in the research process. Service user research also aims to equalise research relationships. However, this occurs within a framework that places users in control and emphasises self-empowerment. This demonstrates a shift from potentially colonialist, participatory community work to community ownership.

It is with emancipatory disability research that service user research has the closest links. Emancipatory disability research has as its key goal the liberation of disabled people, through challenging both dominant ideas of disability and traditional methods of exploration. Similarly, user research does not aim to conduct objective, value-free research, but is committed to empowerment through research participation and output. Such 'emancipatory discourses' fuelled the first service users/survivors to propose the notion of survivor research a little over a decade ago (Rose, 2004).

SERVICE USER/SURVIVOR RESEARCH

WHAT IS SERVICE USER/SURVIVOR RESEARCH?

Although terminology around user research is no more than fifteen years old (Turner & Beresford, 2005), service user research has begun to establish itself on the mental health research landscape. Yet what constitutes user research can be difficult to define. This is partly owing to its infancy and consequent small literature, but also because the nature of consumerist and democratic influences mean that the form it takes can vary. Before attempting to define the emerging picture of user research, we will first look at its chronology.

SURVIVOR RESEARCH IN THE 1980S

The desire to conduct research from a user perspective first began to germinate in the UK in the mid-1980s, when early members of the user movement expressed dissatisfaction at the way current research failed to represent them. Members were using testimonies to tell their stories, embodied in the group Survivors Speak Out. The use of testimonials by the powerless is echoed in the beginnings of other social movements (e.g. Morris, 1991, cited in Stone & Priestley, 1996). They are a vital means of communicating experiences, and how these depart from mainstream knowledge.

A small number of service user movement pioneers also brought together their research expertise and experience of mental distress in a few small, local, often unfunded research projects. This is a form of activism, of ensuring that previously silent voices are heard. But it also represents early attempts to move from testimony and story telling alone to the conduct of research from a user perspective (Beresford & Wallcraft, 1997).

SURVIVOR RESEARCH IN THE 1990S

Through the 1990s, a number of collections of testimonies were published in the mainstream, such as *Speaking Our Minds* (Read & Reynolds, 1996) and *From the Ashes of Experience* (Barker, Campbell & Davidson, 1999). Such publications gave power to service users' voices, whilst mainstream access helped to legitimise what was being said.

Service user research also gained standing with the establishment of two large programmes of research in national mental health charities, User-Focused Monitoring (UFM) at the Sainsbury Centre for Mental Health (Rose, 2001) and Strategies for Living (S4L) at the Mental Health Foundation (Faulkner & Layzell, 2000). Although the research approaches differed, each aimed to represent service users' stories. There was a clear desire to conduct high quality research acceptable to the mainstream. Yet the activist element was not lost, the aims being to generate an alternate knowledge that could challenge mainstream representations and influence services both locally and nationally. Along with a concern with output, both programmes had a strong focus on research *processes*, revealing a concern among user researchers with how research is conducted. Service user research was beginning to take shape.

SURVIVOR RESEARCH FROM 2000

Since the turn of the century, there has been a rapid growth in user research. Conducting research from a user perspective continues to be a feature of the Mental Health Foundation, though S4L no longer exists. More recent initiatives include SURE (the Service User Research Enterprise) based at the Institute of Psychiatry,

King's College London, Suresearch based at the University of Birmingham, and Bristol's SURF (the Service User Research Forum). These represent just a few of the growing number of service user research groups around the country.

SERVICE USER RESEARCH AND USER INVOLVEMENT IN RESEARCH

Alongside the growth in service user research, there has been an increase in user involvement in research. The simple difference between the two is that in service user research, users have control over the process; service users do not have that control when merely involved in research (Faulkner, 2004). In their work, Turner and Beresford (2005) found that focus group participants drew a sharp distinction between service user research and service user involvement, with the former seen positively and the latter as potentially creating tokenism and marginalisation.

This difference in attitude may owe something to the different traditions in which service user research and user involvement have arisen. Where service user research is strongly rooted in the democratic model, service user involvement in research owes more to the consumerist model. This means that involved users typically do not have control over research questions, processes or whether and how outcomes are applied, and this can lead to scepticism.

However, service user research is not always presented and discussed as a research approach that is distinct from service user involvement, and these variations in the understanding and application of terminology can contribute to difficulties in its definition. Instead, involvement is frequently seen as a continuum.

COLLABORATIVE RESEARCH

One of the most frequently cited continuums is that of INVOLVE, which defines three distinct but continuous categories: *control, collaboration* and *consultation* (Haggerty, Reid, Freeman, Starfield, Adair & McKendry, 2003). The second category, collaboration, has also become more common in recent years. This refers to partnerships between service users and most typically academic or clinical collaborators. Turner and Beresford (2005) found that their participants were particularly wary about collaboration, as it is difficult to move from an inherent power imbalance to genuine partnership working.

This uncertainty finds some echoes in Rose (2003a), who describes mainstream scepticism, potentially immutable power differences and partnerships being enacted simply to 'tick the user involvement box'. However, she also describes collaborative projects in which partnership working has enabled professionals to better understand users' experiences. This has led to far stronger research, demonstrating some of the successes of collaborative and partnership working.

Clearly then, service user activity in research is increasing, whether it be through consultation, collaboration or control. This increase in activity means that a clearer picture of what service user research represents is emerging.

THE EMERGING PICTURE OF SERVICE USER RESEARCH

The publication of *The Ethics of Survivor Research* by Alison Faulkner in 2004 represents a step forward in the understanding of service user research. The report was written following consultation with user researchers, and provides a definition of what it means to be a user or survivor exploring the social world. The principles described as underlying user research are:

- *clarity and transparency:* being clear and open with all involved
- *empowerment:* challenging stigma and ensuring participants' voices are heard
- *identity:* disclosing a shared identity with participants
- *commitment to change:* conducting research that in some way contributes to change
- *respect:* respecting participants' views and ensuring they are heard
- *equal opportunities:* ensuring those from diverse or marginal communities are heard
- *theoretical approach:* openness about the theoretical underpinnings of the research
- *accountability:* clarifying the relationship between the research and wider society and taking a sophisticated approach to the understanding of accountability to other users

So we can be clear, then, that service user research is about the empowerment of users at both individual and collective levels (e.g. Wallcraft, 2003). This occurs through both research process and research output. This is because participation in research aims to empower (process), whilst the production of knowledge from a service user perspective challenges mainstream approaches and dominant medical belief systems (output).

There are a number of points of divergence between service user and mainstream research. First, users' priorities for research often differ from that of mainstream researchers. For example, in a consultation exercise of local service users, Thornicroft and colleagues found that the top priority was for involvement in all stages of research (Thornicroft, Rose, Huxley, Dale & Wykes, 2002). This finding was echoed by a service user panel reporting user priorities for research to a Department of Health review of mental health research (Department of Health, 2002).

Second, service user researchers typically approach research questions from a different perspective from that of mainstream researchers. Furthermore, research has found that having users or families ask questions of their peers produces different responses (Rose, 2001).

Third, service user researchers typically define mental distress in a different way from mainstream researchers. Rather than focusing on medical diagnoses, there is a sensitivity and respect for individuals' understandings and interpretations

31

of their own distress. Where broader discourses are used, these are typically based on a social rather than medical model.

Fourth, service user researchers place a greater emphasis on researching alternatives to the psychiatric system (Wallcraft, 1998a), whilst also exploring perspectives and experiences of mainstream services (Lindow, 2001). Experience is seen as a valid and powerful source of evidence, and it is for this reason that users have tended to use qualitative methods. However, quantitative methods are not rejected. For example, UFM used qualitative methods to generate quantitative measures.

THE EPISTEMOLOGY OF SERVICE USER RESEARCH

Some service user researchers now feel that the time is ripe to address deeper questions of epistemology. Epistemology refers to theories of how we come to know. The key user researchers currently writing on this topic are Diana Rose (Rose, 2004), David Armes (Chapter 14 of this book) and Peter Beresford (Beresford, 2003).

It is possible to draw together common principles underlying each author's approach. Each sees service user knowledge as being based on experience (experiential knowledge), with different knowledge being produced from that of mainstream (scientific) knowledge. However, because experiential knowledge is undermined by the science of positivism, dominant knowledge comes to be seen as the 'truth'. This is because of the relationship between knowledge and power. The mainstream has the power to define the best methods to generate knowledge, and therefore what constitutes truth, whilst the knowledge of those with experience is dismissed as unscientific. Each author argues that, in some way, service user-produced knowledge is more complete, more authentic or closer to the truth than the knowledge that is generated in the mainstream.

It is at this point that the approaches diverge. Rose focuses on standpoint epistemology first developed by feminists. In Chapter 4, she argues that users produce different knowledge from that of mainstream researchers. This knowledge may be more complete, as user researchers have access to both the discourses of professional researchers and that of service recipients. Whilst translating between the two is a challenge, working alongside clinical academics may ultimately produce more complete pictures of service users' lives.

Armes believes in a social constructionist project, arguing that perspectives are framed by particular discourses such as the medical model, yet psychiatry's power means that psychiatrists can assert their discourses as reality, with service user discourses being rejected. Service user researchers should work towards developing a social constructionist service user/survivor standpoint, which challenges dominant mental health discourses. From this beginning, users will be able to construct and deconstruct their own realities. The knowledge this creates may be 'better' knowledge, as it comes from the powerless.

Finally, Beresford argues that mainstream thought strives for neutrality, objectivity and distance. This privileging of distance results in those with direct experience being seen as having less credibility than those without. This further marginalises people, as their own knowledge and experience are undermined. User researchers need to reclaim and re-explore the role and value of first-hand experience, whilst mainstream researchers need to explore how they can draw closer to users' experiences. To Beresford, the knowledge produced by users is likely to be the most authentic, because it reduces the distance between experience, interpretation and knowledge.

CHALLENGES FACING SERVICE USER RESEARCH

Knowledge is not static but ever changing, and so generating knowledge from a service user perspective is not a project with an end. It is equally likely that user researchers will continue to debate how best to generate knowledge from the user perspective. This debate in part owes something to the legacy of the user movement, our seemingly fragmented discourses that value self-determination and the differences amongst us. However, our debates will prove meaningless if users continue to experience powerlessness and marginalisation within the mental health system. Tackling this powerlessness is the biggest challenge facing user research and activism.

Service user research continues to be a marginal activity lacking in mainstream acceptance. This often occurs through silent accusations of bias, although some mainstream authors have been more candid in expressing doubt. For example, the current editor of the *British Journal of Psychiatry* described user involvement as lacking an evidence-base, continuing: 'There is a real danger that the engine of user initiatives in mental health services, although positive in principle, will accelerate out of control and drive mental health research into the sand' (Tyrer, 2002: 406).

Such scepticism has contributed to the exclusion of service user research from peer-reviewed journals, although this is beginning to change. The epistemology of user research should provide a firm base from which to challenge further remaining exclusion. In addition, calls to evaluate user involvement in research will enable the development of an evidence base.

An additional challenge is the lack of resources for service user research and user involvement in research, described as 'a key challenge to achieve inclusion for mental health' (Thornicroft & Tansella, 2005). Funding would enable an expansion of the number of user researchers, and enable user researchers to expand their skill base, helping prevent user research being a passing fad.

There are concerns that service user researchers are invited to participate simply to 'tick the box' for user involvement, rather than to make a meaningful contribution. User researchers need to negotiate meaningful participation, whilst mainstream researchers need to be willing to relinquish power.

There is also the challenge of having a 'double identity' (Rose, 2003b). Holding a 'double identity' of service user and researcher enables user researchers to access the discourses of the scientific community, as well as that of service users. Whilst this can produce a more complete knowledge, mainstream researchers may find it difficult to accept users' research expertise. Similarly, service users participating in research may see the user researcher as an expert with all the power of a traditional researcher. Encouraging each group to recognise both identities can be a challenge. However, this double identity also means that user researchers are in a unique position to act as 'agents of change', enabling other users to become more involved in research (Faulkner 2007, personal correspondence).

CONCLUSION

Like all social science approaches, the development of service user research has come about through interaction with the whole of the social world. A flourishing user movement in the 1980s and beyond saw users search for a collective voice, leading to a focus on choice, self-determination and empowerment, and most fundamentally, the right of users to speak for themselves. The rise of consumerism led to a focus on service user involvement. This is in some ways distinct from user research, which has grown from democratic perspectives and can be seen as an alternative to mainstream research. Within academia, critiques of positivism have challenged the silencing of madness, and contributed to the reconceptualisation of the entire research process. Finally, methodological developments have influenced the shape and form that user research takes. However, each of these influences cannot be seen as sharply distinct trends, as each feeds into and affects the other. This chapter has been an attempt to start untangling some of these influences on user research.

Yet the precise shape of service user research can be difficult to grasp, owing to its infancy and predominance in grey rather than peer-reviewed literature. However, we can be clear that the presence of users in research can take a number of forms, including involvement and collaboration. Principles underlying user-controlled research are emerging, and these are fundamentally different from many mainstream research approaches. These differences have contributed to moves to develop an epistemological base for user research. It is hoped that this move will help strengthen the position of user research. Yet there are still a number of challenges facing us, including powerlessness in the mental health system, lack of funding, and the benefits and difficulties of having dual identities. Clearly, we need to address these concerns for user research firmly to establish itself on the mental health services research landscape.

ACKNOWLEDGEMENTS

I am extremely grateful to Peter Beresford, Alison Faulkner, Pete Fleischmann, Louise Morgan, Mary Nettle and Diana Rose for their valuable comments on an earlier version of this chapter.

REFERENCES

Campbell, P (2006) *Some Things You Should Know about User/Survivor Action. A Mind Resource Pack*. London: Mind.

Baker, EA, Homan, S, Schonhoff, R & Kreuter, M (1999) Principles of practice for academic/ practice/community research partnerships. *American Journal of Preventive Medicine, 16*(3S), 86–93.

Barker, P, Campbell, P & Davidson, B (eds) (1999) *From the Ashes of Experience: Reflections on madness, survival and growth*. London: Whurr.

Barnes, C (2001) *'Emancipatory' Disability Research: Project or process?* Public Lecture at City Chambers, Glasgow, 24 October 2001. Available at: www.leeds.ac.uk/disability-studies/ archiveuk/archframe.htm

Barnes, C (2003) What a difference a decade makes: Reflections on doing 'emancipatory' disability research. *Disability and Society, 18*(1), 3–17.

Barnes, C & Mercer, G (1997) Breaking the mould? An introduction to doing disability research. In C Barnes & G Mercer (eds) *Doing Disability Research* (pp. 1–4). Leeds: The Disability Press, University of Leeds.

Bartunek, JM (1993) Scholarly dialogues and participatory action research. *Human Relations, 46*(10), 1221–33.

Beresford, P (2002) User involvement in research and evaluation: Liberation or regulation? *Social Policy and Society, 1*(2), 95–105.

Beresford, P (2003) *It's Our Lives: A short theory of knowledge, distance and experience*. London: OSP for Citizens Press, in Association with Shaping Our Lives.

Beresford, P & Evans, C (1999) Research note: Research and empowerment. *British Journal of Social Work, 29*(5), 671–7.

Beresford, P & Wallcraft, J (1997) Psychiatric system survivors and emancipatory research: Issues, overlaps and differences. In C Barnes & G Mercer (eds) *Doing Disability Research* (pp. 67–87). Leeds: The Disability Press, University of Leeds.

Braye, S (2000) Participation and involvement in social care: An overview. In H Kemshall & R Littlechild (eds) *User Involvement and Participation in Social Care: Research informing practice* (pp. 9–28). London: Jessica Kingsley Publishers.

Brown, LD & Tandon, R (1983) Ideology and political economy in inquiry: Action research and participatory research. *Journal of Applied Behavioral Sciences, 119*(3), 277–94.

Campbell, P (1996) The history of the user movement in the United Kingdom. In T Heller (ed) *Mental Health Matters: A reader* (pp. 218–25). Basingstoke: Macmillan.

Cornwall, A & Jewkes, R (1995) What is participatory research? *Social Science and Medicine, 41*(11), 1667–76.

Department of Health (2002) *Strategic Reviews of Research and Development: Mental health main report*. London: Department of Health.

Elden, M & Chisolm, R (1993) Emerging varieties of action research: Introduction to the special issue. *Human Relations, 46*(2), 121–41.

Faulkner, A (2004) *The Ethics of Survivor Research: Guidelines for the ethical conduct of research carried out by mental health service users and survivors.* Bristol: Policy Press, in association with the Joseph Rowntree Foundation.

Faulkner, A & Layzell, S (2000) *Strategies for Living: A report of user-led research into people's strategies for living with mental distress.* London: Mental Health Foundation.

Foucault, M (1967) *Madness and Civilisation: A history of insanity in the age of reason* (trans, R Howard). London: Tavistock.

Haggerty, J, Reid, R, Freeman, G, Starfield, B, Adair, C & McKendry, R (2003) Continuity of care: A multidisciplinary review. *British Medical Journal, 327,* 1219–21.

Lindow, V (2001) Survivor research. In C Newnes, G Holmes & C Dunn (eds) *This is Madness Too: Critical perspectives on mental health services* (pp. 135–46). Ross-on-Wye: PCCS Books.

Minkler, M & Wallerstein, N (2003) *Community-Based Participatory Research for Health.* San Francisco: Jossey-Bass.

Nicholls, V, Wright, S, Waters, R & Wells, S (2003) *Surviving User-Led Research: Reflections on supporting user-led research projects.* London: Mental Health Foundation.

Oliver, M (1992) Changing the social relations of research production. *Disability, Handicap and Society, 7*(2), 101–15.

Oliver, M (1997) Emancipatory research: Realistic goal or impossible dream? In C Barnes & G Mercer (eds) *Doing Disability Research* (pp. 15–31) Leeds: Disability Press, University of Leeds.

Read, J & Reynolds, J (eds) (1996) *Speaking Our Minds: An anthology of personal experiences of mental distress and its consequences.* Basingstoke: Macmillan/Open University.

Rose, D (2001) *Users' Voices: The perspectives of mental health service users on community and hospital care.* London: Sainsbury Centre for Mental Health.

Rose, D (2003a) Collaborative research between users and professionals: Peaks and pitfalls. *Psychiatric Bulletin, 27,* 404–6.

Rose, D (2003b) Having a diagnosis is a qualification for the job. *BMJ, 326,* 1331.

Rose, D (2004) Telling different stories: User involvement in research. *Research, Policy and Planning, 22*(2), 23–30.

Shaw, I (2000) Just inquiry? Research and evaluation for service users. In H Kemshall & R Littlechild (eds) *User Involvement and Participation in Social Care: Research informing practice* (pp. 29–44). London: Jessica Kingsley.

Stone, E & Priestley, M (1996) Parasites, pawns and partners: Disability research and the role of non-disabled researchers. *British Journal of Sociology, 47*(4), 699–716.

Thornicroft, G, Rose, D, Huxley, P, Dale, G & Wykes, T (2002) What are the research priorities of mental health service users? *Journal of Mental Health, 11*(1), 1–5.

Thornicroft, G & Tansella, M (2005) Growing recognition of the importance of service user involvement in mental health service planning and evaluation. *Epidemiologia e Psichiatria Sociale, 14*(1), 1–3.

Turner, M & Beresford, P (2005) *User Controlled Research: Its meanings and potential.* Final report, Shaping Our Lives and the Centre for Citizen Participation, Brunel University, Eastleigh, INVOLVE.

Tyrer, P (2002) Research into health services needs a new approach. *Psychiatric Bulletin, 26,* 406–7.

Vernon, A (1997) Reflexivity: The dilemmas of researching from the inside. In C Barnes & G Mercer (eds) *Doing Disability Research* (pp. 158–75). Leeds: Disability Press, University of Leeds.

Wallcraft, J (1998a) *Healing Minds: A report on current research, policy and practice concerning the use of complementary and alternative therapies for a wide range of mental health problems.* London: Mental Health Foundation.

Wallcraft, J (1998b) Survivor-led research in human services: Challenging the dominant medical paradigm. In S Baldwin (ed) *Needs Assessment and Community Care: Clinical practice and policy making* (pp. 186–208). Oxford: Butterworth-Heinemann.

Wallcraft, J (2003) Service user-led research: Towards a model of empowerment. Mental Health Foundation online conference. London: Mental Health Foundation.

Wallcraft, J, Read, J & Sweeney, A (2003) *On Our Own Terms: Users and survivors of mental health services working together for support and change.* London: Sainsbury Centre for Mental Health.

CHAPTER 4

SURVIVOR-PRODUCED KNOWLEDGE

DIANA ROSE

INTRODUCTION

This chapter is about user involvement in research and how it produces alternative knowledge. I also address some of the criticisms we may expect from mainstream research in respect of this work, and how we might answer these criticisms. I will concentrate on 'user involvement' in research rather than 'user-led' research as most of my examples come from the unit in which I work – the Service User Research Enterprise (SURE) at the Institute of Psychiatry, King's College London. All the research projects that we carry out are jointly undertaken by user researchers and clinical academics and in that sense are 'collaborative'. This is not to criticise user-led research at all. It is because we see our role as intervening in and trying to shift mainstream psychiatric research and the practices that flow from it. User-led research, which has a broader remit, is also vital (Faulkner & Layzell, 2000). In the second, more theoretical part of the paper, the arguments apply to all kinds of user-focused research.

Michel Foucault, the French philosopher and historian of medicine, has argued that for three centuries psychiatry has constituted a 'monologue of reason *about* madness' (Foucault, 1967: xi, italics in original). This monologue, he continues, has silenced the voice of those designated mad by deeming them non-rational in contrast to the rationalist spirit of the Age of Enlightenment. It is from this spirit of Enlightenment that what we now call 'science' was born. It may be that we are witnessing the end of Enlightenment rationality as some postmodern sociologists have suggested (Lash, 1990). Perhaps psychiatric service users can be part of this as we find our voice and refuse to be silenced any longer. As Faulkner and Thomas (2002) have suggested, the voice of experience is breaking through the barriers of enforced silence, incarceration and compulsion. Increasingly, mental health service users and survivors are coming to be called 'experts by experience'. The National Institute for Mental Health in England (NIMHE) even has an 'experts by experience' group.

What does this mean for user involvement in research? For user-*led* research, it must mean exploring the experience of service users in their own terms and using the experience and the subjectivity of user researchers to do this. For collaborative research, it means this too, but it also means trying to open up a dialogue between user researchers and professional researchers to break open Foucault's monologue.

SOME EXAMPLES

I shall now give an example of user involvement in research, drawing on the work of SURE. The example shows how the involvement of user researchers produced 'different truths' concerning the topic under study. In this example, the collaborative process was relatively smooth, and so I shall also discuss occasions when it has been less so.

The example is from a review of consumers' perspectives on ECT (Rose, Wykes, Leese, Bindman & Fleischmann, 2003). This was commissioned by the Department of Health in England alongside a meta-analysis of trials of the effectiveness and safety of ECT (UK ECT Review Group, 2003). The two empirical researchers on the consumer project had themselves experienced ECT. I was one of them. The team also included a psychiatrist and a psychologist; their role was to help with the analysis and the write-up.

The review relied on existing materials: we did not gather any new information, for example in the form of interviews. We collected 26 articles written by clinical academics and nine authored by consumers or in collaboration with consumers. We also collected 139 'testimonies' or first-hand accounts of receiving ECT; most of these were in electronic form, for example from the internet.

The academic articles reported much higher levels of satisfaction with ECT than either the user-led research or the testimonies. The standard response to this is that the user-led research and the testimonies relied on biased sampling. However, because we had experienced the treatment and also experienced being in hospital and being interviewed as to whether this treatment had helped, it seemed to us that something else was going on. The academic articles that reported the highest levels of satisfaction had a very particular methodology. Satisfaction interviews were conducted as soon as treatment ended, or even during it, and the interviewer was the treating doctor who asked a few simple questions. From our own experience, we thought that under these circumstances, users would not want to complain or might not tell the truth in order either to avoid more treatments or simply to get rid of the doctor who was asking yet more questions! We therefore argued that these academic papers were overestimating user satisfaction with ECT. This use of our experience led to a 'different truth', in contrast to received psychiatric wisdom, being distilled from the material we had to hand. We also produced different results from the meta-analysis of trials.

The non-service user academics in our team helped with the analysis and the write-up. Another of our findings was that even where people signed a consent form for ECT, up to a third felt there was pressure to do so, and hence they did not freely choose to have the treatment. We had a lot of help from our academic colleagues with respect to mental health legislation and case law, and the psychiatric literature on 'perceived coercion'. This is therefore an example of successful collaboration in research.

Not all user involvement in research is so smooth. For example, there are many ways in which power differentials between clinical academics and user researchers can emerge to undercut collaboration. First, even if a user researcher has all the requisite degrees, he or she is unlikely to have the same career track record as a professional. Mental health problems themselves can interrupt careers, but there is also still discrimination and stigma that prevents people seeking or getting research posts. Second, and linked to this, there are salary and status differentials, so that even experienced user researchers in a collaborative project will be perceived as 'junior'. Some user researchers acting as consultants to research projects do not receive a salary at all. They receive small sums of money under 'permitted work' rules, despite substantial input. Finally, and most corrosively, is the overlaying of the user/professional research relationship by an implicit patient/ doctor *clinical* relationship. It is as if some collaborators are regarding user researchers through a double lens – once as a researcher, and secondly as somebody's (or a potential) patient. I have been in research meetings that suddenly felt like a ward round. This brings us back to Foucault's monologue. These kinds of power differentials can mean that the knowledge of the professor is seen as more rational and 'scientific' than that produced by user researchers. We do not just have 'different truths' but 'valid truths' and 'doubtful truths'.

CRITICISMS WE CAN ANTICIPATE

This brings me to criticisms that we can anticipate. Mainstream researchers are likely to criticise the kinds of knowledge that are based on, or influenced by, direct experience as 'subjective', 'biased' and as knowledge produced by people who are 'over-involved'. It will be said that we are too close to the subject and so cannot be objective, that we use methods such as participatory research that will never guarantee an unbiased approach, and that relying on one's own experience in the process of producing knowledge is a recipe for unscientific disaster.

These criticisms rest on a certain view of knowledge production. It is held that scientific knowledge is generated in an unbiased and objective way, and that the subjectivity of the scientist exerts no influence on the knowledge that is produced. Randomised controlled trials are held to be the apex of this method in medicine because there are no biases in the selection of subjects and the outcome measures have been tested for their reliability and validity.

We can question whether this image of science is an accurate reflection or more like a myth. Outcome measures always originate with a scientist or group of scientists, and so their individual and collective ideas are what produce these measures. There is little space to generate outcome measures from the user perspective. Reliability only means that results are replicable between individual investigators, which is hardly surprising as all will have been trained to use them in the same way. Validity is notoriously difficult to assess. The process of 'blinding', where the investigators are supposed not to be aware of who has had an intervention and who has not, always has pitfalls as both 'subject' and investigator can guess who falls into which class.

STANDPOINTS

It can be argued that mainstream research is not the universal rationality that Enlightenment thought promised, but that it comes from a particular standpoint. In psychiatry, that standpoint is the perspective of those who deliver services and treatments and who research them (usually the same people). If this is so, user-focused research is not biased and subjective but comes from a different standpoint – that of those who receive services and treatments.

The above is anathema to some mainstream researchers because it smacks of relativism. There is no 'universal knowledge' but only particular knowledges produced through different standpoints. Different standpoints produce 'different truths'.

The next step is how we evaluate these different truths. Are all equally valid? Is this really relativism? In my view, every piece of research needs to be judged against agreed and specific criteria but there is a general point. It is commonplace in the social sciences and in the philosophy of the social sciences to argue for a fundamental distinction between protocols for producing knowledge about the physical world and protocols for producing knowledge about the human world. It is said that the physical world is one of mechanism and of cause and effect, and that the human world is one of meaning and interpretation. This is over-simplifying but it will do for now.

Psychiatry deals in human matters. Should it not then pay attention to the worlds of meaning that its patients inhabit? Yet it regularly does not do this. The statistical methods used in randomised controlled trials were first used in agriculture to study crop rotation and were then transferred to the field of medicine. Diagnostic processes used in psychiatry attempt consistency with diagnostic processes used in physical medicine. Yet it has been shown that the much-sought-after reliability of diagnostic categories does not exist (Kutchins & Kirk, 1999) and that, ultimately, the categories were arrived at by committee. In this way, the thoughts and opinions of those who designed the diagnostic categories exert a fundamental influence.

I would not deny that there is a place for mainstream research, including randomised controlled trials. I would not take a drug that had not been subject to an RCT, and would demand that the trial was absolutely rigorous about side effects and withdrawal. However, the world is not made up of simple interventions like drugs, much though it might seem like this sometimes. Mainstream research in mental health recognises this when it speaks of 'complex interventions'. Yet the randomised controlled trial is still held to be the best way of assessing these interventions. User-focused research goes far beyond this. When we invoke experience we are invoking the world of meaning, which many argue is at the heart of the human condition. In that sense, the knowledge we produce may rest on stronger theoretical foundations than does knowledge that transfers the methods of the physical sciences into the human world.

EPISTEMOLOGY

We can learn here from feminist epistemology. Epistemology simply means protocols or theories for producing valid truths. Feminists such as Sandra Harding (1993) have argued that women have been marginalised from science. This is because Enlightenment thought rests on certain oppositions: reason/unreason, rational/ irrational, culture/nature, intellect/emotion. Science has elevated the first terms of these oppositions and, of course, these are attributes traditionally ascribed to men. By making male attributes the acme of science, women are excluded. But this is a sleight of hand, as it pretends that male attributes are the universal attributes of thought.

It seems to me that these oppositions also describe the power relations between psychiatrists and service users, probably more so than in the case of power relations between men and women. We are defined by our unreason or irrationality, and our closeness to brute nature, and are deemed to be overwhelmed by our emotions. Rationality and intellect are the province of those who help us and who do research 'into' our condition.

Of course, sometimes we *are* irrational and emotional. But this only matters if the rationalist/intellectual model of science is taken as the only and universal way of producing knowledge. We need to reclaim our voice. Doing this means critiquing a science that rests on a false universality, and producing our own knowledge based upon the meanings that we inhabit. We will not produce the same truths as mainstream research: that much is clear. However, there are two important points. The designated irrationality of mad people must not be allowed to downgrade the knowledge we produce. As feminist epistemologists have shown and I have already said, such downgrading rests on a false view of Enlightenment thought as universally true and of its epistemologies being the only way of producing valid truths. The second point applies mainly to collaborative research. We need to try and open up a dialogue with mainstream researchers. Much of what is written here would horrify them. But in specific projects, where we produce alternative knowledge, there is more room for negotiation and seeing where the lines of both agreement and fracture emerge.

Finally, to return to Foucault. The above arguments show how user researchers can be positioned as the bearers of unreason. And so if it is argued that science is the acme of rationality, what is the fate of knowledge produced by those deemed non-rational? The argument is a vicious circle and the place of the user researcher a contradiction in terms. I would argue that this is implicit in some of the criticisms of user research made by mainstream researchers, although it is never stated explicitly. Nevertheless, it should be something of which we are aware and which we ought to contest as an obstacle to the work we do.

CONCLUSION

In this chapter I have tried to give examples of the production of 'different truths' in the context of collaborative research between user researchers and clinical academics. I have also tried to show that all user-focused research will be subject to certain criticisms from the mainstream, and that these criticisms can be answered by paying attention to some theoretical arguments as well as defending the use of subjectivity and experience in producing knowledge from a user/survivor standpoint.

REFERENCES

Faulkner, A & Layzell, S (2000) *Strategies for Living: A report of user-led research into people's strategies for living with mental distress*. London: Mental Health Foundation.

Faulkner, A & Thomas, P (2002) User-led research and evidence-based medicine. *British Journal of Psychiatry, 180*, 1–3.

Foucault, M (1967) *Madness and Civilisation: A history of insanity in the age of reason* (trans, R Howard). London: Tavistock.

Harding, S (1993) Rethinking standpoint epistemology: What is strong objectivity? In L Alcoff & E Potter (eds) *Feminist Epistemologies* (pp. 67–99). London and New York: Routledge.

Kutchins, H & Kirk, SA (1999) *Making Us Crazy. DSM: The psychiatric bible and the creation of mental disorders*. London: Constable and Company.

Lash, S (1990) *The Sociology of Postmodernism*. London: Routledge.

Rose, D, Wykes, T, Leese, M, Bindman, J & Fleischmann, P (2003) Patients' perspectives on electroconvulsive therapy: Systematic review. *BMJ, 326*, 1363–6.

UK ECT Review Group (2003) Electroconvulsive therapy: Systematic review and meta-analysis of efficacy and safety in depressive disorders. *Lancet, 361*, 799–808.

DEVELOPING A SOCIAL MODEL OF MADNESS AND DISTRESS TO UNDERPIN SURVIVOR RESEARCH

PETER BERESFORD

INTRODUCTION

Survivor research can be seen as one expression of the emergence of and developing interest in service-user-controlled research. This is research that is initiated and owned by the people who have historically tended to be the subjects of research – whether as poor people, older people, disabled people, people with learning difficulties or, as here, mental health service users/survivors. The best known and probably most developed of these research approaches is emancipatory disability research. Study of user-controlled research has highlighted that terms like user-controlled, emancipatory and survivor research are sometimes used almost interchangeably as if they meant the same thing (Turner & Beresford, 2005).

THE SOCIAL MODEL OF DISABILITY

Yet there is one important difference between the mental health service user/survivor movement and disabled people's movement that has an important bearing here and has led to a significant difference in the nature of survivor and emancipatory disability research. It is essential to explore this. It is the development of the social model of disability.

The modern disabled people's movement, whose origins can be traced to the 1960s, has been based on and developed around a big idea that challenges and rejects traditional Western ways in which disability and disabled people have been understood and perceived. The disabled people's movement developed its own, alternative ways of interpreting the situation and experiences of disabled people, which provided a changed basis for responding to both. Its 'big idea', the social model of disability, has had a major impact on public policy and understanding in countries like the UK, leading to major new legislation, new support roles and new approaches to service provision (Barnes, 1991; Oliver, 1996).

The social model of disability draws a distinction between the (perceived) physical, sensory or intellectual *impairment* of the individual and *disability*, the disabling social response to people seen as impaired. It highlights the oppressive nature of the dominant social response to impairment, which excludes, segregates and stigmatises disabled people, creates barriers to their equality and participation, and discriminates against them, restricting their human and civil rights. Thus disabled people are 'disabled' because their perceived 'impairment' results routinely and institutionally in an oppressive and discriminatory response within society. This social approach to understanding has encouraged disabled people to highlight the problems they face as primarily a civil rights (rather than welfare) issue, although there is a keen and ongoing debate about the social model of disability (Barnes, Oliver & Barton, 2002; Corker & Shakespeare, 2002; Thomas, 2007). There is no doubt that the social model of disability has influenced public understanding of disability, as well as many disabled people's own perceptions of themselves. This last is important, because it has made it possible for disabled people to stop feeling 'guilty' about being disabled, as though it were their fault, and to stop thinking of themselves as a 'burden'.

It is important that any discussion like the present one, which approaches the social model of disability from a different perspective, guards against perpetuating a simplistic understanding of the model. It is essential to make clear the dynamic state of discussion about the social model of disability. Disabled people and the disabled movement have subjected it to considerable review and re-evaluation. This analysis has been both supportive and critical of the social model. It has questioned its capacity to address issues of difference in relation to gender, ethnicity, culture and sexuality. It has called into question the ability of the social model's advocates to address equally, and to interrelate, its twin focus on (perceived) impairment and disability, and on direct experience and social barriers. The social model of disability has been critiqued from feminist, cultural, postmodern and post-structural perspectives (Morris, 1996; Thomas, 2007).

However, two key statements can be made here about the social model of disability. First, it is widely accepted within the disabled people's movement, and has exerted a significant influence on the lives of countless disabled people as a result, developing a counter view to traditional, medicalised, individualised models of disability. Second, it has been crucial to the research of disabled people themselves. One of the foundations of emancipatory disability research is the social model of disability. Its advocates regularly identify it as a key characteristic of emancipatory disability research. Thus, instead of focusing on the individual deficiencies of disabled people and trying to find 'cures' for them, such research has been concerned with exploring the barriers they face (which may relate to both impairments and discrimination), and with finding ways of overcoming these consistent with what disabled people themselves want. Emancipatory disability research is therefore part of the process of securing disabled people's rights and challenging the oppression they face.

THE SITUATION FOR SURVIVOR RESEARCH

Survivor research hasn't had as clear a theoretical underpinning as this. This is because the survivor movement itself has not been based on a clear philosophical or value base that is the equivalent of the social model of disability (Beresford & Wallcraft, 1997). This does not mean that survivors have not had a range of key values informing their goals and activities. These have included principles of self-advocacy, participation, inclusion and a commitment to the inherent validity of mental health service users/survivors. But such values and beliefs have not been the equivalent of the explicit and ongoing social model developed by the disabled people's movement.

The reasons for this are not clear. They seem to be linked with two concerns that mental health service users/survivors appear to have. The first of these relates to challenging the underpinning medical model of 'mental illness', in which service users'/survivors' intellects are perceived as inherently 'defective' or 'pathological'. There is a fear that rejecting a medicalised, individual model of their situation and identity would lead to them being ruled out and discounted as simplistic and irrational (Campbell, 1996). The second relates to service users'/survivors' worries about signing up to any kind of monolithic theory or set of principles, for fear that these dominate and subordinate them, and demand an orthodoxy in the same way as professional psychiatric thinking has done for so long. There is a strong libertarian strand in much mental health service user/survivor thinking that resists this.

A further reason may be that the survivor movement, with some exceptions (for example, Mad Pride) has largely sought to work closely with the service system in partnership relationships, reliant on service system funding and trying to improve mainstream services, rather than operating in the more separatist, independent ways that have often characterised the disabled people's movement. For example, major thrusts of the disabled people's movement in relation to services have been to set up direct payment schemes, putting people in control of their own system of support and user-controlled services, both following from the social model of disability. The partnership approach developed by survivor organisations would clearly make it difficult to challenge prevailing thinking within the psychiatric system fundamentally.

The disabled people's movement was spurred on to develop the social model of disability because understandings of and responses to disability were predominantly individualistic, conceiving of the problem in terms of individual 'tragedy', dependence and inadequacy. The dominance of medicalised interpretations of 'mental health' issues and mental health service users/survivors have, if anything, been even stronger. It is important to highlight this issue and it is difficult to overemphasise it.

THE DOMINANCE OF A 'MENTAL ILLNESS' MODEL

Most people in the West, including, it should be said, most mental health service users, still seem primarily to understand madness and distress in terms of something being 'wrong' with them, of being 'ill', or as some sort of 'disorder'. This is not surprising. It is accepted in prevailing public, political, media, cultural and therapeutic understandings. This is how we have been taught, and it is still the main approach of most organisations working in this field. At the same time, mental health problems are not generally accepted as the same as other kinds of 'illness', so that good quality 'treatment' is not always seen as a priority, and allowances are not always made when people cannot function as they ordinarily might. Instead, mental health services have become a stigmatised area of low priority in public policy and political understanding.

It can come as a surprise, on careful scrutiny, to see just how little in essence mental health policy and practice have changed over the years. In the case of physical health, there has been a growing recognition of the importance of public health approaches, prevention, self-management and social factors. Yet the mental health field is still heavily reliant upon an individualised, medical model of 'mental illness'. Mental illness is still the dominating key concept in this field. This is still how issues are defined and shaped. It is an approach that focuses on and is framed in terms of:

- an emphasis on the inclusion of individuals in particular, medicalised diagnostic categories
- ideas of 'treatment', care and 'cure' for such illness
- medicalised responses to 'mental illness' which are still centred on medicalised roles, hospital provision, and admission for long-term problems
- 'treatments' consistent with a medical model that are predominantly based on drugs and mechanical treatments
- mental health legislation that is increasingly focused on the extension of restrictions to people's rights

The underlying approach remains essentially unchanged since the first half of the twentieth century. The big change in this period has been the shift from large institutions to major reliance, with new pharmaceutical discoveries, on drug therapy and smaller residential and day institutional settings. However, broader shifts in social understandings of social problems have had a limited impact on the core medical base of mental health policy and provision.

Instead, new groups and problems have been incorporated into such medicalised understanding as the influence of psychiatry has widened. These include children and young people with problems and (vulnerable) older people, and the problems of trauma, violence and sexual abuse. Social issues have been reframed as individual psychiatric problems. Policy and public attitudes are still significantly based on a view of mental distress as a form of individualised pathology. This has been reinforced by increased concerns recently about the potential 'dangerousness' of mental health service users, and a renewal of interest in biological, physiological and chemical causes of 'mental illness'.

THE RESULTANT PROBLEMS FOR SURVIVORS

All this has been despite the reality that this traditional psychiatric approach to mental and emotional distress does not have a good record of success, 'recovery' and reintegration for many service users. Instead, its negative associations with pathology and individual problems have encouraged the wide attribution of negative characteristics to mental health service users and encouraged their negative stereotyping, social exclusion and marginalisation. To sum up:

- the 'mental illness' framework for madness and distress does not seem to offer a workable basis for interpretation and effective responses to the issues it includes;
- it can make things worse for individuals and perpetuate their problems;
- the psychiatric system is frequently a negative experience for service users, and widespread abuse and neglect has regularly been identified within it;
- its inability to attract adequate funding means that services are frequently of poor quality, unreliable, inadequately accessible and sometimes unsafe;
- it has led to the association between mental health service users and dangerousness and perceived risk, although there is no evidence that this is true for the great majority;
- it has been associated with an over-reliance on chemical/pharmaceutical responses, which are not always carefully used and which have frequently been linked with negative 'side effects';
- the medical model routinely pathologises service users, leading to stigma and discrimination;
- it has struggled to address issues of difference and equal opportunities effectively, and in particular has failed to address issues of race equality among service users. Evidence repeatedly highlights the inferior treatment of members of black and minority ethnic service users in the psychiatric system.

EMERGING INTEREST IN SOCIAL APPROACHES

The fact that so far, for whatever reason, the mental health service user/survivor movement has not developed or widely adopted a social model of madness and distress comparable to the social model of disability has meant, first, that the dominant medical model has not yet been subjected to any major challenge, and, second, that there is not yet an alternative framework available to service users and others to reframe their thinking and activities. The massive expansion of user involvement in mental health services over the last 20 years has not in itself challenged this dominance of traditional medical thinking. Nor is there any consensus about these issues among service users as yet. This leaves an important gap, which can be seen to create problems both for the survivor movement and survivor research. It can be argued that neither as yet has clear philosophical underpinnings. Without these, it is not clear how service users/survivors can work out and focus on what goals they want to achieve, and identify the most effective strategies to achieve them. Given survivors' and their movement's limited resources, this is likely to pose particular problems.

Yet there has been some awareness of the social factors associated with madness and mental distress for some time. However, with the emphasis on individual illness, these have often been overlooked. Recently, though, there has been a rebirth of interest in social approaches to and understandings of madness and distress from both professionals and service users.

This interest is still early on in its development. In 2002–3, two conferences focusing on a social model of madness and distress were organised by Greater London Action on Disability. There was significant interest in these events from a wide range of service users/survivors. Over the same period, however, there has been the development of a parallel (professionalised) national discussion, convened by a new Social Perspectives Network. Contributions to this discussion have, so far, significantly come from professionals, and have been based on an understanding of 'social' that seeks to take account of social factors in explanation rather than reflecting the rights-based approach of the social model of disability (Duggan, with Cooper & Foster, 2002). This network has also been publicly described by the Department of Health's head of mental health legislation (responsible for taking forward the new Mental Health Bill with extended provisions for compulsion) as 'a network of professionals funded over two years to ensure a social care presence in the National Institute for Mental Health England (NIMHE)' (Sieff, 2003).

This seems to be some way away from some service users'/survivors' understanding of a social approach. At most, it represents a social approach only in the sense of taking account of broader factors contributing to people's distress in society. It does not necessarily challenge the dominant mental illness model, merely accepting the need to consider broader environmental relations, as well as individual personal causes.

TOWARDS A SOCIAL MODEL OF MADNESS AND DISTRESS

Discussion about social models among mental health service users/survivors is still at an early stage. The development of such thinking has also been encouraged in recent years by government attempts to further restrict the rights of mental health service users, by extending the compulsory powers of proposed new mental health legislation beyond the hospital 'into the community'. This has focused attention and interest on survivors' rights. Some key issues pertaining to a social model have been highlighted (Beresford, 2002). First, there is an interest among service users/survivors in a social model that is located within a framework of the social model of disability, but which would also have transformational implications for the social model of disability itself. It is important to remember this, since the social model of disability was not originally developed with issues relating to madness and distress being taken into account. Such a social model would highlight both issues of personal experience and social oppression.

There is an unwillingness among many survivors to see 'impairment' as an objective part of their identity or situation – they do not necessarily see their experience/perceptions as problematic – and so the discussion demands consideration of the socially constructed nature of 'impairment'. Such a model would also have to take account of the strong sense that many survivors have that their processing in the psychiatric system is related not only to them being seen as defective but also frequently dissident, non-conformist and different in their values from dominant societal values (Plumb, 1994, 1999). These are all issues for further and broader discussion among mental health service users/survivors. Such a social model of madness and distress would have the potential to take account of issues of individual difference and experience, and the negative social responses to them that exist in society, and to seek to address both of these and to take account of their complex interrelations. Parallels to this development can be seen in the way in which social understandings of disability, developed by the disabled people's movement, have profoundly and positively influenced disability policy and disabled people's lives.

TOWARDS A RIGHTS-BASED APPROACH TO MENTAL HEALTH

Such a social model of madness and distress, like the social model of disability before it, provides a basis both for developing survivor collective action, and for survivor research as part of such action. It provides a basis for a more holistic understanding and approach to madness and distress, and to being a mental health service user/survivor. For example, it highlights the barriers that restrict the rights of mental health service users, and the need to address these strategically as well as individually. Challenging social barriers emerges as a traditionally neglected but key task. The 2004 Social Exclusion Unit report on social exclusion and mental health represents the first official recognition in England of the importance of such barriers (Social Exclusion Unit, 2004). A social approach offers a powerful framework for pulling together the growing, but so far frequently ad hoc recognition of such barriers in mental health. These include barriers of:

- *stigma and negative stereotyping:* identified by mental health service users as a key obstacle to their well-being;
- *poverty and low income:* these continue to be the common condition of a majority of long-term mental health service users;
- *social isolation:* damaged and weakened social networks mean that many mental health service users have reduced social support, contacts and networks on which to rely;
- *institutionalised racism:* this includes its effects on the mental health of black and minority ethnic people, and its operation within the mental health system;
- *high levels of unemployment:* many mental health service users are denied a key route to a decent income, and to meaning and purpose in their lives;
- *relationship breakdown:* intimate and friendship relationships are undermined. This is encouraged by the lack of adequate and appropriate support that many service users and their loved ones have. Such relationships are identified by service users as central to their well-being and happiness.

Such barriers operate individually and collectively to perpetuate mental health service users' distress and social exclusion, and to undermine their opportunities to restore and maintain their well-being and social integration. Emerging government priorities and policies provide levers for challenging such barriers.

A PHILOSOPHICAL GROUNDING FOR SURVIVOR RESEARCH

This chapter has argued that research based on a social model of madness and distress is likely to have the capacity to prioritise issues such as the barriers facing mental health service users/survivors and ways of overcoming them, thus supporting the advancement of service users'/survivors' civil and human rights.

It is unlikely that undertaking survivor research that merely follows the dominant medical mental illness agenda will be particularly helpful for survivors in the long term. It is more likely to mirror traditional research priorities, focuses and preoccupations. There is no doubt that this is happening now to some extent when survivors do not have clear control over the research agendas to which they have to subscribe, for example, when they are located in non-survivor-controlled settings. Without a clear philosophical framework to guide it, survivor research may only identify and offer responses to an overly narrow range of individualised issues affecting mental health service users/survivors. If this risk is to be avoided, then it is important that research is undertaken using a clear value and theory base, which not only spells out the nature of its process, but also of its objectives. (And this needs to be at a more specific level than something like 'supporting the empowerment of survivors'.) The social model of disability has provided a cornerstone for disabled people's research to develop effectively in this way. It is not unreasonable to expect that the development of a social model of madness and distress could serve the same purpose for survivor research.

REFERENCES

Barnes, C (1991) *Disabled People in Britain and Discrimination*. London: Hurst and Co., in association with the British Council of Organisations of Disabled People.

Barnes, C, Oliver, M & Barton, L (eds) (2002) *Disability Studies Today*. Cambridge: Polity.

Beresford, P (2002) Thinking about 'mental health': Towards a social model. *Journal of Mental Health, 11*(6), 581–4.

Beresford, P & Wallcraft, J (1997) Psychiatric system survivors and emancipatory research: Issues, overlaps and differences. In C Barnes & G Mercer (eds) *Doing Disability Research* (pp. 67–87). Leeds: The Disability Press, University of Leeds.

Campbell, P (1996) The history of the user movement in the United Kingdom. In T Heller, J Reynolds, R Gomm, R Muston & S Pattison (eds) *Mental Health Matters: A reader* (pp. 218–25). Basingstoke: Macmillan/Open University.

Corker, M & Shakespeare, T (eds) (2002) *Disability/Postmodernity: Embodying disability theory*. London and New York: Continuum.

Duggan, M, with Cooper, A & Foster, J (2002) Modernising the social model in mental health: A discussion paper. Leeds: Social Perspectives Network, Topss (Training Organisation for the Personal Social Services) England.

Morris, J (1996) *Encounters with Strangers: Feminism and disability*. London: Women's Press.

Oliver, M (1996) *Understanding Disability*. Basingstoke: Macmillan.

Plumb, A (1994) Distress or Disability? A discussion document. Manchester: Greater Manchester Coalition of Disabled People.

Plumb, A (1999) New mental health legislation. A lifesaver? Changing paradigm and practice. *Social Work Education, 18*(4), 450–78.

Sieff, A (2003) The Mental Health Bill – The right prescription? Plenary presentation, Community Care Live, 21 May, London, Community Care.

Social Exclusion Unit (2004) *Mental Health and Social Exclusion*. London: Office of the Deputy Prime Minister, Social Exclusion Unit.

Thomas, C (2007) *Sociologies of Disability and Illness: Contested ideas in disability studies and Medical Sociology*. Basingstoke: Palgrave Macmillan.

Turner, M & Beresford, P (2005) *User Controlled Research: Its meanings and potential*. Final report, Shaping Our Lives and the Centre for Citizen Participation, Brunel University, Eastleigh, INVOLVE.

SURVIVOR RESEARCH
ETHICS APPROVAL AND ETHICAL PRACTICE

ALISON FAULKNER

AND

DEBBIE TALLIS

PART ONE: ALISON FAULKNER
ETHICAL PRACTICE

As this book demonstrates, there has been a considerable increase in both local and national research projects and initiatives involving (or led by) mental health service users and survivors. The Mental Health Foundation's Strategies for Living programme was one such initiative, providing support and training to a number of small user-led projects across the UK from 1997 to 2004–5. The Sainsbury Centre for Mental Health has been the base for the User-Focused Monitoring (UFM) network for some years now, having developed a methodology in UFM that could be replicated and developed for local service needs. Shaping Our Lives has developed a more distinctly user-controlled model for social care research. And the last few years has also seen the successful establishment of SURE (the Service User Research Enterprise) at the Institute of Psychiatry, King's College London.

There are many more such projects and initiatives across the UK, from SURF (Service User Research Forum) in Bristol to Suresearch in Birmingham and Direct Impact in Wakefield. I have been involved in a number of projects in Leeds, including the user-led evaluation of a crisis service, and have been working with the Academic Unit of Psychiatry at the University of Leeds to engage service users and carers in research through running a series of seminars. My recent involvement in interviewing for service user interviewer posts revealed to me the extent and diversity of our experience and expertise as service users, activists, researchers and interviewers.

All of this is very encouraging and has, to some extent, been supported by government policy. For example, the Department of Health Research Governance Framework for Health and Social Care, originally published in 2001 (Department of Health, 2001) and revised in 2005 (Department of Health, 2005), explicitly encourages consumer involvement in all stages of the research process.

THE ETHICS OF SURVIVOR RESEARCH

With all of this activity taking place, it has been difficult to stop and reflect on what we – as service users or survivors – mean by good practice principles and practices, and to explore what has been developed by different groups and projects. This was the concern of Viv Lindow, mental health activist and survivor researcher, when she put her proposal to the Joseph Rowntree Foundation in 2002. I was fortunate enough to inherit her project when she decided that she was unable to carry it out. The aim of the project was to develop an accessible manual on ethical practice for researchers, trainers and interviewers working from the perspective of mental health service users and survivors.

One of the issues that emerged at an early stage was the clear distinction to be made between 'ethical practice' and 'ethics approval'. Researchers working within the health and social care context often need to gain approval from a Research Ethics Committee (REC) before they can proceed to approach service users to take part in their research. This is universally regarded as a bureaucratic hoop for researchers to jump through, and tends to focus on the protection of research participants. As lead researcher, you need to demonstrate, amongst other things, that you have considered all of the potential risks to participants, and have clear procedures in place for obtaining informed consent and maintaining confidentiality. Debbie Tallis describes one perspective on this process below.

In contrast to this formal process, I am interested in exploring what principles and practices those of us involved in doing survivor research have developed. Were we all engaged in difficult discussions about the limits to confidentiality? The importance of providing feedback to participants? The provision of clear and accessible information to participants at all stages of the research? The respectful consideration of how best to interview people? The project funded by the Joseph Rowntree Foundation gave me the opportunity to find out more.

The project employed a combination of methods: interviews and focus groups carried out around the UK, a literature review, and questionnaires distributed to a sample of survivor researchers. The idea was to learn from practical experience, as well as to incorporate elements of existing research codes of practice developed by various professional groups, where we believed these to be appropriate. The project had a reference group of survivor researchers convened from people with differing perspectives to guide the consultation process.

The findings demonstrate the considerable care and concern shown by service user and survivor researchers in undertaking research. Many based their current practice on their own experiences of 'being researched' and treated as research fodder without the respect for others that they would now advocate. It was clear also that discussion of 'ethical practice' extended far more widely than the issues considered by RECs. The latter were seen as a hurdle to be jumped over, but not a source of useful guidance for ethical practice in research.

The issues covered in the guidelines (Faulkner, 2004) cover the research process in a broadly chronological order, with topics of relevance for both survivor researchers and for research participants. The guidelines consist of the following sections:

1. underlying principles
2. planning and design
3. recruitment and involvement
4. training, support and supervision
5. involving participants
6. analysis and feedback
7. dissemination and implementation
8. Research Ethics Committees

ETHICAL RESEARCH: THE FINDINGS

The following section summarises the themes that emerged from the research, complemented by quotations from service user and survivor researchers.

> Survivor research should attempt to counter the stigma and discrimination experienced by survivors in society.

Firstly, we explored the underlying principles inherent in survivor research, and found that survivors valued principles of clarity and transparency, respect and equal opportunities, with a commitment to change and opportunities for empowerment.

> The more control you have over research, the more chance it will be empowering and you will find you have benefited. If you don't have any control, then the more chance you will find it harmful.

There was general agreement that service users should be involved from the start of a research project, and that there should be adequate funding for involvement and a flexible approach to allow for the involvement of people subject to periods of distress or illness.

> There needs to be some more flexibility but on the other hand we want to be able to work properly. That takes some help and training and that bit of extra support.

Most people felt that, whilst upholding standards of ethics and quality, research should aim to be inclusive, giving everyone a role in the process, with some open negotiation taking place around particular skills.

> We like to involve as many people as possible – be inclusive, find a role for anybody, but that does need time and money.

There were strong feelings that payment should be available to all those who take part, except where people in receipt of benefits might find themselves compromised, or people choose not to receive payment. There should also be other incentives where possible; for example, people should be offered training, support and supervision with adequate account taken of researcher safety.

> One of the criteria we came up with is that all those involved in a project, including the coordinator, should have access to support and supervision and this should be set up at the beginning.

Where research participants are concerned, informed consent and confidentiality are of paramount concern: the guidelines explore these issues in some depth. Support should also be offered or available to participants in the event of distress, and payments should be made where feasible. There were strong feelings that feedback should be given to all participants in the research:

> It's important because in my experience you never used to get any feedback and it really gets to you and so you never wanted to take part any more ... you have a duty to share the results back.

Service users should be engaged fully in the analysis and report writing, and dissemination of the research should take account of all of the groups or stakeholders involved in the research. Finally, all reasonable attempts should be made to ensure that the results of the research are implemented. People felt strongly that survivor research should set out with a commitment to change based on research findings. After all:

> What is the point of doing research if it's not implementable?

PROTECTION FROM HARM

Historically, Research Ethics Committees were developed in order to protect patients from research that might be harmful to them in a variety of ways. 'Protection from harm' is a principle behind most professional research guidelines. It became clear from the discussions that took place for these guidelines that most people regarded ethical practice in research as quite distinct from the need to gain ethical approval from RECs, hence the breadth of issues covered. In this project, it was of concern to some people that protecting mental health service users from harm can at times be patronising and inappropriate. As a couple of people said, people can be distressed by an interview and can nevertheless wish to continue and to contribute. Distress is not necessarily equivalent to harm:

> In a palliative care project people got upset but it was positive for them. Becoming distressed is not the same as harm. There must be routes for follow-up. It's not an excuse for going round upsetting people ...

Survivor researchers were sensitive to the needs of interviewees for support, both during and after a distressing interview, but also reflected on the need for people to tell their story. So often, people do not listen to those experiencing mental health problems, and their stories are not given due respect. The consultation for these guidelines demonstrated that many people valued the role of research in enabling service users and survivors to tell their own stories in their own words.

POWER AND EMPOWERMENT

To be a patient is to be powerless, and to be a research subject is to be doubly so. Many of the principles and practices reflected here are about service users and survivors taking back some power and doing some of the thinking and theorising for ourselves. To be in the position of researcher is to take on some power, and yet there may be people who are powerless in the relationship if the research is being done on or to others. Again, some of these principles and practices aim to adjust that relationship, to include more people within the thinking and doing that constitutes research, and to give participants more rights within an overall framework that is more respectful and ultimately more empowering.

However, there may well be different levels of power within different manifestations of user/survivor research, depending on who is funding and managing the research. This will influence the degree to which user/survivor researchers can determine the direction of the research and the way in which it can be carried out.

THE ETHICS OF SURVIVOR RESEARCH: IN PRACTICE

The guidelines – *The Ethics of Survivor Research* (Faulkner, 2004) – are based on research and the experience and expertise of many other survivor and professional research groups and organisations. They are intended to present helpful guidance on issues to be considered prior to the design and conduct of any survivor research project or research training programme. In some cases, a particular view is given by the author on behalf of the research undertaken; in other cases, it is made clear that the issue in question needs to be discussed and decided upon by the research team or individual researcher(s) involved.

The primary audience when developing the guidelines comprised service user/ survivor researchers, trainers and interviewers actively engaged in research over which they had some influence or control. However, the guidelines may also be useful for service users involved in an academic research project where they and their co-workers are seeking some good practice guidance. The guidelines may also provide useful information and ideas for academic (non-survivor) researchers looking to involve service users in their research, for Research Ethics Committees, and for NHS Research and Development Committees.

It is hoped that the guidelines form part of the overall movement towards gaining a greater say in what happens in research and what kind of research happens:

> Undertaking emancipatory research has been part of the survivor movement's project of survivors speaking and acting for themselves; improving their lives and liberating themselves from an oppressive psychiatric system; of changing and equalising relationships between research and research subjects; and developing survivors' own knowledge collectively. (Beresford & Wallcraft, 1997: 77)

PART TWO: DEBBIE TALLIS
ETHICS COMMITTEES – FROM AN INDIVIDUAL PERSPECTIVE

It is good to have ethics committees to protect people from any potential harm that research may pose. But is the process that an ethics committee goes through fair for all who wish to carry out research? The following describes my experience of the journey to carry out research, which involved applications to ethics committees.

THE SCIENTIFIC BIAS OF ETHICS COMMITTEES

I have had to go through RECs several times. The first time was easy: I suppose I was naive in research, and so the 'power' that such committees held was not impressed upon me. I had no problem getting my research approved at that time, about fourteen years ago. It was to take blood samples from people, to stick their hand in a bucket of iced water, and then to take another blood sample: how could this have any negative effect on anyone? Looking back, I suppose that because this research – which was for my Masters dissertation – was able to measure something in a so-called scientific manner, there would have been no reason why the local ethics committee would not have accepted it.

At the time, I was working as a research psychologist in a hospital setting amongst medical staff and researchers. I was not aware that getting ethical approval could be difficult, although I was aware that patient interests were paramount. The ethics committee to which I had to apply was hospital based and made up mostly of medics. The form that had to be completed asked many questions, such as whether it was a randomised controlled trial (RCT – this is usually used to measure the effectiveness of different treatments); whether there would be any administration of drugs or taking of bodily fluids; and the extent to which my research would be of value to the scientific community. Again, I was not fazed by this, as I believed that what I wanted to do was of great scientific value and that the people who volunteered to take part would believe so too!

Ten years later when I started my doctorate, going through ethics committees was a very different story. My research had changed significantly, in that I wanted to interview people in secure hospitals to find out how they felt about having a psychiatric label. The forms that had to be filled out were written in a way that implied you would be doing a randomised controlled trial (one which is objective and measurable ['quantitative'], as opposed to 'qualitative' [subjective, and exploring the thoughts, feelings and experiences of individuals]). The forms were not in any way 'user friendly', and did not seem to be designed for research that might want to 'measure' people's thoughts and feelings around something they had experienced. Just reading the forms gave me the impression of excluding many people who may want to carry out research. The process of applying to gain ethical permission was not in a user-friendly format at all.

USER/SURVIVOR RESEARCH AND ETHICS COMMITTEES

This does not mean that I do not believe that we need ethics committees *and procedures*, but I think that they need to come more into line with real people and acknowledge that 'real' people can do – and do do – research! For example, the National Service Framework for Mental Health (Department of Health, 1999) states: 'The External Reference Group recommended that people with mental health problems should be able to expect that services will ... involve service users and their carers in planning and delivery of care' (p. 4).

So, why aren't things changing? In an article on his experience of being part of a research project, Burke (2002) discusses the effect of the proposal going through a local Ethics Committee and states that 'the end result seems to have turned a valuable, well overdue and relatively simple project into a convoluted, and unnecessarily complicated piece of research' (p. 6). Burke is describing a project in which mental health service users were trained to do research through a university, but were subjected to having to get permission from their care coordinators before they were allowed by the ethics committee to take part in the research. Would this happen if someone had physical disease, I wonder? Would an ethics committee ask someone who had multiple sclerosis, for example, to get permission from their consultant to take part in interviewing other people with the same disorder?

The Department of Health consulted from September to December 2004 on an *Ethics Review of Social Care Research* (Department of Health, 2004), which followed on from the *Research Governance Framework for Health and Social Care* (Department of Health, 2001). This framework aims to protect the public and improve research quality, but as Howarth and Kneafsey (2005: 675) state, a number of complex issues have arisen. They cite Smith (2000, in Howarth and Kneafsey, 2005), however, as suggesting that the governance 'could potentially stifle research innovation'. One organisation that responded to the 2004 consultation, INVOLVE (which 'promot[es] public involvement in NHS, public health and social care research'), commented that:

> we are aware of a number of research proposals which we regarded as having good quality involvement that have encountered difficulties because of the perceptions of Research Ethics Committees (RECs) as to the vulnerability and capability of the active participants. What those committees have probably regarded as appropriate protective considerations have often been seen by those who are the subject of ethic review decisions as being overly paternalistic, ill informed, and disempowering. (INVOLVE, 2004)

Tschudin (2001) concurs with INVOLVE when he writes about European experiences of ethics committees as 'perhaps creating a climate of paternalism that has tended to exclude other views and other frameworks' (p. 44). This seems to be the problem at present, in that the majority of professionals on ethics committees are medical rather than experts in social care. Perhaps ethics committees should get more users of services on board? As most individuals are users and/or carers in some form, then this could give another dimension to what exists at present. There has been user representation on an ethics committee in London, but the people involved found it hard to be heard at times. This is a start, but we need to have more user voices on these committees, so that social research can be carried out and seen as equally valid as that which is based on randomised controlled trials.

My latest experience of discussing a project with members of an ethics committee along with two of my colleagues turned out to be a very fraught one. The lay person on the committee was a nurse, and so one would expect that perhaps she would have an understanding of mental health. However, it was this person who said that we would need the researchers who did the training with the user researchers to be present when they (the user researcher) interviewed other people with mental health problems 'in case there was a problem and someone became ill'. Again, I doubt that this would happen if someone had a physical illness. The training of user researchers had indeed discussed the issue of what to do if either the participant was too unwell to take part or that they themselves were unwell – the decision was that the interview would not go ahead.

I believe that what ethics committees do not realise is that people who have experienced emotional distress quite often find it cathartic to talk about their experiences. If this is in the form of being interviewed with their permission, then I do not see it as a problem. I cannot see that this is a risk, or that the participant might be likely to sue the hospital trust for allowing this form of research to take place. Part of the research process is to make sure that there is backup for those who take part in the study as well as for those working as researchers. Jacomb, Jorm, Rodgers et al. (1999) found, following a mental health survey, that:

> despite the sensitive nature of many of the questions, only a small percentage of respondents reported distress, while many found that the questionnaire had made them feel good about themselves. This is important information to present to Institutional Ethics Committees and to future participants in such studies. (p. 80)

Maybe I ought to send these results to the local ethics committee with which I was involved?

REFERENCES

Beresford, P & Wallcraft, J (1997) Psychiatric system survivors and emancipatory research: Issues, overlaps and differences. In C Barnes & G Mercer (eds) *Doing Disability Research* (pp. 67–87). Leeds: The Disability Press, University of Leeds.

Burke, M (2002) A service user/researcher's experience with an ethics committee. *Consumers in NHS Research Support Unit News*, Spring.

Department of Health (1999) *National Service Framework for Mental Health. Modern Standards and Service Models.* London: Department of Health.

Department of Health (2001) *Research Governance Framework for Health and Social Care.* London: Department of Health.

Department of Health (2004) *Ethics Review of Social Care Research: Options appraisal and guidelines. Public consultation 1 September 2004 to December 31 2004.* London: Department of Health.

Department of Health (2005) *Research Governance Framework for Health and Social Care* (2nd edn). London: Department of Health.

Faulkner, A (2004) *The Ethics of Survivor Research: Guidelines for the ethical conduct of research carried out by mental health service users and survivors.* Bristol: Policy Press, in association with the Joseph Rowntree Foundation. (Also available online: http://www.jrf.org.uk/bookshop/eBooks/1861346662.pdf)

Howarth, ML & Kneafsey, R (2005) The impact of research governance in healthcare and higher education organizations. *Journal of Advanced Nursing, 49*(6), 675–83.

INVOLVE (2004) *Ethics Review in Social Care Research: Option appraisal and guidelines by Jan Pahl: a response from INVOLVE.* Available from http://www.invo.org.uk/pdfs/INVOLVE_response_to_DH_consultation_on_social_care_ethics_review_December_2004.pdf (Accessed 17 December 2008).

Jacomb, PA, Jorm, AF, Rodgers, B, Korten, AE, Henderson, AS & Cristensen, H (1999) Emotional response of participants to a mental health survey. *Social Psychiatry and Psychiatric Epidemiology, 34*(2), 80–4.

Tschudin, V (2001) European experiences of ethics committees. *Nursing Ethics, 8*(2), 142–51.

IDENTITY ISSUES IN MENTAL HEALTH RESEARCH

KARAN ESSIEN

Identity is important for mental health, as it bestows upon the bearer a sense of belonging with others who share similar experiences. Service users retain the right to describe themselves and their problems in a system that has continuously undermined and labelled their mental health status as being different from the norm.

This chapter looks at identity issues with women in the Rainbow Nation study, which was a user-led research project that aimed to understand and raise awareness of black African and African Caribbean women's experiences of mental distress. (The study was supported by the Mental Health Foundation's Strategies for Living programme.) The women present examples of how their different experiences of mental distress affected their lives, and how they continue to struggle as service users. Within the interview, the participants identified with the researcher on a personal and a social level, as black women in mental distress within a mental health system that keeps them oppressed.

The researcher felt that being open about her own ethnicity, gender and service user status would equalise the power imbalance in the interviews and lead to more interesting discussions with the women. Furthermore, the women disclosed that their ethnicity was more significant than their service user identity, which may indicate why black and minority ethnic people in mental distress are under-represented in the user movement.

WHAT IS IDENTITY?

Our identity is the set of personal and behavioural characteristics by which we identify ourselves as belonging to a social group. It is formed first within the family, or substitute family, and later on through our life experiences. Our identity, therefore, is socially constructed, and is understood to be based on shared experiences and relationships with other people whom the individual identifies as belonging to the same group and sharing the same practices. In any individual several identities overlap, and what is important to one person may not be to another.

In a postmodern world, we no longer have to conform as strictly to traditional modernist identities, such as those we are assigned at birth. Identities are not as rigid as they used to be. They are more fluid than fixed, and can be bought through the accumulation of consumer products. Identities are less about geography and more about meeting people through networks such as interest and user groups. How we react to our situations is dependent upon many factors, including how we see ourselves in this world.

SERVICE USER IDENTITY

Mental ill health is defined by professionals on the basis of the medical construction of illness, which tends to pathologise individuals. They define certain behaviours as problems that can be treated in much the same way as physical illnesses. Williams (1999) suggests, however, that rather than being an illness, 'behaviours defined as symptoms and disorders are best understood as creative responses to difficult personal and social histories, rooted in a person's experience of oppression' (p. 31). Mental illness can be seen as a stigmatising label, as 'other' and as not belonging to the norm. One of the defining features of the user movement has been the belief in the right of users/survivors to identify themselves on their own terms. My definition of a service user is someone who has experience of mental distress and identifies with others who have similar experiences of mental health services, whether they are in the voluntary, private or statutory sector.

Service users with mental health problems are as diverse as other social groups in society. However, group identity is not as straightforward as it may seem. Some service users choose not to be recognised as having mental health problems because of stigma, the fear of isolation, and the negative consequences these can have on employment, housing and personal relationships:

> Within our community, and when I say 'our community', in the black African or black Caribbean community, they do not mm, see depression as a mental health [problem] they don't see it and they do deny it when it actually happen to them because it is seen as something that is no good. (Essien, 2003b)

Yet, some service users embrace this label and become active members of user groups. These service users are predominantly white, perhaps because it is easier to 'come out' as a service user and it is less detrimental than it is to experience racism, which is more pervasive.

Many service users meet collectively through these shared experiences, in user or action groups, in settings such as Mind organisations where group identity based on service user involvement is formed. Some groups may, for example, raise awareness about issues affecting service users such as medication or campaigning for rights under the Mental Health Act. They may be seen as actively attempting to redress the balance of negativity and discrimination towards service users. Some mental health service users may not define themselves as service users, and may prefer to address themselves as survivors of the mental health system.

BLACK AND MINORITY ETHNIC (BME) IDENTITY

Mental health service users groups are just one part of the mental health culture fighting for the right to identify themselves on their own terms. BME communities in mental distress also feel that their needs are not being addressed. They seek reparation against injustices relating to racism within Western psychiatry, and there is evidence that they receive more coercive treatment than their white counterparts (Keating, Robertson, McCulloch & Francis, 2002). They may not, first and foremost, want to identify as service users, because their ethnic identity may be more important to them. Some BME organisations, such as Diverse Minds, have formed alongside the main mental health organisations, and aim to raise the profile of people in mental distress from BME communities.

Our identity is an important element of self-esteem and positive mental health, and for black people it can serve to externalise stress, and can provide a sense of meaning, history and group affiliation (Keating et al., 2002).

Because of the way [black people] have been treated in this society. They say: Have I been treated this way simply because of my skin colour? [Racism] actually contributes to mental health problems and depression and leads to many people having low self-esteem. (Essien, 2003b)

Many BME communities are identified by others on the basis of physical appearance, namely skin tone. Generally speaking, many BME women are described as 'black', but there is a wide range of women subsumed within this category: they are by no means a homogeneous group, as suggested by the research literature on the mental health status of the black population in Britain. As Rassool (1998: 188) has argued, 'Black identities are not linear constructions but rather they reflect a tapestry of interwoven life experiences having their origins within different socio-historical epochs.' In the Rainbow Nation study, women described themselves as black British, mixed parentage, African and African Caribbean: their black identities are not fixed. However, politically they did see themselves as belonging to one 'black' social group.

My ethnic identity was perceived to be along similar lines to the women in the study. One woman who identified with me said: 'We are from the same place, the same blood' (Essien, 2003b). I specifically targeted black African and African Caribbean women in a city where the black African and African Caribbean population is in the minority within a larger minority ethnic population. Whereas the larger minority community had specific mental health support groups, the black population had no explicit services to meet their basic needs; they used services designed with the majority population in mind. Women in general have specific needs within the mental health system, and black women have unmet needs, but little has been achieved in the recent past to accommodate their requirements.

FEMINIST PERSPECTIVES

Feminist researchers have politically tried to meet the needs of women in different social and political spheres. A basic tenet of feminist research is the importance of listening to women's voices. Feminist research focuses on gender issues and how these affect women. It differs from traditional male-dominated research in that it is research conducted by and for women, similar in principle to user-led research. Some feminist researchers are recognised to have 'sided' with marginalised groups like women and children (Warner, 2001). My stance is similar, because I believe the researcher is not neutral in the research process. She brings to the research her own impressions of life and multifaceted experiences, and needs to be aware of her cultural background and how this might influence the perceptions of those being interviewed. With my experiences of being an inpatient, of racism, abuse, gender discrimination, and with my explicit feminist and user/survivor stance, I thought that I would be able understand the women better. Feminist researchers realised that the best way to learn more about how women view themselves in the world was through interviewing them about their lives. Semi-structured interviews are used as a way to allow social interaction between both researcher and participant.

There are gender differences in the distribution of mental distress in both the population as a whole and those in black communities. Indeed, sexual abuse is more prevalent in women, and it is known that it has affected a large percentage of women in psychiatric hospitals. Again, some feminist researchers have taken these issues on board for women generally, but it has been left largely to black feminist researchers to conduct research on black women's circumstances. Some research has focused on inequalities in health and social care for black women, and how these disparities may be reversed.

THE SOCIAL CONSTRUCTION OF BLACK WOMEN

The social construction of black women in mental distress is based on Western models of psychiatry and Eurocentric preconceptions and pre-existing ideas of black people in general. As a result, these myths and stereotypes still exist in the minds of some professionals. This leads to inappropriate care and treatment, and to black women's needs not being addressed. The impact these presumed identities have on black women affects their self-esteem and the way they present to others. For example, one woman said:

> They look down on you because you are a black person, they look down on you because you are a woman ... they have already judged you before they even know you. That you can't do it, no matter how good you are at work there is a label there that being a black person that actually subjects you to a life sentence of not being able to do it. So the discrimination is still there, it's still going on, and when you are a woman you face double discrimination and double oppression. (Essien, 2003b)

This participant viewed her black cultural identity as being more important than her gender and mental health identity, which highlights that while we may be able to disguise some aspects of our personhood, for example our sexuality and our mental health status, it is not possible for women from BME communities to hide their 'blackness'. BME women are physically much more visible than women in white communities, and those with mental health problems suffer double discrimination. This is one reason why policies concerning social inclusion within BME communities have been prominent of late in the mental health arena.

> The needs of black African or African Caribbean are not important but we are part of this community and I'm a citizen of this country, my children are citizens of this country, so we deserve a better service, as other people are going through. So we want the same service, a quality service, a service that is culturally aware, that is very sensitive, a friendly environment. (Essien, 2003a: 27)

THE IMPORTANCE OF RESEARCH WITH BLACK WOMEN

Black women in mental distress often have complex problems, owing to their life experiences and circumstances prior to the onset of their mental distress. They are among one of the most socially excluded groups in society, and many black women are potentially marginalised in mental health care and treatment (Essien, 2003a).

In particular, black African and African Caribbean women are over-represented in the mental health system, but they are invisible: when the mental health concerns of black people are researched, it usually means black men, and when the mental health of women is researched, it generally means white women. They face discrimination both within their communities and wider society, and are regarded as second-class citizens.

Black women are often not consulted about their mental health needs despite their susceptibility to mental distress. Several studies indicate that people living in inner cities have higher levels of mental health problems (Thornicroft, 1991) owing to adverse circumstances such as poverty, unemployment and bad housing. Women from these communities see their position in society mirrored in the mental health system, and feel socially excluded from mental health services. It is important that any research conducted with these women must acknowledge these inequalities and aim to enhance empowerment.

POWER RELATIONSHIPS IN THE INTERVIEWS

Black women are often seen as lacking power within research. They are under-represented as researchers and as participants. There is generally an imbalance of power between the researcher and the participants that can affect the outcome of the study, but there are countless ways of enhancing the balance of power. For example, actively encouraging black women to participate in the research and, indeed, to take the lead in the interview situation and direct the flow of discussion to areas within which they feel comfortable. It is generally assumed in research that the researcher has ultimate power within the interview relationship, but in this user-led research the service users were actively involved in deciding on the nature of the topic studied from its inception through to its end. As the user researcher, I ultimately decided on the research topic and guided the questions in a certain direction, but, at the same time, the participants had their say in discussing the issues important to them. For example, two women talked about the impact of racism on their lives. The researcher had not considered racism as being one of the most important issues affecting their mental health, but, because it emerged in this way, subsequent interviews were expanded to accommodate this issue.

Some women stated that the language used in the mental health field served to keep them marginalised. The language in the interviews was informal, and the intention was not to oppress the women in any way. If there were differences, these were discussed and brought out into the open. This occurred on one occasion when a young participant was trying to tell me about the types of services she received without divulging too much personal information. I tried to be sympathetic and supportive and let her know that she did not have to tell me anything about it as it was clearly painful. Some participants even saw the researcher as an ambassador for black women who had the power to ensure their issues were addressed; they considered their cultural needs were being neglected by the health and social care sectors. One woman stated:

> Because we look across the district there is nobody working on the aetiology of black African or black Caribbean ... You know, I am very happy about the research you are doing because there is a very big gap in the service provision [for black women] and those people who have been funded for mental health they don't actually serve our needs. (Essien, 2003b)

LIMITATIONS OF IDENTIFICATION

However, I was wary of assuming that we shared the same language and understanding as each other and saw things in the same way, because there were many differences between us. We came from different socio-economic backgrounds, and indeed we each had different perceptions of our mental distress and did not share our strategies for living. Whilst some interviewees viewed themselves as service users, others were adamant that they were survivors and indeed that they no longer had mental distress. I acknowledge, on reflection, that I implicitly made a few assumptions about the women I interviewed. The survivor in me assumed that they would be coping in the community, when in fact many were struggling to 'keep it together'. However, these women were not passive recipients of racism, sexism and structural oppression. They had coping strategies that kept them going, and they had many strengths in different areas despite their mental distress.

On the whole, participants tended to value the matching of participants and interviewer across gender, ethnicity and service user background. There may, however, have been problems with over-identification. One woman described us as 'sisters' fighting for black African and African Caribbean women's rights to equality in the mental health system, but I did not always share her vision. I also wondered whether my approach was any different from that of a European interviewer, given my previous formal research training. However, I felt overall that we had a lot more in common with each other, and we were able to rise above our differences in the interviews.

CONCLUSION

The participants in this study described their personal mental health histories as black women and discussed their location in the mental health system. However they are defined, black women in mental distress remain marginalised and are invisible. Identity is important for our mental health and can provide us with positive feelings of belonging, whether these are based on ethnicity, service user and/or gender identity. The women identified as black women first and then as service users. Some black women in mental distress identified with the researcher with respect to racism and gender inequalities in mental health, and this was used as a springboard for dialogue between participants and researcher prior to, within and after the interviews. Although other studies warn of over-identifying with participants, the interviewer felt that sharing her experiences with the participants meant she was more sensitive to their needs, which may have led to a more equal power relationship. However, we should not be complacent with this view of the interview, because there are situations that may unintentionally harm the participants. Finally, as it was such a small sample, the characteristic features of this study may not be replicated, because I believe we all continually create the situation, and it exists only in this context in time.

REFERENCES

Essien, K (2003a) *Rainbow Nation: Black women speak out.* London: The Mental Health Foundation.

Essien, K (2003b) Transcripts from the Rainbow Nation: black women speak out research. London: The Mental Health Foundation.

Keating, F, Robertson, D, McCulloch, A & Francis, E (2002) *Breaking the Circles of Fear: Review of the relationship between mental health services and the African and Caribbean communities.* London: Sainsbury Centre for Mental Health.

Rassool, N (1998) Fractured or flexible identities? Life histories of 'black' diasporic women in Britain. In HS Mirza (ed) *Black British Feminism: A reader* (pp. 187–204). London: Routledge.

Thornicroft, G (1991) Social deprivation and rates of treated mental disorder. *British Journal of Psychiatry 158,* 475–84.

Warner, S (2001) Disrupting identity through visible therapy: A feminist post-structuralist approach to working with women who have experienced child sexual abuse. *Feminist Review, 68,* 115–39.

Williams, J (1999) Social inequalities and mental health. In C Newnes, G Holmes & C Dunn (eds) *This is Madness: A critical look at psychiatry and the future of mental health services* (pp 29–50). Ross-on-Wye: PCCS Books.

FIRST-HAND EXPERIENCES OF DIFFERENT APPROACHES TO COLLABORATIVE RESEARCH

CAREY OSTRER

AND

BRIGID MORRIS

In this chapter, we are going to compare and contrast our two experiences of collaborative research. First, Carey will outline her experience of being a service user advisor to a research project undertaken by a department of community psychiatry in a medical school. Then Brigid will describe a project in which she supported a group of service user researchers to carry out a study in their local inpatient hospital. Following a brief description of the two projects, we will extract what we feel are the key issues. We hope that this will be useful food for thought for any readers thinking about undertaking collaborative work.

Collaborative research is a term that means different things to different people, and can encompass a wide spectrum of user involvement. In the two examples that we are going to share with you, one project involved a group of academics inviting service users to take part in their research, whilst the other involved a service user organisation approaching an academic department for their assistance. In the former study, the decisions were ultimately made by the academics, whilst in the latter, the decision-making was in the control of the service users. These two examples of collaboration, which perhaps could be regarded as two extremes – one academic-controlled and one user-controlled – highlight the importance of being aware of where the power lies within collaborative work. It is more usual for power to be located with professionals, be they academics, research commissioners or service providers. All those engaging in collaborative work, particularly those with status and authority, need to be conscious and active with regard to ensuring that service users involved in their projects can contribute as fully as possible and, crucially, have an opportunity truly to change the research process.

CAREY'S EXPERIENCE

HOW I BECAME INVOLVED

I was invited to be involved in research whilst attending outpatient services at my local hospital. I had already been involved for two years in my mental health trust's service user consultation group, and had done some voluntary work in the research and development department.

A consultant psychiatrist and senior academic working at the trust's medical school wanted to put a bid together for funding from the NHS executive. One of the criteria for funding was that there needed to be user involvement, which was very new at the time. An appointment was arranged for me to meet with the consultant psychiatrist and a clinical psychologist (who was to be the project manager). The meeting seemed a little like an assessment of me and I felt quite intimidated. But I was really keen to be involved, as I had already developed a growing interest in research and had been reading the work of some of the service user researcher authors in this book – which I had found truly inspirational. As I remember, an outline of the project was explained to me, as well as how they were going to bid for funding. I do not think that any of us knew then what form my 'involvement' would take, but one thing was certain: I did not have personal experience of the diagnosis being researched. I said that I felt unable to give a direct service user perspective on it, but what I could do was give some advice about how to involve those who had. I suggested that we search for a voluntary sector group with specialist service user knowledge, and this was agreed.

I think it is useful to say that it was all quite nerve-wracking at the start. Not only was I unfamiliar with academic mental health research, but also I felt strange in what seemed, at the time, to be like a new form of doctor–patient relationship. I was suddenly in a group of mental health professionals (both clinicians and researchers) – god-like creatures – and I felt a bit like a raggedy old alley cat being suddenly dropped into a pack of lions. My driving force, however, was that I strongly believed that the results of the research would be more relevant and grounded if there were good user involvement. I was going to try as hard as I could to bring service user voices and their experiences to the project, in as powerful a way as I could, because I felt that to be my role and my responsibility.

WHAT WAS GOOD ABOUT THE PROJECT

The first twelve months were wonderful. A number of building blocks were put in place to facilitate strong user involvement. First, a national voluntary sector organisation was represented on the steering committee by one of their managers and counsellors. This woman had fifteen years' experience of working in the field with other women with this diagnosis. Initially she was sceptical about being involved, as she already had other experiences of research where she had been asked to advise, but in the final event had little influence. And she was a busy woman. She was persuaded to take part by virtue of the fact that the overall research question focused on the issue of recovery. In addition, she felt that the user involvement in the research process appeared to be meaningful. Later on in the research process, this woman was absolutely crucial in encouraging service users from her own organisation to participate. She agreed to attend monthly steering group meetings and to have input into the interim and final reports. She promoted the project to the organisation's membership, and encouraged them to become participants by completing the postal questionnaire that was to form the second stage of the research. She was generous with her time and expertise in between steering group meetings. She would be a named author on the final report and be paid a consultancy fee – payable to her organisation.

Secondly, my suggestion that a woman who had herself recovered from the condition being explored should be employed as the research worker was agreed. Her role was to collect the qualitative data through one-to-one interviews with other 'recovered' women. This data would then be used to develop a second stage postal questionnaire that would be sent to the voluntary sector organisation's membership. In other words, ten women would be asked in individual interviews to list the things that had helped them personally to recover from their condition. The findings of this first stage of the research would be collated, and then the women recruited from the voluntary sector organisation would be asked which items on the list they agreed had helped them to recover, and which had not.

Thirdly, the two-stage Delphi design[1] would be supplemented by a third stage, which would comprise a group of the women interviewed in stage one coming together to help shed light on the amalgamation of the collected data. As a group, then, they would inform the final analysis. Fourthly, all participants who were interviewees and participated in the group analysis meeting would be paid for their time and contribution and have their childcare expenses reimbursed.

My own role developed over time. At first, the principal investigator spent about one hour a week with me explaining the research process and discussing ideas around user involvement. I was terribly aware that he was extremely busy, and that this hour was a lot of time out of his week. However, he was generous and helpful, and I came to appreciate him greatly. In addition to suggesting the points mentioned above, I was the main link to the service user organisation, wrote articles for its newsletter and did literature searches. I also linked up with professional service user researchers for their advice on everything from recruitment through to service user definitions of recovery. In short, I put my heart and soul into trying to

---

1. The Delphi Method may be characterised as a technique for structuring a group communication process so that the process is effective in allowing a group of individuals, as a whole, to deal with a complex problem. To accomplish this 'structured communication' there is provided: some feedback of individual contributions of information and knowledge; some assessment of the group judgement or view; some opportunity for individuals to revise views; and some degree of anonymity for the individual responses. For more information see http://www.is.njit.edu/pubs/delphibook/

In this case the Delphi Method was chosen to explore expert opinion and develop agreement on what would help women recover from post-natal depression. Stage 1 comprised 12 interviews with women who had recovered from postnatal depression, gathering opinion on what helped them, and formulating statements. In Stage 2 these statements were circulated by mail to a much larger group of recovered women, members of the The Association for Post-Natal Illness (APNI), who were asked to rate them for importance. These rated scores were analysed by an experienced Delphi researcher for what was agreed and fed back to the original group of 12 women in Stage 3 for final comment.

make this project really relevant to service users, and I was one hundred per cent enthused by the process! I was given a desk and a computer, and though I was not paid because I was still receiving incapacity benefit, my expenses were covered with a little extra. On a more personal level, I had spent years of feeling useless and being made to feel useless – particularly by the indignity of the benefits agency. I had been very poor and very ill. Now I was slowly becoming reacquainted with my old working life, I was feeling better, and I was part of a team.

WHAT WAS DIFFICULT

About one year into the project, someone said that we could not ask the key research question that we had planned, because if we did, the research would not constitute a pure Delphi research method. We had already asked participants in the one-to-one interviews the first version of the question, but would have to change the question in the postal questionnaire. For the pure Delphi method, the question needed to be changed from asking women about what had helped them to recover, from their own personal experience, to asking them what they felt might help other women to recover. The representative of the voluntary sector organisation, the service user worker and I felt that this would be hugely confusing for women. We believed that they would be able to answer only from their own experience. As if that were not shocking enough, some senior team members proceeded to deny that they had ever intended to ask the question in the initial way. We all felt very angry for a number of reasons:

- the responses to the two different research questions would produce confused findings
- the service user organisation representative had convinced her management team to allow access to the membership based on the original research question (i.e. to ask about their personal experience)
- we felt that we had been lied to, or that the senior researchers had not been careful enough to identify this issue at the beginning

As a matter of fact, it was only when I managed to find the plain language summary stating the original question in black and white – submitted to the NHS for funding – that the senior researchers stopped denying that there was a change in the question being asked. At the time of the change in the research question, it did not cross my mind that I could have approached the funding body about my concerns. I would not have known whom to approach, nor felt that I had the authority to do so.

I did not know what to do. I decided that my role was to support my voluntary sector partner in whatever she chose to do. The service user researcher was told in no uncertain terms that her opinions were irrelevant and that she should keep quiet. She agreed because, as she told me, she needed a positive reference at the end of the job.

The principal investigator and the Delphi expert asked for a meeting with the representative of the service user organisation. She agreed to this and asked me to accompany her to support her at this. She felt as if she had misled her organisation's membership, and was considering pulling out of the project. To cut a long story short, at the end of an exhausting and challenging four-hour meeting, we felt that we had a duty to continue with the project, and agreed to a compromise that, in reality, we were unhappy with. It scarred the team's relationships for the rest of the period and it affected the quality of the research. In my opinion, the service user organisation could have carried out a better study if had they been funded to do it themselves.

Interestingly, when the research was peer reviewed, one of the reviewers picked up on the Delphi issue and said that problems had unnecessarily risen out of the Delphi expert's insistence in sticking to a purist version of Delphi design.

Ultimately, the power imbalance and my and the service user organisation's lack of knowledge about a Delphi design transformed what was potentially a very good project into one of lower quality. I felt that I had failed the service user participants, as well as those service users who might be affected by the research findings in the future.

Lessons I drew from the experience cover nuts-and-bolts issues around design, social issues around relationships and hierarchy, as well as the old question of how knowledge is created and by whom. This is all useful learning for the future. However, I have to be honest: I have worryingly little faith in academics responding to the fundamental concerns of people who use mental health services. We are light years away from being taken seriously by them, and I wonder how much this is owing to the sheer competitive ruthlessness of the research world in academia.

BRIGID'S EXPERIENCE

DEVELOPING THE RESEARCH PROPOSAL

In April 2003, I was recruited and employed by a local service user organisation based in north London. My job as research coordinator was to support its team of researchers to undertake a study on the wards of its local inpatient unit. The idea for the research had initially come from this organisation. It had collected many anecdotal accounts from its service user membership about the inadequate conditions for those staying on the wards. The organisation now wanted to carry out a research project to obtain systematically collected evidence that it could then present to its local mental health trust (MHT) and primary care trust (PCT) to ensure that improvements on the wards would become a priority.

The service user group, at the point of writing its research proposal, approached the mental health department of its local university to ask staff if they would be interested in working alongside it. The group was keen to get the university on board as it felt that it would help provide the research with credibility. Collaboration with a university would not only be likely to help them to gain funding: it would, additionally, enable the group to gain easier access to the views of patients and staff on the wards, and, it was hoped, help the group to produce a research report at the end of the project that the two local trusts would not be able to dismiss. The service user researchers were adamant that the research they undertook should lead to real improvement for people needing to stay on the inpatient wards in the future.

In addition to feeling that the research required the cachet of university backing, members of the research team were keen to develop their interviewing skills and to learn about new ways in which to design interview schedules and written questionnaires. This group had carried out research before, and were aware that they had gaps in their skills and knowledge. They were keen to gain ideas about a wider range of ways in which they could undertake their work.

A third reason for asking a university to become involved was to have access to a non-service user – an independent researcher who could interview ward staff. The aim of the study was to gain a picture of life on the wards from the perspective of both current inpatients and staff. The team of service user researchers would interview inpatients, and the university researcher would interview staff. The service user group felt that this design would provide a rich description of what it was like to stay and work on the wards, as well as enabling staff to feel that they were being taken into account and thus not to feel threatened by the idea that inpatients were being asked for their opinions.

The research proposal was submitted to the local PCT and MHT, and funding was agreed. The funding provided the money for my part-time post, for payment to the service user researchers, for their expenses including lunch and refreshments on the days of the research meetings, to buy in training and research advice and time from the university researcher, and to provide inpatients with a financial thank you for their participation.

THE POSITIVE ROLE OF THE STEERING GROUP

It was at this point that I was recruited into my role as project coordinator, and a steering group was established. The steering group was the cornerstone of the project in many ways. It was the forum in which representatives from each of the research partner organisations could meet and contribute to the design, process and impact of the research. The steering group had a consistent membership throughout the one-year lifespan of the research, met approximately every two months, and included the coordinator of the service user organisation, at least two members of the service user research team, myself, the university researcher, the mental health commissioner from the PCT, senior consultant psychiatrists and the senior inpatient manager from the MHT. Thus in many ways the collaborative nature of this research project stretched beyond that of a service user group and academic department undertaking research together. The collaboration involved local service users (the service user research team, the service user-led group to which they belonged, and the service users on whose behalf this organisation worked), a university, a PCT and a MHT. The research project that was carried out was ambitious and successful. Its success needs to be attributed to the input of all of the partner organisations.

The importance of the steering group lay not just in the fact that it existed. It lay instead in the specific way in which it functioned. Indeed the steering group was enabling and supportive of the research process – and crucially of the service user research team. It was not a forum where the researchers (service user researchers from the service user organisation, myself and the university researcher) were told what they could and could not do. Instead it was a forum where the researchers reported on their progress, flagged up any decision-making that needed discussion, and heard the views of the partner organisations. This positive interaction between the service user perspective and those of the professionals – the academic, the mental health service provider and commissioner – occurred, I believe, for a number of reasons.

The service user research team would always meet together prior to the steering group meeting, and at this meeting the whole team would determine which issues should be taken to the steering group. In this way, the wider service user research team felt that their views and opinions were present at the steering group meetings. In addition, those members of the service user research team attending the meetings could feel that they were truly there on behalf of the wider group. The service user research team representatives would always fully feed back what was discussed at this meeting to their colleagues, and the representatives would rotate so that everyone, who wanted to, could have the chance to attend and take on this role. In addition, members of the service user research team felt supported by the wider service user organisation to which they belonged. There was much passion, support and motivation from workers within this organisation – for the research to take place and to bring fully to light service users' inpatient experiences.

ATTITUDES OF THE NON-SERVICE USER PARTNERS

The university researcher was insistent throughout her contact with the service user research team, during the training sessions she provided, and in her ongoing role as research advisor, that all the decisions made about the research design and process should ultimately be made by the service user research team. She saw her role as providing members of the service user research team with an opportunity to develop their skills and knowledge. She encouraged them to use this widened knowledge of research methods, and crucially their experience as mental health service users, to make decisions – for example, about which questions should be asked of the research participants and, crucially, how they should be asked. She was keen fully to exploit the unique and valuable expertise that the service user research team had – namely their experience of using mental health services and of living with their mental health problems. This was particularly important for thinking through the ways in which to collect information from the current inpatients on the ward. The service user research team was keen to collect the views of a wide range of inpatients – both those with shorter and longer attention spans – and in a way that was as comfortable and meaningful to them as possible.

Finally, the people representing the PCT and MHT were forward thinking, were respectful of the personal experience of the service user research team, and were committed to improving the conditions on the wards. Like the university researcher, they were open to research that was innovative, creative and was really addressing how best to collect the data, particularly the views of current patients on the wards. They were also supportive in practical ways. They actively helped to get ward managers on board, which enabled smooth enough access on to the wards for the service user researchers for their interviews. A comfortable room with computers and a locked filing cabinet was provided on the hospital site for the service user research team to meet in and work from. In addition, trust and respect developed over time between the partners and was mutual. This took place as a result of the PCT and MHT staff observing the careful and thorough work of the service user research team, and the service user research team experiencing the practical assistance, respect and commitment to change of the representatives of the two trusts.

POSITIVE OUTCOMES

The project did not always run smoothly. Such projects rarely do. Throughout the year in which we undertook the research, we encountered resistance from some ward staff, illness within the service user research team and tiredness due to undertaking a large project on a very part-time basis. The research team and I were funded to work only one day a week together, and the university researcher also worked very intensely. However, we were very pleased with what we managed to achieve. The service user research team interviewed 61 current inpatients across five acute wards and one intensive care ward. The university researcher interviewed 38 members of staff from the same wards, ranging from cleaning staff through to consultant psychiatrists, and collected 50 staff-completed written questionnaires. Both quantitative and qualitative data were collected and analysed, and the service user research team, the university researcher and I jointly wrote a report. The findings were well received by a wide range of staff within the hospital, and the key recommendations were directly taken up by the MHT in their formal action plan for improving inpatient care.

The project was also successful in that members of the service user research team spoke of how they had personally developed. Team members spoke of how they had enjoyed the mental stimulation of the research process, had enjoyed meeting as a team, and had surprised themselves with regard to the skills and experience they had gained during the year. Some people proved to themselves that they were effective interviewers, whilst others entered data into an Excel spreadsheet for the first time. Members of the service user research team were invited to take part in as many different aspects of the research process as they wished to, were interested in, or felt able to. A few research team members bravely and successfully agreed to present the process and findings of the project at a couple of conferences packed full of academics.

Overall, I feel that the study was completed successfully and relatively smoothly, owing to all the partners being open to innovation, change and challenge. I believe that there is not much point in involving service users in research if you are not going to question traditional ways of doing research and consider how you can use their expertise to improve the research methods you are using, and vice versa. The academic involved in this study was open to and encouraging of adapting the research tools and methods used to fit the purpose of the research. She felt that modification of the research tools used, particularly with regard to collecting the views of the vulnerable and 'unwell' service users on the wards, was crucial in order to collect meaningful and indeed valid data. Conversely, the service user researchers also needed to be open to the opinions and experience of the academic researcher and the mental health professionals involved. The questions asked of ward staff were improved following suggestions from members of the trusts. The research repertoire of the service user researchers was much enhanced as a result of the training and advice received from the university academic.

The full report of this research project's process and findings can be found in Burns, George, Holmshaw, Johnson, Kisosonkole et al. (2004).

LEARNING FROM OUR EXPERIENCES

From our two experiences, we feel that the following issues are crucial when considering undertaking the challenge of collaborative research:

1. That the *power imbalance* between service users and academic researchers is acknowledged throughout the collaborative research process. Researchers have a high status within society, while those who use mental health services often experience stigma and discrimination. Mental health service users frequently experience low self-esteem and feel unskilled, often because they have been out of the workplace for many years. Not all service users have had a positive experience of education or have achieved academic qualifications at school, college or university. The world and language of academia can sometimes feel very intimidating. Service users frequently require active and ongoing encouragement and support to engage fully with academics and to feel that

their contribution is valuable. Undoubtedly, the personality of researchers and their underlying motivations for working alongside service users will affect where the balance of power lies.

2. The *lack of user-friendliness of the benefits system* may also contribute to the low self-esteem experienced by some service users attempting to get involved in research projects whilst on benefits. Benefits agency staff rarely appreciate the therapeutic nature of such work. Service users often need to move in and out of this type of activity, depending on their experience of 'wellness' or mental distress at the time. Such fluctuation in distress is not well understood by the benefits agency – whose systems are very inflexible. Service users who get involved in collaborative research may not only experience challenges within their research projects, but in addition may face obstacles and difficulties in being permitted to undertake such involvement.

3. That full consideration is given by researchers about *why they wish to involve service users* in their research. It is more common for academics to approach service users to take part in their research than vice versa. Researchers need to be aware that involving service users in their research will require them to be reflective and creative. Researchers need truly to understand and value the insights that service users can bring to the research process. Crucially, they need to be open to reviewing and adapting their research methods. Ideally, researchers and service users undertaking work together will have the common goal of wanting to design and undertake research in the most effective and sensitive way possible. Service user involvement in research should not simply be undertaken in order to 'tick the box' on a commissioning form, or for approval by a local research governance department. Real collaborative research is time consuming and challenging, and there needs to be real comprehension about and commitment to the process.

4. *Service user research is usually not considered to have enough status or credibility* if it is developed and carried out by service users alone. Conversely, academic research is frequently carried out and taken seriously without service user involvement. It is likely that most academics view service user involvement in research as being an interesting add-on if you have the time, rather than something that is essential. Many service users would argue that it is essential that mental health research is thoroughly embedded in first-hand experience of living with a mental health problem. Involving service users in research alters which research is undertaken and how it is carried out.

5. In academic institutions *it is a real challenge to establish meaningful user involvement,* owing to the constraints of time and money. The current funding environment is very competitive, and encourages academics to submit bids

that often offer too much and for not enough money. As a result, adequate user involvement can be hugely compromised. The worry is that if user involvement is under-funded and not carried out well, it will add negligible value to research projects, and so may eventually be rejected altogether by academics, funding bodies and indeed service users.

6. That meetings where service users and academics come together to share their ideas and discuss ways forward need to be well thought out:

   - The locations of meetings need to be comfortable for service users. For example, in the project Brigid described, the steering group meetings took place on the territory of the service user researchers – the office space where the service user research team undertook its work.

   - Pre-meetings can be helpful to service users attending steering group or project meetings to enable them to plan – with supporters or service users they are speaking on behalf of – what they want to raise and discuss in the meeting with partner organisations.

   - Meetings need to be well chaired in order that the service user perspective can be fully heard and utilised to inform decision-making. Research meetings can feel formal and intimidating to those unused to them. The language used can sometimes be alienating. All those attending should be mindful that it is essential to create an environment in which service users feel comfortable and valued enough to express their views and share their experience. In addition, it is important that a forum is created in which open debate and discussion from all perspectives can, though possibly uncomfortable at times, take place.

Collaborative research is resource intensive and challenging to all. However when undertaken with appropriate thought, time, shared understanding and mutual respect, we believe that the process and findings can be greater than the sum of its parts – academic training and service user expertise – and can lead to what we believe is innovative, meaningful and effective research.

REFERENCE

Burns, T, George, L, Holmshaw, J, Johnson, P, Kisosonkole, P, Koroma, A, Morris, B, Trifourkis, M & Vincent, Z (2004) *Life on the Wards: Patient and staff views and experiences of acute mental health care in Haringey.* Undertaken by Researchers from Matrix Service User Group and Middlesex University. London: Matrix / Barnet, Enfield and Haringey Mental Health Trust / Middlesex University. http://www.spn.org.uk/fileadmin/SPN_uploads/Documents/Final.pdf (Accessed 17 December 2008).

CHAPTER 9

LITERATURE REVIEWS
AN EXAMPLE OF MAKING TRADITIONAL
RESEARCH METHODS USER FOCUSED

PETE FLEISCHMANN

INTRODUCTION

It is vital that service users/survivors understand and are involved in systematic reviews, as they are becoming ever more important in determining mental health policy and practice. Systematic reviews are about being thoughtful and systematic in how we approach the investigation of what is already known about a specific issue.

The aim of this chapter is to enable service users/survivors to start thinking about how they can conduct their own reviews, collaborate meaningfully in academic-led reviews, and also to begin to look critically at published reviews.

The chapter briefly sets out the context and history of systematic reviewing. Then some key issues for people considering undertaking a review are discussed. Finally, the characteristics of user-led reviews are described. Also included are case studies of two user-led reviews.

WHAT IS A SYSTEMATIC REVIEW?

At the most basic level, a review consists of investigating a research question or issue by looking at what has been written to date on the subject. Literature reviewing is a form of secondary research. This is in contrast to primary research, which involves investigating an issue by having direct or indirect contact with research participants or research phenomena. Literature reviews are variously known as narrative reviews, rapid reviews, knowledge reviews, meta-analyses and systematic reviews (see below for glossary box, Table 1).

The methodologies used to assemble and analyse the data, and generate results and conclusions have their parallels with the sampling, data gathering, analysis and conclusion generation of primary research. Not until relatively recently, however, has there been an emphasis on transparency, rigour and replicability in the field of literature reviewing.

Table 1: *Literature review definitions*

Term	Definition
Literature review	General term referring to reviewing written material. This term gives no indication of what kind of review is being referred to, or what kind of methodology has been used.
Narrative or descriptive review	These terms tend to indicate a review of literature on a particular area or topic that is unlikely to have made any attempt to be comprehensive, rigorous or to synthesise the material.
Rapid review	This term indicates a quick dip into the literature with no attempt to be especially comprehensive or rigorous, and it is unlikely that any attempt has be made to synthesise the material.
Systematic review	This term indicates that the review authors consider their review to be comprehensive, rigorous and transparent.
Meta-analysis	Typically this term refers to a systematic review that uses statistical methods to combine and summarise the results of a set of randomised controlled trials (RCTs). So, despite being traditionally considered the most scientific and rigorous of methods, a meta-analysis will automatically exclude a lot of research and other material. However, it should be noted that there are meta-analytic methods for qualitative data and this is a developing field.
Knowledge review	This term is used by the Social Care Institute for Excellence (SCIE) to indicate that the reviews that it conducts and commissions will aim to include a wide range of literature, including research, grey literature (literature not published in peer-reviewed journals), policy documents and testimony. In addition, a survey of practitioners or focus group with users might also be included.

Review authors sometimes refer to their work as systematic reviews. This is commonly understood to indicate that, firstly, the review includes only randomised controlled trials (RCTs) and, secondly, that the review has been conducted rigorously and with methodological transparency. This chapter will use this term to indicate rigour and transparency, but without the implication that only randomised controlled trials have been included.

THE CONTEXT OF SYSTEMATIC REVIEWS

THE PEER REVIEW SYSTEM

The majority of systematic reviews consider only research that has been published in peer-reviewed journals, and is therefore accessible via medical and scientific databases (more about these later). The peer review system aims to ensure that the research published in scientific journals is of high quality. In order to be published, every paper has to be favourably reviewed by at least two other academics, who are considered experts in the field. It is questionable how effectively the system functions as a form of quality control; it is also possible that the system constrains innovation (Smith, 1997). It is therefore currently unusual for user research to be published in peer-reviewed journals.

Many researchers and policy makers see systematic reviews as the key decision-making tool in many areas of policy and practice. Systematic reviews now occupy the top place in the traditional hierarchy of evidence (see Figure 1). Three factors have arguably produced this position. Firstly, the development of more rigorous methods of reviewing; secondly, the demand from government for evidence to support policy; and thirdly, the development of powerful search engines which make possible the searching of research databases at the touch of a button.

THE DADDY OF ALL SYSTEMATIC REVIEWS

In the early 1970s, Dr Archie Cochrane developed the idea that medical knowledge was not being approached in a systematic or coordinated manner: 'It is surely a great criticism of our profession that we have not organised a critical summary, by specialty or subspecialty, adapted periodically, of all relevant randomised controlled trials' (Cochrane, 1979: 9). This insight was the genesis of the development of The UK Cochrane Centre (see http://www.cochrane.co.uk), which was established in 1992 to oversee the collation of systematic reviews of randomised controlled trials of health care treatments. In 2003, the Centre became part of an international network. The Cochrane methodology emphasises the need for unbiased comparisons of treatments, and requires that reviews are comprehensive, include all the high quality trials available, and are constantly updated. The Campbell

Collaboration (see http://www.campbellcollaboration.org) serves a parallel function to Cochrane, focusing mainly on criminal justice, social care and education. Campbell reviews tend to include a wider range of research.

NEW LABOUR, NEW EVIDENCE

'If No. 10 says bloody "evidence-based policy" to me once more I'll deck them one', Louise Casey, National Director, Anti-Social Behaviour Unit (ASBU) (cited in Branigan, 2005).

The current government has emphasised and re-emphasised that policy should be based on evidence not ideology. For example, David Blunkett, speaking in 2002 as Home Secretary, said the administration wished to:

> be guided not by dogma but by an open-minded approach to what works and why. This is central to our agenda for modernising government: using information and knowledge more effectively and creatively at the heart of policy making and policy delivery. (Blunkett, 2000)

This policy emphasis has found expression in the health and social care field in the creation of the National Institute for Health and Clinical Excellence (NICE) (see http://www.nice.org.uk) in 1999 and the Social Care Institute for Excellence (SCIE) (see http://www.scie.org.uk) in 2001. Central to both NICE's and SCIE's core activities are reviews of evidence designed to inform good practice and policy.

THE RISE OF THE SEARCH ENGINES

Databases such as Medline, PsycINFO, EMBASE, PubMed and Social Science Citation Index are basically computerised indexes of published, peer-reviewed scientific articles. Using databases, it is possible to search quite specifically for all articles that mention, for example, mental health and social exclusion. The database will produce a list of all the articles that refer to mental health and social exclusion. The quantity of articles the engine brings up is commonly referred to as the number of 'hits'. The search engine can be asked to produce synonyms of search terms. For example some databases can produce a list of similar or related terms to the one you have entered; others provide subject 'trees' that are lists of linked items or themes. Some databases will also allow users to limit the search by items such as date, language, research subject, gender, age and geographical area.

These databases have made literature searching much quicker and easier than previously could be imagined. Using databases, lists of references and abstracts can be retrieved. In some cases, access to the full papers is also possible.

Figure 1: *Traditional hierarchy of evidence*[1]

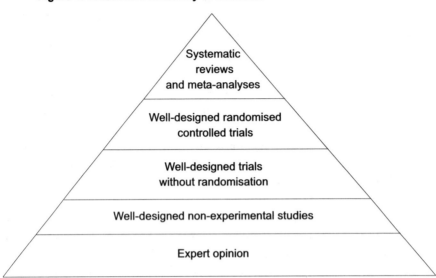

Notes to Figure 1

• *Systematic reviews and meta-analyses* These synthesise all randomised controlled trials (RCTS) on a particular issue.

• *Well-designed randomised controlled trials* Although much criticised from user and social scientist perspectives, RCTs remain the gold standard of medical research. An RCT will randomly allocate its sample to a group who try the new treatment and a group of people who do not.

• *Well-designed trials without randomisation* These are trials that do not select their samples randomly.

• *Well-designed non-experimental studies* RCTs and trials are experiments: they aim to test hypotheses by setting up artificial situations. Non-experimental studies ask people about their lives, or observe and try to draw conclusions, rather than setting up scientific tests.

• *Expert opinion* The opinion of respected authorities, reports of expert committees, or doctors' opinions based on case studies. In this context, the opinions of users do not figure at all. However, some traditional academics will say that user opinion should be included here.

KEY ISSUES IN UNDERTAKING A SYSTEMATIC REVIEW

There is not enough space in this chapter to discuss fully the nuts and bolts of undertaking a review. There is a no shortage of tools and guides that describe how to undertake a review (e.g. see the resources provided by the Evidence for Policy

1. See http://www.shef.ac.uk/scharr/ir/units/systrev/hierarchy.htm and https://carmenwiki.osu.edu/display/imresidency/Evidence+Based+Medicine

and Practice Information and Co-ordinating Centre (EPPI-Centre) at the Institute of Education, University of London [http://www.eppi.ioe.ac.uk/cms/], SCIE [http://www.scie.org.uk], the Evidence Network at King's College London [http://www.evidencenetwork.org], and Campbell Collaboration [http://www.campbell collaboration.org]). In addition, Suzy Braye and Michael Preston-Shoot (2005) have written a useful account of the issues surrounding user and carer involvement in systematic reviews. Reviews generally progress in stages: from assembling the team, to deciding the scope of the review, setting research questions and protocols, searching and assembling the material for review, some sort of quality assessment of materials, analysis, results and finally drawing conclusions. There are four critical issues for any review, especially those that are either user led or are aiming to have a high level of user involvement:

1. THE TEAM

Assembling the right team is obviously crucial. Many reviews consist of a core research team, who actually do the work, and a reference group – who consist of academics with an interest in the area of study, and possibly users, carers and other stakeholders. In order for user involvement to be effective, it is advisable to have people with direct experience of using services, both as part of the review core team and as a major presence on the advisory group. The ideal team will have a combination of technical and methodological know-how and direct experience. As there are not currently many service user researchers with skills in systematic reviewing, it may be necessary for teams to consider offering training for individual members, and also to think strategically about supporting service user partner organisations to capacity build in this area.

2. THE MATERIAL FOR REVIEW

Locating the literature is a key element. Most reviews initially search using databases. A hand search of journals that are not indexed in databases may also be included. The references of included papers may also be looked at to cross-check. This is sometimes known as snowball searching. The search strategy may include consulting experts in the field, and talking to libraries and information specialists. A user-led review may also wish to include users' personal testimonies, and a separate search strategy may need to be developed to locate this material. SCIE calls its reviews 'systematic knowledge reviews'. This is because they usually include a practice survey and aim to include a broad range of different sources of knowledge. SCIE has identified five sources of knowledge (see Table 2 below) within social care, and argues that all of them need to included in knowledge reviews.

Table 2: *SCIE Sources of knowledge in social care*

Source 1	Source 2	Source 3	Source 4	Source 5
Organisational	Practitioner	Policy community	Research	User and carer
Knowledge gained from organising social care	Knowledge gained from doing social care	Knowledge gained from wider policy context	Knowledge gathered systematically with a planned design	Knowledge gained from experience of and reflection on service use

One particular problem with the incorporation of user-generated knowledge is that it does not currently have wide coverage, especially in terms of research. Therefore reviewers need to be highly imaginative in accessing this material. Strategies to incorporate a user perspective should also be in place in the eventuality that there is not a user-generated research literature on the topic. Such strategies could include: consideration of non-research literature such as personal testimony, looking at user research in other allied fields or internationally, and/or a strengthening of other arrangements for user involvement.

3. HOW TO JUDGE THE MATERIAL'S QUALITY

Once a body of material has been assembled, it is necessary to assess the quality of material. For traditional reviews, this a comparatively simple process, as the scientific standards for RCTs are well established. (For example, the CONSORT Statement [see Moher, Schulz & Altman (2001)] is a consensus protocol for conducting RCTs.) Judging the quality of qualitative research presents more problems, as there are no comparable, universally agreed standards. Different inclusion and exclusion criteria may need to be used for different sources of material. SCIE has developed a framework called TAPUPAS (see Table 3), which proposes a method of accessing

Table 3: *TAPUPAS system for quality appraisal (Social Care Institute for Excellence)*

Transparency – is it open to scrutiny?

Accuracy – is it well-grounded?

Purposivity – is it fit for purpose?

Utility – is it fit for use?

Propriety – is it legal and ethical?

Accessibilty – is it intelligible?

Specificity – does it meet source-specificstandards?

the quality of a wide range of materials (Pawson, Boaz, Grayson, Long, & Barnes, 2003). Most reviews employ some form of inter-rater reliability testing. This means that a sub-sample of all the papers will be read and assessed by two members of the research team. The results will be compared to determine the level of agreement, which will be expressed as a percentage.

4. SYNTHESISING THE RESULTS

Synthesising the results of material from a range of sources also presents challenges. Conventional systematic reviews applying the Cochrane model, for example, are able to provide answers to specific questions by taking an average of averages from all the included trials. A user-led review, which is likely to include material from a wide range of sources, will not be able to follow the Cochrane model. However, there is a developing body of methodological work that concerns the synthesis of qualitative material (Popay & Roen, 2003; Fisher, Qureshi, Hardyman & Homewood, 2006). Furthermore, there is an example of a review that 'integrates in a rigorous and systematic way, the findings of a statistical meta-analysis with the findings from a qualitative review' (Thomas, Sutcliffe, Harden, Oakley, Oliver et al., 2003). The methodological tools are therefore available for non-traditional reviews to synthesise data from a range of sources.

THE CHARACTERISTICS OF USER-LED REVIEWS

User-led reviews are currently rare. However, a methodology has emerged from the Service User Research Enterprise (SURE) at the Institute of Psychiatry, King's College London. SURE has undertaken two user-led systemic reviews (see Table 4). A user-led review will generally have the following characteristics:

MORE FLEXIBLE IN THE DATA THEY ADMIT

User-led reviews will make use of peer-reviewed literature, but only if it asks users directly what they think about a treatment or service. User-led reviews will include 'grey' literature, and will be especially interested in reports authored by users. A user-led review may also look at first-hand accounts of direct experience, sometimes known as testimonies.

TEAM COMPOSITION

Several members of the core research team will have received the intervention or a comparable intervention to that which is being considered by the review. This gives the research team 'insider knowledge', and will bestow the team with credibility with the user movement, which may enhance access to user-generated knowledge.

Table 4: Two case studies of user-led systematic reviews (conducted by SURE, Institute of Psychiatry, King's College London)

Study title	Review of consumers' perspectives on ECT	**User and carer involvement in change management in a mental health context: Review of the literature**
Authors	Dr Diana Rose, Co-Director, Service User Research Enterprise (SURE) Pete Fleischmann, Researcher, SURE Professor Til Wykes, Co-Director, SURE Dr Jonathan Bindman, Senior Lecturer, Institute of Psychiatry	Dr Diana Rose Co-Director, Service User Research Enterprise (SURE) Pete Fleischmann, Researcher, SURE Dr Fran Tonkiss, Goldmiths College Peter Campbell, Independent user consultant Professor Til Wykes Co-Director, Service User Research Enterprise (SURE)
Funding	Department of Health	National Co-ordinating Centre for NHS Service Delivery and Organisation R&D (SDO)
Available online	http://www.ect.org/resources/consumerperspectives.pdf	http://www.sdo.nihr.ac.uk/files/project/17-final-report.pdf
METHOD **Research question/aims**	Systematically to describe and summarise consumers' perspectives on ECT	Examines literature about user and/or carer involvement in managing organisational change within mental health services.
Team composition	The lead researcher Diana Rose and second author Pete Fleischmann both have direct ECT experience. Other team members are clinical academics.	The lead researcher Diana Rose and authors Pete Fleischmann and Peter Campbell all have direct experience of using mental health services and have been active in user involvement since the 1980s. Fran Tonkiss is a sociologist; Til Wykes a clinical academic.

Reference group	An advisory group meet twice during the project. It was formed of representatives of user and voluntary groups with a stake in ECT research and researchers with an interest in user perspectives on ECT. The reference group had a simple majority of people with direct ECT experience. The reference group advised on the location of literature, thematic issues and reviewed drafts of the report.	A reference group consisting of users and carers who are active in user/carer involvement and academic researchers with an interest in user/carer involvement. The main input of the group was in the development of the coding frame used to analyse the literature, helping to specify different types of change, and factors tending to facilitate or impede effective change.
Search terms	The following search terms and all available synonyms were used: Electroconvulsive therapy, Patient attitudes, Patient satisfaction, Client rights, Memory loss, Benefit/helpfulness, Information, Consent, Treatment drop-outs.	The following search terms and all available synonyms were used: user, carer, involvement, mental health, health care services, service delivery, organisational culture, innovation, change management.
Data sources	The review considered three type of evidence: academic research studies, user/voluntary group studies, user testimony. *Academic research studies* Databases were searched: PsycINFO, MedLine, Web of Science and King's Fund Library. *User/voluntary group studies* The researchers used own prior knowledge and contacts to assemble this part of the research database and asked the reference group for assistance. Nine consumer-led or collaborative studies were identified. *Testimony* 'Testimonies' or first-hand accounts of the experience of receiving ECT were sourced from internet sites, various print media and a video archive.	The literature reviewed for this report was assembled from five sources: 1. Electronic databases including:· • MedLine • PsycINFO • EMBASE • HMIC • Social Sciences Citation Index • King's Fund Library 2. An existing research archive on a similar topic was purposefully searched 3. Reference group recommendation 4. A comparative sub-sample of articles in two key journals 5. Snowball searching.

Inclusion/exclusion criteria

The following inclusion criteria were used:

- Research participants and all consumers who provide testimony have received ECT.
- The research ascertains consumer views by asking directly about experience of ECT
- Papers have a publication date of 1975 or after.
- All materials are in the English language.

Exclusion criteria

- literature published before 1987
- literature in languages other than English
- literature concerning people aged under 18 years or over 65 years
- literature concerning user or carer involvement in auditing or
- evaluating services, where changes following the audit or evaluation are not described

Inclusion criteria

- Date: 1987–2002
- Language: English
- User and/or carer involvement
- Mental health
- Change

Data extraction

For the research studies an SPSS file was used to log the studies' variables. Testimony was logged using a specially designed grid.

A coding frame was used to rate all the literature in terms of its relevance to the key research concepts, and as the basis for preliminary analysis of the literature. The coding frame was designed to incorporate for analysis the main themes of the review: as well as recording the type and source of the paper, coding categories covered modes of user/carer involvement, forms and drivers of organisational change, and factors facilitating or impeding involvement.

Inter-rater reliability

The inter-rater reliability of allocating testimonies to categories in the grid was assessed with a sub-set of 25 testimonies coded independently by two raters. Agreement was high at 83 per cent.

The inter-rater reliability of the coding of papers was assessed with a sub-set of 30 papers. Two raters coded the material independently. Agreement was high at 79.9 per cent. Additionally, every paper or report was assessed by at least two readers to check for any inconsistencies or oversights in rating.

Methodological evaluation

All the studies were reviewed in terms of their methodology and found to be very diverse and of variable quality. All the studies start with certain assumptions and values concerning ECT and this leads to both differences in the participant selection and interpretation of data.

Testimony data is now available in a wide variety of formats including a video archive and 'threads' of correspondence sourced from email forums. Email forums introduce the arena of group discussion or beliefs into the data. The contexts in which the testimonies are elicited do constrain what can be expressed and how it is expressed. However the different sources each provide checks on the perspectives expressed in the other formats.

Two readers read approximately 850 abstracts yielded by electronic and purposive searches. Full papers were then accessed where abstracts met the inclusion criteria:

156 papers were read in full and coded for inclusion on a four-point scale:

1. Recommend inclusion
2. Consider inclusion
3. Marginal – some insights
4. Reject.

The final number of papers included for analysis was 112.

Analysis

A template for analysing the substantive themes was developed which ensured that no single approach to ascertaining consumers' views on ECT was privileged. Where research studies using a range of methodologies produce similar results, the review makes a statement of the form 'at least X per cent of consumers experience Y'. Where different methodological contexts produce different results, conclusions cannot be drawn with confidence. The different

In order to 'map the terrain' of the literature, the coding sheets for each paper, report or book were entered into an SPSS data file. Frequency counts were reported for the different categories and some cross-tabulations. Cross-tabulations were tested with chi-square to assess the significance of co-occurrence of categories. A significance level of $p < 0.05$ was used.

Through this exercise three clusters of types of change management were identified:

1. Promoting democracy and representation and/or cultural change
2. Strategic planning, restructuring and policy initiatives
3. New service provision and the employment of service users in organisation

For each cluster, approximately one-third of the literature is discussed in substantive detail. Papers were selected for this more detailed analysis on the basis of readers' assessment of quality and research relevance, with an emphasis on papers with an empirical, evidential or practical orientation. Some papers were also included because they reported on specific issues of critical relevance – for example, papers that reflected issues of equality and diversity.

The literature assembled presents a complex picture of user and carer involvement in change management. It is very diverse and of variable quality. The review suggests that the role of organisational culture is key in both facilitating and impeding user/carer involvement in change management. The review details factors that facilitate and hinder user involvement in change management.

strategies used by clinical and consumer research to summarise data are also examined to see how diverse conclusions may be reached on the basis of very similar data.

The testimony data was analysed using a form of qualitative analysis that occupies a middle ground between formal content analysis and discourse analysis. It takes from content analysis the existence of a set of themes decided in advance of examination of the data. At the same time, discourse analytic methods allow the content and detail of themes to emerge from the data and attend to the interactive nature of e-mail forums and interviews.

Combining research and testimony data gives more confidence when similarities of results are disclosed. Conversely, discrepant data from a range of sources must be treated with caution.

Conclusions

Consumers who are opposed to ECT are often characterised as a vocal minority. However, this review found that dissatisfaction with ECT may be more widespread than is often supposed. Consumers' views are not simple and there is no one 'consumer perspective' on ECT. However, of those providing testimonies, few were equivocal about the treatment. In all types of information gathered for the review it is evident that memory loss is a persistent reported side effect for at least one-third of recipients of ECT. For some people, memory loss causes great distress and profoundly affects their sense of identity.

Dissemination

Academic Journal articles including:
British Medical Journal [1], *British Journal of Psychiatry* [2], *Journal of Mental Health* [3]

Article in *Open Mind* [4]

Media coverage including *All in the Mind*, BBC Radio 4 and *Shocking Treatment* ITV West

Numerous Talks including Royal College of Psychiatrists Annual Conference 2003

Full report available online (http://www.ect.org/resources/consumerperspectives.pdf)

The report had an impact on NICE's ECT guidance [5] and drafting of new Mental Health Act provisions on ECT.

The funder SDO commissioned a briefing paper which is available online and in hard copy. Full text is also available online (http://www.sdo.nihr.ac.uk/files/project/17-final-report.pdf)The review is widely cited most recently in the report of an evaluation of the National Institute for Mental Health England's (NIMHE) user involvement structures. [6]

The review was one of six reviews that formed the basis for the Social Care Institute for Excellence's position paper 3: Has Service User Participation Made a Difference to Social Care Services?

1. Rose, D, Wykes, T, Leese, M, Bindman, J & Fleischmann, P (2003) Patients' perspectives on electroconvulsive therapy: systematic review. *BMJ, 326,* 1363–6.
2. Rose, D, Wykes, T, Bindman, J & Fleischmann, P (2005) Information, consent and perceived coercion: Consumers' views on ECT. *British Journal of Psychiatry, 186,* 54–9.
3. Rose, D, Fleischmann, P & Wykes, T (2004) Consumers' perspectives on ECT: A qualitative analysis. *Journal of Mental Health, 13*(3), 285–94.
4. Fleischmann P, Rose, D & Wykes T (2003) Life saver or memory eraser? User dissatisfaction with ECT. *Openmind, 122,* 12–13.
5. Available online http://www.nice.org.uk/page.aspx?o=68305
6. Health and Social Care Advisory Service (2005) *Making a Real Difference: Strengthening service user and carer involvement in NIMHE:* final report. Leeds: NIMHE. http://www.letsrespect.csip.org.uk/viewdocument.php?action=viewdox&pid=0&doc=33488&grp=1

Secondly, the review will convene a reference group largely made up of those who have received the intervention in question. The reference group will be especially helpful in framing the review themes and conceptual approach, ensuring that this is relevant to direct experience of the treatment.

WIDER DISSEMINATION

A user-led review may adopt a different dissemination strategy. It is less likely that the only form of dissemination will be papers in peer-reviewed journals. Authors of user-led reviews will be especially keen to reach the user audience, and will try to place articles in media that are known to have a high user readership. They may also wish to look at strategies to ensure that the results of the review are available and accessible to the widest possible audience.

CONCLUSION

Systematic reviewing is one of the last areas of research to be subject to the wider democratisation movement in research. User involvement in systematic reviewing is in its infancy. Systematic reviews are extremely important in shaping mental health services, and it is likely that they will become more so in the future. Systematic reviewing is commonly perceived as a highly technical form of research that can only be conducted by experts, and one that has little relevance to the daily lives of mental health service users/survivors. The challenge for user/survivors and academic reviewers is to ensure that systematic reviewing is demystified and that a truly participative model is developed. It is vital that users and survivors do get involved in systematic reviews as an important and powerful way of grounding reviews in lived experience.

REFERENCES

Blunkett, D (2000) Influence or irrelevance: Can social science improve government? Secretary of State's ESRC Lecture Speech, London: 2 February.

Branigan, T (2005) 'Deck 'em' adviser made head of respect drive by Blair and Clarke. *Guardian*. 3 September. http://www.guardian.co.uk/politics/2005/sep/03/ukcrime.prisonsandprobation#article_continue (Accessed 17 December 2008).

Braye, S & Preston-Shoot, M (2005) Emerging from out of the shadows? Service user and carer involvement systematic reviews. *Evidence and Policy, 2*, 173–93.

Cochrane, AL (1979) *Medicines for the Year 2000*. London: Office of Health Economics.

Fisher, M, Qureshi, H, Hardyman, W & Homewood, J (2006) *Using Qualitative Research in Systematic Reviews: Older people's views of hospital discharge*. How Knowledge Works in Social Care: Report 9. London: Social Care Institute for Excellence. http://

www.scie.org.uk/publications/reports/report09.pdf (Accessed 17 December 2008).

Moher, D, Schulz, KF & Altman, DG (2001) The CONSORT statement: Revised recommendations for improving the quality of reports of parallel group randomized trials. *BMC Medical Research Methodology, 1*:2. http://www.biomedcentral.com/1471-2288/1/2 (Accessed 17 December 2008).

Pawson, R, Boaz, A, Grayson, L, Long, A & Barnes, C (2003) *Types and Quality of Knowledge in Social Care*. SCIE Knowledge Review 3. London: Social Care Institute for Excellence. http://www.scie.org.uk/publications/knowledgereviews/kr03.pdf (Accessed 17 December 2008).

Popay, J & Roen, K (2003) *Using Evidence from Diverse Research Designs: A preliminary review of methodological work*. SCIE Reports No. 3. London: Social Care Institute for Excellence.

Smith, R (1997) Peer review: Reform or revolution? Time to open up the black box of peer review. *BMJ, 315*, 759–60.

Thomas, J, Sutcliffe, K, Harden, A, Oakley, A, Oliver S, Rees, R, Brunton, G & Kavanagh, J (2003) *Children and Healthy Eating: A systematic review of barriers and facilitators*. London: EPPI-Centre, Social Science Research Unit, Institute of Education, University of London.

INFLUENCING CHANGE

OUTCOMES FROM USER-FOCUSED MONITORING (UFM)
INPATIENT RESEARCH IN BRISTOL IN 2002

ROSIE DAVIES

This chapter reflects on the outcomes of a User-Focused Monitoring (UFM)[1] study in Bristol. The first part of the chapter provides some background information on the research and what happened afterwards; the rest of the chapter reflects on the implementation process.

This is inevitably a personal perspective. I was heavily involved in the implementation work and built relationships with a whole range of people as a result. I am sure that my reflections differ from those of others involved.

BACKGROUND INFORMATION

A UFM project was set up in Bristol in 2001, based at Bristol Mind. It was fortunate to be funded on an ongoing basis by the two Primary Care Trusts (PCTs) in Bristol at the time; the funding provided a paid UFM development worker – who was also required to be a service user – and an office base with space to meet and work for the other service users involved in the research.

Although my own involvement in service user activity started in 2001, Bristol has had a number of active service user groups for many years, and there has been a background of activity in campaigning for better services and service user involvement in the local trust, the Avon and Wiltshire Mental Health Partnership NHS Trust (AWP).

The first UFM study in Bristol was on inpatient services (Bristol Mind UFM Project, 2002). It included current and recent inpatients from three local hospitals: Barrow, Southmead and Blackberry Hill. Seventy-six people were interviewed in all, and eighteen service users carried out the research. The questionnaire covered many different aspects of inpatient care, and the study produced a large report with many recommendations. There were different levels of service user satisfaction with inpatient services reported in the study. However, key findings were:

---

1. User-Focused Monitoring is a research model where service users decide the subject of research, develop the instruments, administer the research and interpret the results. It aims to provide service user recommendations for service development.

- a poor physical and psychological environment for care
- insufficient information
- lack of service user involvement in the planning and reviewing of care and treatment
- not enough staff contact
- insufficient attention to ethnicity and gender and protection from harassment/ abuse
- lack of meaningful activities
- poor links with other agencies

After the report was produced it was widely disseminated to service users and staff in the area.

The UFM development worker and the senior nurse for clinical governance in Bristol set up a UFM Action Group to consider the findings and recommendations from the report. This was a key development, and included service user representatives from the UFM project, other service user groups, and staff and managers from inpatient services. The UFM Action Group was a sub-group of the Bristol Clinical Governance Forum. It aimed at collaborative working between staff and service users.

The Group agreed a number of areas to focus on: the admission process, allocation of named nurses, time spent with doctors and nurses, lack of activities on the wards, lack of safety, and involvement in care planning. On a practical front, work was initiated to improve access to drinks and kitchens at night, and on the availability of nightclothes and bedding supplies for the wards.

I had been involved in interviewing for this study, and in writing the report. I also became a member of the UFM Action Group. There were discussions about the need both to improve the admissions process and to provide more information to people on the wards. I was interested in these pieces of work because they felt tangible and practical. In some of the other areas of interest identified by the Group, it was difficult to see how action might be taken that fell within the scope and resources of those involved.

I was appointed to chair an Admissions Sub-Group, which was duly formed. This was a small working group, which included on average three service users and three staff. The main staff involved were the modern matron at Barrow Hospital, one of the ward managers and a nurse from one of the acute wards. It was formed in October 2002, usually met monthly, and the last meeting took place in April 2004. Membership over this period was quite stable, and people remained committed to the process. The Admissions Sub-Group reported back to the UFM Action Group, and sought guidance there. The Action Group reported the Sub-Group's activities from time to time to Bristol's Clinical Governance Forum.

At about the same time AWP formed an acute inpatient forum and I was invited to become a member. As a result of discussions there, what had started as a Bristol initiative became a trust-wide initiative. The Admissions Sub-Group decided to produce a patient information booklet for adult acute wards, which set standards of care and a service user-oriented admissions checklist. Getting these documents agreed as trust-wide policy meant I became involved in other committees in the trust, and in liaison and consultation on a much broader basis. The director of nursing and the deputy director of nursing were key allies in this process. The patient information booklet and the admissions checklist were circulated to all relevant staff in the trust and all service user groups in the area for two rounds of feedback.

In the spring of 2004, the Admissions Sub-Group successfully produced a patient information booklet and an admissions checklist for all the adult mental health wards in AWP. Because it was geared to a number of hospitals and wards over a large area, the patient information booklet included a list of suggestions of site-specific information that should also be available to service users.

The trust funded the printing of the booklet, and also put on six launch events in the first half of 2004. Each ward was asked to send representatives to these events so that they could see what had been produced and consider how they might introduce these new resources to the wards, including time to consider any difficulties that they might envisage in the process. Representatives were also asked to feed back to the deputy director of nursing on their implementation process, and on how they were going to monitor and evaluate the use of the two documents on their wards.

In the Avon sector of AWP at the time there were service user involvement workers. A separate initiative had started with service users in Bath and North East Somerset to address certain issues on the inpatient wards in Bath. The nurse consultant for acute care was based in Bath at that time, and she worked with the lead service user involvement worker on these issues. This led to some training being designed for inpatient staff, which included input from service users and carers, and discussion of the patient information booklet and the admissions checklist. I helped to facilitate some of this training. Parts of this training – which focused on the admissions checklist and patient information booklet – continued to be offered within the trust to inpatient staff after I ceased to be involved. This training was supported by the service user involvement worker and other service user facilitators.

AWP was also in the process of building a new hospital to replace Barrow. It may be that some of the learning from the UFM inpatient study had some indirect influence on the design or operational policies for this hospital, alongside other service user input.

So in theory everyone in AWP is now being admitted to acute wards using the admissions checklist, and will receive a copy of the patient information booklet with the names of their key workers written in for them. This has been achieved as a result of the UFM inpatient study. However, in reality, we know from anecdotal feedback that this is not necessarily happening everywhere.

REFLECTIONS ON THE IMPLEMENTATION PROCESS

KEY ALLIES

When I reflect back on the implementation process, one of the most important factors was having some key allies. One vital step in the process was the alliance between the UFM development worker and the senior nurse for clinical governance in setting up the UFM Action Group. I am not exactly sure how this happened, but my perception of the process was that it was dependent on the relationship itself and on personal commitment to the aim of collaborative working between service users and staff. The development worker and senior nurse co-chaired the Action Group for at least eighteen months, and provided stable support for the Admissions Sub-Group. They also coped with conflict within the Action Group between service users and staff. However, both these workers have moved on and the Group no longer meets.

It was also important that the Admissions Sub-Group had a fairly consistent membership, and that it was small, usually six or fewer. We agreed to discuss sections and content of the booklet. I then wrote drafts, which we all worked on. We took questions back to the Action Group for guidance. I think that people remained committed because we were doing something tangible, because we made progress, and because we developed good working relationships where everyone's contributions were respected.

Other important alliances were formed as the work became a trust-wide initiative via the acute inpatient forum. It was helpful that some suggestions from the UFM inpatient research project dovetailed with guidance that had been published by the Department of Health on acute care (Department of Health, 2002). The deputy director of nursing and the director of nursing supported the work and also the production of a carers information pack. I worked quite closely with the deputy director of nursing, who helped me to navigate my way through formal processes in the trust, and we worked together on the printing of the booklet.

Two other people were important in the process: the consultant nurse for acute care and the lead service user involvement worker for Avon. Through these connections, the work of producing and launching the booklets was linked to training of inpatient staff, initially in Bath and then in other areas. Although the consultant nurse moved on, the service user involvement worker continued to provide training on the admissions checklist and booklet for some time.

In my view, for the implementation to be successful, the training needs to be consistent around the trust, and the use of the checklist and booklet need to be audited and evaluated, which indicates the need for further work. However, it is unclear who might be involved in this process.

The implementation process has been reliant on key people working in alliance. This was not a planned process; it was based on commitment and goodwill.

MY ROLE AND NEEDS

When I took on this work, I had no idea what I had let myself in for. In retrospect, I know that I played a key role, effectively one of project management. I was involved in all aspects of the work; I made links and pulled things together. I did a lot of work. I had relevant skills and experience, and was able to work on my own initiative. However, I also needed a lot of support. What I mainly needed was to be able to talk things through, to get advice and to feel valued. I did not need or seek much practical support; for example, I did most of the typing and administration myself.

My main support came from the UFM development worker, though the senior nurse for clinical governance was also very helpful in the UFM Action Group. We were asked to take on other, related tasks along the way. For example, it was suggested that we develop an admissions care pathway! I needed help to maintain some boundaries and contain the work of the Admissions Sub-Group, so that all feedback came via the consultation process and was dealt with in the Sub-Group, rather than people trying to have particular things changed via discussions with me. It was also difficult not to be drawn into more work, such as a translation of the booklet, when it was not at all clear that anyone else would do it if we did not.

I was paid for some of the work I did, and could have been paid for much more of it. I did not feel exploited, and was challenged on how much time and energy I was investing, which I think was very important. However, I think it is potentially quite easy for UFM Projects to exploit their workers unintentionally, particularly if service users are keen to get things done.

I was also supported by the other allies described above, and by the feeling I had from people that what I was doing was valued and appreciated. It was difficult when the work was being criticised, particularly when it was criticised by service users.

At the time this was happening, I was able to put a lot of time into the project, and I was willing to do this because it generally felt productive and gave me a sense of achievement. This project came at the right time for me in my own recovery, when I was functioning fairly well and wanting to be active. I had gained some confidence from other voluntary roles that I had taken on, and wanted to stretch myself further. My needs and the projects needs coincided. Of course, this was not planned for or resourced in the UFM budget.

TIME AND RESOURCES

Implementation takes a long time and a lot of resources. Formation of the UFM Action Group and initial discussions took several months, and so it took at least two years actually to produce the booklet and checklist. After they were produced, there was still a further process of introduction to the wards at the launch events, and ongoing training for inpatient staff, which went on for at least another eighteen months. Commitment and sustained input was needed over a long period from a number of people. There is potentially still work to be done to audit and evaluate the use of the booklet and checklist, and so the implementation work does not have a clear end. Audit and evaluation could trigger further work. Also, the work I have described was only one part of work initially identified by the UFM Action Group that could be followed up as a result of the inpatient study.

The amount of time and investment needed from both service users and staff to support this kind of process is large, and therefore has to be seen to be important and worthwhile for all involved. In this case, a lot happened because the right people were available at the right time, and the inpatient study coincided with new guidance on inpatient care from the Department of Health. But, again, this was good fortune, not planning. If service user research projects want to include implementation in a more planned way, there is obviously a significant implication for ongoing funding. Getting support for implementation from the trust is also important if staff are to become involved, and they were essential in our project.

For me, it felt important that this work spread out to include staff training and other kinds of service user involvement, and was linked up to other initiatives. If service user-led research were to have more systematic links to other service user involvement work, again there would be implications for funding and resources.

LOCAL FACTORS

Bristol and the surrounding areas have well-established service user groups, which had been trying to improve mental health services in a number of different ways, including involvement with the trust. The UFM project at Bristol Mind was, therefore, established in already fertile ground, with links to other kinds of complementary service user involvement. This has many advantages. However, at times there was conflict, and the UFM project was seen as trying to steal the limelight when other groups had been trying to work on similar issues for years.

The fact that the UFM project had and has ongoing funding, a secure and independent base and a paid worker are clearly very important in supporting both the research process and any follow up and implementation. I feel it is particularly important that the project is based outside the trust, in an independent service user-led organisation.

However, it is clear that there is more work to be done on audit and evaluation. Since the inpatient study, the Bristol UFM Project has completed a study on crisis

(Bristol Mind UFM Project, 2004) and another on care planning. Having the capacity to support ongoing research *and* implementation is clearly a critical issue if such research projects are to lead to change. The Bristol UFM Project has also been approached to take on other pieces of work, which is very positive. There is, however, still only one paid worker. (And I am aware that the Bristol UFM Project is well resourced in comparison to many service user research projects.)

BEING PART OF THE TRUST'S FORMAL STRUCTURES

It was important for the implementation process that it was located in the trust's formal structures. The UFM Action Group created an important forum for staff and service users to discuss the report and start the process of deciding what could be tackled. It was important that this group included people from other service user groups in Bristol, because there could be some friction and rivalry between the older, established groups and the newer UFM Project. The Action Group managed to contain this friction and to cope with conflict between staff and service users, which at one time threatened the survival of the Group. Another difficulty was that it was very hard to get many inpatient staff to attend, particularly from different hospitals.

Through the Action Group we were linked into the Bristol Clinical Governance Forum, and later also to the Acute Care Forum. Trust committee structures were initially rather difficult to understand, and it was also hard to work out where particular decisions had to be taken – hence the need for allies. The Admissions Sub-Group needed formal status in this process, and to function within trust procedures.

CONSULTATION AND FINDING RELEVANT INFORMATION

Being part of the trust's formal structure also meant that the drafts produced in the Admissions Sub-Group went through two rounds of consultation through the trust intranet and the whole service user network. This was potentially very positive. However, consultation in such a big organisation and geographical area[3] seemed rather remote, and it was difficult to know if it was very meaningful. In theory, everyone who might have had an interest should have had the opportunity to see the drafts. Senior staff 'cascade' information to team members, and all service user groups were sent copies, but I am not sure the process was very effective. We did receive some comments and suggestions, but my feeling is that it would have been difficult for anyone to feel very involved without more tangible contact – and that was not really viable with the resources available in the Admissions Sub-Group. For example, we did not have the time or energy to go round to meet up with service user groups all around the trust, or to visit all the inpatient units.

---

3. The AWP Trust covers Bath and North East Somerset, Bristol, North Somerset, South Gloucestershire and all of Wiltshire, including Salisbury and Swindon.

It was also difficult to find other similar leaflets that had been produced, both locally and nationally. When the booklet was almost finished, I discovered that some national work was being done on how to produce patient information, but despite several attempts to acquire it, I did not succeed. Quite late in the process I discovered that another part of the trust had been doing something similar for their inpatient wards, and were somewhat disgruntled that the work we were doing was being done for the whole trust. I felt quite frustrated, as I was sure that other people must have been through a similar process and that we could have benefited from that experience.

In the shift from being a Bristol initiative to a trust-wide initiative other issues emerged. The area served by AWP had previously been organised into different trusts and, in particular, the Avon and Wiltshire areas had different histories, cultures and ways of working. Service user involvement was also very different in different areas of the trust. I know that people from outside Bristol complained because a lot of things were based in Bristol, however the UFM office is in Bristol, and I live there too.

CONCLUSION

I feel satisfied that there are tangible products from the inpatient study, which embody a stronger service user focus and standards for admission and inpatient care in our trust. Something new is happening as a result of the research. Because, in my view, most service users get involved in research to improve services, this feels really important, and, I hope, encourages others to get involved.

Implementation takes a long time and lot of effort. It was a very complex process, and I had to be resilient to stick with it. I was fortunate to have people who helped me to maintain boundaries and contain the work; without this I would not have survived.

In this implementation process a lot of what happened was partly owing to good luck and coincidence. Those of us involved took hold of those opportunities and used them to advantage, creating something positive as a result. In the absence of sufficient funding to follow up on research, my feeling is that to see change we need to seek alliances wherever we can, and seize any opportunities where different interests converge, so as to find ways to make a difference.

However, in the end I do not think that good fortune and informal networks are a reliable support for the implementation of research. I think more reliable outcomes need resources, capacity, leadership and planning. I think service user-led research projects need to develop more capacity to support research and implementation on an ongoing basis, and be linked into practice and service development processes within NHS trusts.

I am also left with concerns that the admissions checklist and patient information booklet are not necessarily being used fully, despite everything we have done. This indicates the need for audit and evaluation, which points back to having the capacity to follow up further on this work. Supporting change means participating in an ongoing process of service development and review that seems to have no end!

REFERENCES

Department of Health (2002) *Mental Health Policy Implementation Guide: Adult acute inpatient care provision.* London: Department of Health.
Bristol Mind UFM Report (2002) *User Focused Study of Inpatient Services in Three Bristol Hospitals.* Available on Bristol Mind's website, www.bristolmind.org.uk
Bristol Mind UFM Report (2004) *Crisis What Crisis?* Available on Bristol Mind's website www.bristolmind.org.uk

CHAPTER 11

INFLUENCING CHANGE
USER OR RESEARCHER? ELITISM IN RESEARCH

HEATHER JOHNSON STRAUGHAN

SOCIETY EXPECTS QUALIFICATIONS

Whether we like it or not, society demands and expects qualifications that attest to the level of education or training required to do a job well. It is usual in whatever field to expect a certain experience and competence in the skill acquired. When we speak of putting 'our lives in their hands', I know of no one who would go happily into the operating room without the assurance that their surgeon is suitably qualified, having previously carried out the procedure with success for several years. Undertaking research has these same implicit expectations.

Whether it is research from a user perspective or not, research must stand by the quality of the work, not by the quality or meaning of the standpoint alone. That we make a distinction at all might lead non-user researchers into considering that our work, although worthwhile and perhaps slightly fashionable at the moment, lacks the traditionally accepted standards, levels of training and competence of traditional research, and hence the quality of the outcome might be doubted. The distinction might wrongly mislead others into considering that user research is a somewhat subordinate, second-class field, whereas the phrase 'researching from a user standpoint' simply announces our values plainly where all can see them.

Whether we like it or not, when users and mental health professional teams meet together, although the user viewpoint might be given weight in the debate, the conclusions are often drawn by the professionals with their status of 'doctor', their extended knowledge of training in mental health, and their experience in the field. Whilst user expertise is viewed as a useful, although perhaps rare, contribution to a client's case review meeting, it is the professional who takes the direction, leads the debate and makes the conclusions. How, then, as users, can we meet professionals on equal terms and ensure that our standpoint is not put aside, albeit with reasoned politeness, in the final summing up?

LIVING THE HYPOTHESIS

I had never considered retraining in the field of mental health until I was diagnosed with bipolar disorder. Taking an honours degree in psychology seemed a cheaper and more convenient way to work through issues of mental health whilst gaining a qualification than three years of private counselling would have offered. I had never considered pursuing a masters in social research methods, nor undertaking a doctorate, until I realised that my ideas for living a more balanced and happier life with the illness might be put to the test and, if successful, might be made available to others to enable them, too, to live more fruitful lives.

It seemed that since I had put my life back on track after two manic episodes with psychotic features, lost four stones in weight and stopped drinking for a year whilst building a new life in England after fourteen years spent abroad, I was effectively living this healthier lifestyle. It also seemed plausible that I could formulate my ideas for a lifestyle development training into a course manual that could be taught to others. It seemed a plausible hypothesis that this might also result in tangible benefits for the group participants. It seemed reasonable that if I could change for the better, the training, if successful, could help others to change, and I might influence the adoption of the training by services so that it could be offered more widely to those who might benefit from it.

This, then, was my aim: to influence change from a standpoint of equality, from within the group not from without, and equipped with tools to make that influence stronger. Effectively, to win them over or to beat them, I had to join them. I had to achieve the similarly highly held status of 'doctor'. In order to influence change, I had to take account of the perspective they had in evaluating the research they considered worthy. I also had to sell my perspective by being a walking advertisement for it. I had to ensure a presence amongst them.

RESEARCHING WITH AN EYE ON OTHERS' PERCEPTIONS

A number of issues naturally cropped up: design, methodology, outcome measures, analysis, my own standpoint, validity of findings, etc., and how the training would be presented to both participants and mental health professionals I intended to engage in the study. All these issues were considered with an eye on what I considered to be of value, but also what would be considered of value by the 'professionals', both in the field of research and of mental health, so that the study would be taken not only as a piece of user research but as a piece of research in its own right.

Indeed, why make the distinction of user research as opposed to just plain research from a user standpoint? I do not see this as advancing our work from a user perspective, only damning us to a separate, perhaps subordinate sub-group of researchers. All research is value laden. Whether we admit it or not, we all start with a history, a perspective, a hypothesis. Research from a user perspective is still research, but with the twist of penetrating that world where academia and mental health care professionals have until recently been allowed free rein. Research is research, and I was determined that my work would stand or fall on the quality of the work, not from its standpoint alone. Indeed, whilst reading this, some might question whether I am a 'user researcher' at all.

THE TRAINING: NOT THROWING THE BABY OUT WITH THE BATH WATER

In writing the training, I took the view that whilst considering which techniques users had found helpful in dealing with bipolar disorder, I must also look further afield at which techniques were being used by professionals in their work with clients with the disorder. A variety of therapies was on offer from professionals – social rhythm, interpersonal, cognitive behavioural therapy, family, medication, etc. – but user groups provided only illness management or more 'soft' self-help. I felt that it was a didactic or taught training encompassing a more holistic or 'whole life' approach to a person's life that was needed, as it touched all areas of life. I had decided on a more concrete taught approach as, with learning any other new skill for the first time, like driving a car for example, it is traditionally accepted, indeed required by law, that best results are acquired after a period of learning, assimilation and practice with feedback.

Additional 'common sense' techniques derived through my own personal experiences of getting the most out of life were incorporated, so that the training now addressed a person's whole life. Whilst this seemed sensible to me, having had to rebuild my own from scratch, it also seemed wise to incorporate tried and tested professional methods. Rebuttals as to the acceptability of the training would be fewer, as effectively many of the methods employed in the training are currently available, although not widely on offer, from services, and to date are not presented in this more holistic form.

Called 'In-Sight', my training for people with bipolar disorder was named with a view to helping others achieve greater awareness of the illness and a practical 'can-do' approach to managing it. It was also so named because, from a professional standpoint, loss or maintenance of insight is often taken as a vital gauge in the assessment of a person's mental health or ill health.

INSIDER'S VIEW OUTWARD: OUTSIDER'S VIEW INWARD

A case study approach was chosen for the overall design as, working on my own, this allowed for a minimum number of participants for the study. It also allowed multiple sources of data: questionnaires and interviews from clients, professional interviews, medical notes, and my own observations. Triangulation of these sources of data would allow an overall picture to be built up to establish any change in participants following the training. I was conscious that whilst my aim was to clarify participant change through their own accounts, I wanted this change to be confirmed (or not) by mental health professionals, especially consultant psychiatrists as team leaders, to act as a sort of 'external validity' to the findings. It was important to me that both a subjective perspective from the participants, and an objective perspective from the mental health professionals, triangulate to confirm validity, and that I would attempt to explain any discrepancies in reports.

Whilst both professionals' and participants' reports on any change might be considered subjective, this standpoint is taken to mean that 'objectivity' derives from the outsider's perspective looking in on the participant, and 'subjectivity' from the insider's perspective of the participant looking outward. In this way, external validity could be likened to an objective view on what is a subjective state of mind, and reports would likely describe detailed behaviours, rather than changes in mood states or associated feelings or meanings connected to these. It was also possible that participants might report changes that were not observable by or reported to their team, and professionals report changes that had gone unnoticed by participants.

Again, as a researcher, and even more so as a researcher working from a user standpoint, I needed this confirmation of findings in order to give more weight to my work and increase the likelihood of having the training adopted by services, should it prove successful. This aim of incorporating mental health professionals' views would be encompassed within what was a user-led piece of research, with my own participant observations making sense of the whole. This sense of directing and making sense of the whole project is, I believe, vital to the final understanding and emphasis that is placed on the findings. I hoped that this, coupled with the research being carried out with the aim of achieving doctoral status, would rule out any objections about the work being a second-class or weaker piece of research due to its user standpoint.

INCORPORATING OTHERS' STANDARDS
FOR GREATER CHANGE

Within this case study approach, an experimental design was adopted for the research. This was both strategic and through choice. Society awards high status to randomised controlled trials. Randomly allocating participants to either the training group or a control group ('care as usual') seemed the best way of appealing to those who would judge this work with an eye on that benchmark. So, whilst the pilot group had eight participants with no controls owing to poor recruitment, the main study group started with eight participants and a control group of six. It was also my personal choice to use an experimental design: I know of no one who would consider taking medications in any area of health without the assurance that these had been tested rigorously and been found more effective than sugar pills alone.

Data collection methods were similarly chosen on the basis of techniques that are nowadays given more weight, i.e. quantitative data methods (here, questionnaires) were used, together with user-friendlier, qualitative data methods (here, interviews, my own observations and medical notes). Interestingly, I chose subjective participant views collected by quantitative methods, and objective professionals' views collected by qualitative methods.

Outcome measures for questionnaires covered aspects of mood, coping, empowerment and quality of life. It seemed that whilst mood stability and coping were essential to managing the illness, quality of life was equally essential to gauge how the training might positively influence many different areas of life impacted upon by the illness. Empowerment, the only user-constructed measure, indicated for me enhanced belief in coping and personal development.

Whilst quantitative analysis with Statistical Package for the Social Sciences (SPSS) for the questionnaires gave a good overall 'group snapshot' on overall change following the training, the qualitative analysis with NUD*IST[1] for the texts enabled a more detailed and personal picture to build up for each participant and for the group as a whole. Effectively, the quantitative data gave me the broad brush strokes, whereas the texts, some 160 in all, enabled me to fill these brush strokes in. All the data informed both the case study and the emergence of an overarching model of how the training appeared to impact on positive change.

Whilst working on the study, it was interesting that my two supervisors came from two different backgrounds and different epistemologies. One, an academic, favoured a more phenomenological approach and qualitative textual data; the other, a psychiatrist, favoured a more positivist, quantitative, experimental approach. During the past few years, I have happily sat in the middle of them and made up my own mind that both approaches and epistemologies are useful and have much to add, hence a more eclectic approach to my work. My own initial eclecticism, and also the need to explore the different 'tools of the trade' of a researcher, were great motivators for putting this eclecticism into practice.

---

1. NUD*IST is qualitative data analysis software.

VALIDITY OF FINDINGS

I was conscious of the fact that this research was 'user led'; in fact, it was user inspired, user developed, user written, user delivered, user analysed and user reported – it could indeed be viewed as 'user invented'. I wanted to dispel any doubt as to the validity of my findings and, as a student learning new research tools, have a second pair of eyes to check for any mistakes. I therefore decided to have my quantitative data audited for the pilot and checked thoroughly for the main study by unbiased university researchers (i.e. 'objective' researchers in that they were outsiders looking in on the work). With one or two data errors, which resulted in no changes to the findings, my findings were confirmed.

In a similar manner, I had the opportunity to take on a research assistant during the study, with whom I compared my analysis of the texts for one participant who was followed for eighteen months. The similarities of our categories and of the emphasis we had given to changes were noticeable, as were changes that were ongoing. Joint interview preparation and joint interviewing with this non-user research assistant, and confirmation from a consultant psychiatrist on changes in this participant, confirmed the validity of findings emerging from the textual analysis.

SOME INTERESTING RESULTS, FROM WITHIN AND WITHOUT

You may be wondering what the study results showed? I am pleased to say that those who participated in the training groups reported more stable mood, more good coping strategies (such as instrumental and emotional support, positive reframing) and fewer bad coping strategies (such as denial, substance abuse). They reported greater empowerment and improved quality of life post training, in comparison to pre-course scores. The control group showed no changes in these areas. Further, participants generally reported improvements in the 'skills' area of the course (better communication, greater assertiveness and anger management), which impacted on better relationships in general and, interestingly, on a change in attitude towards their mental health professional team. Improvements were also reported in the 'lifestyle' area of the course (more structure and balance, awareness of healthy eating and weight management, more exercise and an improvement in living conditions). Participants also reported a greater understanding and a more positive approach to viewing past traumas in their lives, and how this had impacted on their current behaviour.

They took more responsibility for themselves and less responsibility for others, leading to what one participant called 'stepping a different way' in her life. The majority of participants experienced a mood swing during the period of the study. All of those who experienced a mood swing coped successfully, and these improved coping strategies were fed into and reinforced by improved skills, lifestyle development and the positive reframing of past trauma. These improvements in coping serve to maintain mood stability, help a person stay well for longer, and serve to move a person on in their own development where he or she then starts to renegotiate the system to move on further. The interaction between these improvements led to a sense of greater empowerment, improved sense of self, a brighter future outlook and improvements in quality of life, which in turn fed back into the areas that would confirm the continued use of adaptive coping strategies, helping to maintain greater mood stability and personal development.

Interestingly, mental health professionals also reported that participants showed a greater understanding and acceptance of the illness, and were more able to articulate their feelings and differentiate between what was the illness and what were their 'normal' feelings. They reported that participants were more stable in mood, more rapidly recognised signs of illness onset, and quicker at putting into practice adaptive coping techniques, thereby attenuating a major mood swing. Professionals reported that participants acted more responsibly towards themselves and towards medication, and some were noted as having developed their relationship with their professional team towards a more constructive partnership and away from needing a more directive approach. Participants reported through their mental health team that they had enjoyed the course and the vital 'time out' for themselves, and had found the group of similarly diagnosed people to be supportive, de-stigmatising and enabling greater socialisation.

Some mental health professionals reported that participants were more aware of symptoms. This initial post-course reaction to learning about mood management and gaining more insight into the condition appeared to take a natural course: it later faded as this new awareness was integrated into a person's own standards of what was 'normal' for him or her, and what was not. Like learning to drive a car, when every gear shift is a conscious action, participants took time before assimilating this new knowledge into a more automatic and less thought-demanding process. Whilst some mental health professionals were delighted that their participants were more responsible for themselves after the course, others needed their participants' reassurance that they would not be sidelined in the event of a mood swing. As the coping strategies also included consulting mental health professionals in the event of becoming unwell, this had been incorporated into the training. Finally, it is worth mentioning that in progressing along their own individual paths towards recovery, participants had to renegotiate their further progress with their mental health professionals, and these professionals had to step back in order to give this process of development and responsibility room to grow. Needless to say, the timing of this renegotiation of progress was not always synchronised.

When researching for change, these 'positive for the insider' and 'observable as positive by the outsider' perspectives triangulate to confirm benefits – both for the participants in the progress they wanted to make in their lives, and for the mental health professionals in the improved quality of their therapeutic alliance, and progress in the approach to the care they might now offer. These double benefits are more likely to lead to the training being offered to those with the illness. In research terms at least, it would appear that 'further study' is indeed warranted with a larger study sample. The fact that I have remained mood stable for the last twelve years whilst living and writing this training might be considered by some researchers as irrelevant. However, it might be considered by others to be the very crux of the hypothesis itself and illustrative of what research from a user standpoint is all about.

USER RESEARCHERS AS PIONEERS IN THE 'GREY ZONE'

Whilst I was conscious of working in an environment that might be difficult to penetrate as a lone user researcher, I was also conscious that I was crossing into some sort of grey area, some pioneering zone that stretched between the users and the professionals, especially in the field of mental health and mental health research. It was for this reason that, whilst I had chosen for my base a day centre run by the voluntary sector, and had gained permission to use their address on my personally created letterhead, I also felt I needed the logos of both the university and the county NHS trust. I felt that this piece of research would have a greater potential for change if it were perceived to be interdisciplinary and collaborative. In addition, as a prerequisite of doing the study, I signed an honorary contract with the trust, and the title of clinical research fellow was duly added under my name. To influence change, I believe there has to be change. This initial change gave me status, and my trust identity badge gave me membership of a closed circle that initially did not take to my presence comfortably at their weekly case study meetings.

However, attend them I did. These doctors would be those who would give me their feedback on changes in participants (their patients), and I was aware I had to work at this goodwill to win them over. Several were welcoming from the start; one or two took years of my presence to accept me; thankfully a hostile response was rare. I knew that since I had crossed over the professional boundary into the area called 'mental health service user', I would always be perceived as the user first, and the researcher second. Unfortunately, some people's perceptions would implicitly seek to prevent a person ever to make the 'return journey'.

I felt I needed to achieve doctoral status to make the user perspective somehow more valid, for it to carry more weight in the debate, and possibly to enable me to challenge this incongruence from a viewpoint of equality. Being called 'doctor' would just make things simpler and cut through all the status issues, making my point of view as important as anyone else's in the room, at the summing up of the case study meeting. I wanted the user standpoint to have equality, but that meant refusing the 'user' label, brushing off others' perceptions as inadequate and outdated, and trying to cross back over the boundary to re-enter the 'researcher' area.

I was grateful that my own consultant psychiatrist, who encouraged me in my work, was comfortable with a patient who was fast becoming more of a work colleague. In my discussions with him, I often referred to this as the 'pioneering grey zone', and we both acknowledged that some were not as comfortable as others with this new challenge. Fundamentally, though, I believe it is very much their problem, not mine. Even as I am writing this, I am aware that the us/them dichotomy is still being imposed upon me; other people are uncomfortable about allowing me to look any differently on an opportunity that might not only be helpful for me in my own personal development, but might open up the possibility of development in research in general.

USER RESEARCHER: SECOND-CLASS RESEARCHER OR IDEAL TRAVEL GUIDE?

From the very beginning, I was conscious of this 'user/researcher' dichotomy: to professionals, I was the user; to my participants, I was the researcher. This no man's land between the two became what I perceived to be a perfect bridge and place of unique insight that could bring the two together to influence change. I believe that a more rounded and detailed work can be rendered by users who are researching – more complete for having the knowledge of the sensations, depths of feelings and meanings, and the abject horrors of how illness can impact on one's life. Textbooks on research can be read; personal experience is lived, real experience. No reading or memorising of texts or testimonials can ever hope to make this a living and breathing experience for non-user researchers.

Schutz's researcher takes on the viewpoint of a 'stranger'[2] who arrives for the

---

2. Schutz considered that there were three types or mental constructs which help us understand behaviour around us. In an urban setting, there are (1) the person on the street, getting by without much deep reflection, i.e. having lived experience of a topic; (2) the cartographer with expertise to map environments, who is detached, i.e. an academic researcher without lived experience; and (3) the stranger who needs to have a sufficient understanding of the environment but is neither without reflection nor trapped within a narrow viewpoint of a specialism. According to Schutz, the 'stranger' is likened to 'a bridge' between the two distinct vantage points.

However, what is proposed by the author is that by being informed by experiential knowledge and lived experience, the scientific study of the stranger would be enhanced in its deeper understanding of the events observed. This is developed further by the idea of the cross-cultural travel guide (academically trained user researchers) whose lived experience of mental ill health and knowledge of research methods provide the combination of both detached academia and first time in a town and builds up his understanding of people's actions through noting patterns of behaviour through close observation. In contrast, I believe that the user researcher is the perfect translator of understanding and meaning from a user perspective. The user researcher is the person who would guide Schutz's stranger as he alights to take his tour of the town, would show him local colour that he would miss in the recommended guidebook, and would explore with him the importance of the town and meanings for its people with the appropriate vocabulary that he would not otherwise experience or indeed ever hope truly to understand.

Some might liken being a user researcher to the stance of a native ethnographer who bridges two cultures. Native ethnography again draws on the theme of crossing between two differing cultures, serving as a bridge between two worlds – or being what I like to call the ideal, cross-cultural 'translator travel guide'. If we are to be mindful that academia may be elitist, we must also allow for the possibility that as user researchers working in this rare, pioneering age of cross-culturalism, we could also find ourselves as a somewhat small sub-group or 'elite'. Does this actually serve our purposes?

USER RESEARCHERS: THEIR OWN ELITE?

In calling ourselves 'user researchers', we are not well served by distinguishing ourselves as a race of researchers apart from the rest. For this implies that we would tend to put our standpoint first, rather than the quality of the work that would seek to emphasise this very standpoint. We do not need to do this, as our work is already doing that for us.

When we are perceived firstly as service users with the research quotient tacked on behind, we risk being viewed by some as dabbling in research, rather than as being competent, trained and experienced researchers who stand by the quality of their work. We risk being sidelined into a sub-group whilst mainstream research maintains its superordinate status, into which we are denying ourselves entry.

In announcing our standpoint first, we are perhaps unaware that the outcome of our work will be initially considered on the basis of that standpoint and viewed from that perspective alone. Resultant outcomes, like behaviours emitted from a person with a mental health diagnosis, are then perceived in the light of this overriding theme, and the actual competence and quality of the work, like clients' behaviours, are only explained within the confines of this limited view. We in turn might find this limiting. If we do not remove this primary emphasis, we are not

lived experience, which the 'stranger' cannot ever hope to have. It is therefore this cross-cultural translator travel guide, situated between the two domains and richly connected to both, that user researchers offer to a greater extent than any one of the two on their own, or indeed the stranger's viewpoint.

likely to achieve much, nor very quickly, as we are in fact boxing ourselves in, just as any diagnostic label might inhibit the person from achieving any more than the label will allow. By standing outside that which we wish to influence, and not putting our research skills first, we are probably not making a good long-term choice. In as much as we try to refrain from using nouns to describe people's mental illnesses, i.e. we replace 'schizophrenic' with 'a person experiencing schizophrenia', likewise, I feel we might be better served if the phrase 'user researcher' was reversed to 'researcher from a service user standpoint' – or, as no work is value free, simply 'researcher'. I feel we would get more mileage out of that.

Whilst we may fear being assimilated into the overriding 'traditional research' identity, or being sidelined by more traditional approaches not favouring our own, we are not allowing ourselves the possibility of belonging to the wider research community. This participation does not mean giving up our own user standpoint identity, but being both within the wider research community and separate from it in our own standpoint group. I find it interesting that, at a time when the different sections of psychology are going through a period of change, researchers engaged in work from a user standpoint might also benefit from the more positive approaches to conflict and diversity management that are emerging, so that we might position our work for maximum benefit within a more organic, pluralist approach. This would seem to allow for the wider research community housing many different standpoints, involving all in the change and developmental processes which I feel sure we would wish to influence.

When we speak about engendering change, it is also the change of the whole group of researchers from a user standpoint. We must be aware that if our work is to have real effects on mainstream research, we must influence it by participating in it. We must allow ourselves to enter that wider 'research' group, not stand outside of it by announcing our differences, rather than our similarities, first. As in my own research study, it is not easy to be allowed by mental health professionals to cross back over the boundary and leave the 'service user' subordinate to the 'researcher', but it is a necessary journey for real change, for both service users and mental health professionals.

FOR CHANGE, THERE MUST BE CHANGE

I thought it a testimony to my consultant's forward thinking that he was aware that these were pioneering days in user involvement and research, and that he was comfortable with this. For those who were not so at ease, my attendance at these case study meetings had apparently changed the tone of them. But I was aware that to engender change, there must be change. Coming from two different perspectives, two different standpoints, one medical, one user, could mean that we would meet somewhere in the middle of this grey pioneering area, but still remain with our two different and opposing views. That is not what I hoped for, nor how I see this story ending, if we are indeed all to move forward together. I wanted to start not from the 'user perspective', but from a different one, a fresh one that I hoped would be more constructive. However, how to start from this fresh perspective if others are more comfortable viewing you as the service user with its inherent standpoint? I realised that I would meet professionals coming from their standpoint, and defending their values, their training and personal experience, their way of how things might be done, and, up until then, how things had been done. Effectively, they would be defending their power, unable to choose from other more constructive behaviours.

It seems to me that we have a choice of how users, and researchers from a user standpoint, might proceed. Either we start from opposing sides and achieve equality through hard-bitten struggles, and we win out, as win out we undoubtedly will; or, we start from a new perspective, which I hope my research is testimony to. Such a perspective incorporates both positions to move forward together. Therein lies the challenge: whilst some are willing to work in this new pioneering area that lacks clarity, that makes you question what you do and how you do it, some are unwilling or unable to leave their past behind, whether professional or user, to go a new way. As my own research participant reminded me, it is a case of 'stepping a different way'. For me, that means change for all of us, as researchers from whatever standpoint, and for mental health professionals and service users in general, else we limit our own potential for real change.

DO WE WANT CHANGE OR TRANSFORMATION?

In these pioneering days of researching from a service user standpoint, a standpoint that is theoretically at the heart of mental health services, those who have the skills and tools and the lived experience, as well as the insight into the meaning and value attached to that lived experience, have the chance to engender real change. The question is whether researchers engaged in user standpoint work would wish for permanent transformation, and to lead on good practice in allowing us all to 'step a different way'?

In my work, in as much as I have incorporated both the outsider and insider perspective to note changes resulting from my training, I also think that choosing one perspective above the other is not much of a choice at all. It is neither the user viewpoint nor the more medical, traditional research perspective that should be given more weight than the other. As services become increasingly 'client-centred' and indeed 'client-commissioned', it seems clear which perspective will eventually win out. However, as in my own research, not throwing the baby out with the bath water would mean improving on the old, not simply disregarding it. Whichever route research from a user standpoint takes to develop and engender what I hope will be permanent transformation, it is all hard work!

LIKE ANYTHING WORTH DOING, ACADEMIA MEANS WORK!

Academia is all hard work, and that means that anyone can do it if they are prepared to put the effort into it and want it enough. That means you. It is certainly not easy: working as a lone researcher can be isolating, and your self-reliance and thinking processes are always developing, but it is never boring. It is never without value, and it never loses its motivating forces for you, as you aim to drive through change in an environment that may seek to question every move you make or decision you take, and whose behaviours you naturally question in turn. Your ultimate responsibility for the project resides with you. Whether the work gets done or not is up to you, but ultimately the greatest motivator is that your work, now validated as effective, may be offered (as in my case) to all the other service users with bipolar disorder. The final act for change must be the aim to make practical use of your study in making it available to all: hence my current challenge of establishing a new service where the training might be offered – not another object on my shelf to dust!

As my study is concluding, there is a great sense of personal satisfaction that I have worked hard at developing my skills and thinking processes to gain the status of a recognised, trained professional researcher with doctoral status. I feel that, as the ideal 'translator tour guide', I am able to offer a deeper understanding of the user perspective to those who will always be without this vital component. As you may imagine, this has also been a time of much personal development. The final impact of influencing change and increasing the swiftness with which we have become accustomed to see this change take place is, I hope, also likely to be brought about. As I have consistently worked with this aim in mind, I would certainly hope that to be the case. I find that an interesting hypothesis that I hope many of you reading this would like to explore further. I wish you all the best in your future doctoral work!

REFERENCE

Schutz, A (1944) The stranger: An essay in social psychology, *American Journal of Sociology*, *49*(6), 409–507.

CHAPTER 12

A ROUGH GUIDE TO
GETTING STARTED

ALISON FAULKNER

The aim of this chapter is to provide a few ideas, questions and resources to help you if you want to undertake a piece of research yourself. It is a reasonably quick walk through the issues, and is not intended as a comprehensive guide to undertaking research.

1. WHY RESEARCH?

It is helpful to be clear about why you want to carry out a piece of research (as against, for example, writing, training or campaigning about an issue). You may wish to find out something new; to evaluate a service or group; to explore the extent of local interest in an issue or new service development; to describe something about a population. Research can be a valuable tool in providing evidence for a campaign, but it is a slow process and cannot provide you with that evidence instantly. Carrying out research in an inclusive way with a service user group can also be a route to improving or increasing user involvement.

There is a difference, in research governance terms, between *research* and *audit*. If obtaining people's views about a service can be categorised as 'audit', then it may not need to go through all of the formal procedures to which research with patients as participants is subject to (e.g. obtaining Research Ethics Committee approval).

It is helpful to know the kind of 'research' that you want to do – although this will depend on the particular question being asked (see below).

RESEARCH

This word is often used to refer to some of the others in this list. Strictly speaking, research refers to the process of investigating something new, perhaps expecting participants in the research to respond to a questionnaire or interview schedule that measures them or their attitudes in some way. Sometimes, participants may give their permission for researchers to investigate records kept about them. They may be 'measured' before and after an intervention. Research may be quantitative or qualitative or a combination of the two (see below).

EVALUATION

This term is usually used to refer to the process of evaluating a service or intervention against certain standards, or against the aims and objectives established at the start of its provision. Has the [service] met its objectives? Does it meet the standard criteria for such a service? Typically, evaluation involves a combination of quantitative and qualitative approaches, as there are some things that will need to be counted (e.g. the number of people passing through a service in a specified time period), and some things that need to be explored (e.g. reasons for providing the service in a particular way). Evaluation of a service might include measures of people's mental health or well-being in order to explore whether the service has been instrumental in bringing about change or improvement.

AUDIT (OR MONITORING)

Audit tends to be somewhat more straightforward than evaluation, in that it is focused on finding out if a service is doing what it says it is doing – and in finding out if the people using it are satisfied with it. Audit is expected to take place in NHS trusts on a regular basis.

CONSULTATION

Consultation tends to take place at an early stage in developing a service, at the beginning of research, or perhaps with a view to finding out the views of a particular section of a population to determine if their needs are being met. Typically, a consultation might involve a combination of face-to-face methods (e.g. interviews or focus groups) and a survey in order to capture the views of a larger number of people.

2. WHAT RESEARCH DO YOU WANT TO DO?

The following questions may help you to make some decisions about your research (although see section three, below, for additional hints).

- *Write down your idea for research.*
- *What is it you want to find out?* What is the overall aim of your research?
- *Why do you want to do this research?* Who will benefit? Has anyone done something similar before?
- *What theory or theories are underlying this research?* What thoughts and ideas do you have about the situation you want to research? Do you have a 'theoretical framework' for it?

- *What are your research objectives?* E.g. by the end of your research, you will have demonstrated ... x, y, z. Objectives need to be *precise, realistic, achievable, measurable ... PRAM.*
- *Who will do it?* Do you want to carry out the research yourself, or as part of a team? If the latter, what sort of people might you need to join you?

3. DEFINING AND REFINING YOUR RESEARCH QUESTION

This is an important step in the process. If you can refine your research question well, many other things (e.g. the methods and the kind of participants) may emerge from it. In Table 1, there is an example to help you in this process. In this example, a series of questions are asked of almost every word in the original research idea, in order to help refine the research question and hence the research project.

Table 1: *Refining your research question*

Does providing an advocacy service[1] for people[2] who come to A&E[3] after self-harming[4] improve their outcomes[5]?

1. What do you mean by an advocacy service?
2. Who do you want to include in your research? Are there any people you want to exclude?
3. What stage in admission to A&E are you interested in? When and where will the advocacy service be provided?
4. What do you mean by self-harm in this study? Are there any exclusions?
5. What 'outcomes' are you interested in? How will you know if they are improved?

With thanks to Professor Allan House, Leeds University

---

4. WHICH METHODS WILL YOU USE?

The first question to ask is: which methods are best suited to the question/s you are asking? For example, do you need to count how often something occurs, measure something, or ask in-depth questions of people to find out about people's views, feelings or attitudes about the issue/s? The methods need to fit the aims and objectives, although there may be other factors affecting them, such as time constraints or resources.

Research tends to be divided into *quantitative* (i.e. predominantly about numbers) and *qualitative* approaches (predominantly about meanings). Both approaches have their strengths and weaknesses, and can be used in combination to good effect. However, in the wider research world, quantitative approaches have established a higher status because they can more readily feed into society's need for evidence. In the survivor research world, there has been a tendency to prefer qualitative methods, often because we place a higher value on hearing people's stories and understanding their own meanings. This is by no means universal however, and both methods have their contribution to make.

If you wish to gain the views of a large number of people, then you are likely to need a questionnaire approach, whereas if you wish to find out more in-depth information about people's experiences or feelings about an issue, then face-to-face interviews with a smaller number of people will be appropriate. Either way, the careful design of the questions is of paramount importance. Good research depends on good design from the outset. If you need further advice about choosing your research method, then we would suggest approaching one of the organisations listed at the end of this chapter or your local university or trust R&D department, and obtaining one of the research guides recommended (e.g. Faulkner & Nicholls, 1999; Denscombe, 2007).

5. VALUES AND ETHICS

A vital part of the process of planning your research is thinking about the values and ethics underlying it. Ethics in research is not simply about the need to gain approval from a Research Ethics Committee; it is about how you conduct your research and yourself, the context in which you are doing the research, and – crucially – how you treat and involve your research participants. It is also about the underlying theoretical perspectives that you hold, and how you communicate these to your co-workers and research participants. There are two useful guides to help you in this respect, and both are available for download online: *The Ethics of Survivor Research* (Faulkner, 2004) and *Values and Methodologies for Social Research in Mental Health* (Tew, Gould, Abankwa, Barnes, Beresford et al., 2006).

The Ethics of Survivor Research, which was based on interviews and focus groups with service user and survivor researchers, identified the following underlying principles for survivor research:

- clarity and transparency
- empowerment (see emancipatory purpose, below)
- identity
- commitment to change
- respect
- equal opportunities

- theoretical approach
- accountability

The report proceeds to take each stage in the research process in turn and to consider the ethical issues surrounding it:

1. planning and design
2. recruitment and involvement (of fellow researchers)
3. training, support and supervision
4. involving participants
5. analysis and feedback
6. dissemination and implementation
7. Research Ethics Committees

Values and Methodologies for Social Research in Mental Health, in a complementary approach, explores five themes 'that may help to define the value base of social research in mental health' (Tew et al., 2006: 5):

1. *Partnerships:* How relevant stakeholders, such as service users, carers and practitioners can be meaningfully involved as partners in key aspects of the research process.
2. *Standpoints and distance:* Good research needs to combine the 'insider' (experientially based) knowledge and insights of service users and carers with frameworks that give space for rigorous analysis, so that a clear and authoritative picture can emerge.
3. *Holism not reductionism:* Looking at a person's experience as part of their wider context.
4. *Recognition of social diversity:* Acknowledging the impact of social divisions on people's experience and opportunities, and being cautious about applying research findings from one social or cultural group to another.
5. *Emancipatory purpose:* How will research outputs enable people to attain fuller social and economic participation and exercise more informed choice in relation to the services they receive?

6. PLANNING YOUR RESEARCH PROJECT

There are a great many things to think about when planning your research project. The following suggestions are based on those given in Faulkner (2004).

SUGGESTIONS FOR PLANNING AND DESIGN

1. Think about whom you want to involve in your research: do you need to approach research partners, service user group(s) or university researchers?

2. Access to research participants and services may need to be negotiated at an early stage. Whilst the need to rely on professional gatekeepers may raise problems, it may also be an asset to negotiate with someone who can offer support from within the service.

3. The potential for flexibility needs to be built in from the start: issues such as support, rescheduling the timetable or scope of the research, and anticipating the need for extra time at the end of the project may need to be considered.

4. Find out if your project needs to have the approval of your local Research Ethics Committee: this will need extra time and resources to negotiate. Contact your trust Research & Development department for assistance with this and with other permissions you may need (such as obtaining a Criminal Records Bureau [CRB] check).

5. Plan in some time and resources for the dissemination of your findings and feedback to research participants.

6. Finally, put together a budget outline for obtaining funding.

SUGGESTED CHECKLIST FOR FUNDING

- support for co-researchers and interviewers (may be an additional support worker or alternative)
- external supervision, e.g. to coordinator of a project
- enough funding to include more people than the project needs, to cover for periods of absence
- physical resources, such as space and communications technology
- training of researchers, interviewers, etc.
- social events/time to meet with each other if you are working with a group
- dissemination: in different formats relevant to your project (e.g. language, accessible, written and oral presentations)
- insurance – liability
- fees for participants*
- payment to researchers*

> * PAYING PEOPLE
> One important part of the design and planning of your project is to think about who is involved in the research and how they might be paid (assuming that you have found a source of funding – see section seven below!). There are

some useful resources available that provide advice and information on how to pay people who are currently receiving benefits.

- INVOLVE (2006) *A Guide to Reimbursing and Paying Members of the Public Who Are Actively Involved in Research: For researchers and research commissioners (who may also be people who use services).* First published February 2002. http://www.invo.org.uk/pdfs/Payment_Guidefinal 240806.pdf (Accessed 17 December 2008)

- Mental Health Foundation (2003) *A Fair Day's Pay: A guide to benefits, service user involvement and payments.* Available from http:// www.mentalhealth.org.uk/publications/?entryid5=67804

- Turner, M & Beresford, P (2005) *Contributing on Equal Terms: Service user involvement and the benefits system.* Adult Services Report 08. Shaping Our Lives. London: Social Care Institute for Excellence. http:// www.shapingourlives.org.uk/downloads/publications/benefitsreport oct05.pdf (Accessed 17 December 2008). Also available from http:// www.scie.org.uk

7. FUNDING

This is not an easy part of the process! Sometimes, it is possible that a call for proposals from the Department of Health may cover a topic close to your heart and you have found a possible funder. However, since these funders/commissioners of research are likely to prioritise larger and academic organisations, you are likely to need a research partner in order to proceed. If this is the case, it is well worth approaching your local university or trust to see if there may be interested partners. The INVOLVE website (www.invo.org.uk) also provides information on people who are interested in undertaking collaborative research.

Another route to finding research partners is through accessing the National Academic Mailing List Service, known as JISCmail. This has a 'User Involvement Research' mailing list, which 'aims to bring together people with expertise in user involvement and public participation in the evaluation and delivery of public services' and 'seek to take forward theoretical, conceptual and practical thinking around different types and mechanisms of user involvement. We seek to promote engagement with researchers, providers, policy makers across the higher education, voluntary and public sectors.' If you have an academic contact, you can join the list or search the archives at http://www.jiscmail.ac.uk/archives/user-involvement.html

There are other research funders who fund research in this field, and some of them are listed below. They tend to have their own funding priorities, which change from year to year, and will announce funding rounds as they occur. Nevertheless, you can contact them to find out if they have any forthcoming funding rounds.

- *Mental Health Foundation* www.mentalhealth.org.uk (020 7803 1101)
- *Joseph Rowntree Foundation* www.jrf.org.uk (01904 629241)
- *National Lottery* To find out about applying for funding visit the National Lottery Funding website at www.lotteryfunding.org.uk or call 0845 275 0000

Sometimes, local sources of funding are the most appropriate and convenient way forward.

8. USEFUL RESOURCES[1]

SOURCES OF ADVICE AND INFORMATION

INVOLVE
Part of the National Institute for Health Research, INVOLVE exists to promote public involvement in NHS, public health and social care research.

INVOLVE
Wessex House
Upper Market Street
Eastleigh
Hampshire
SO50 9FD

Email: admin@invo.org.uk
Telephone: 02380 651088
Textphone: 02380 626239
Fax: 02380 652 885
www.invo.org.uk

SHAPING OUR LIVES
Shaping Our Lives National User Network is an independent user-controlled organisation. It started as a research and development project but became an independent organisation in 2002.

Shaping Our Lives
BM Box 4845
London
WC1N 3XX

---

1. Details correct at time of going to press.

Email: information@shapingourlives.org.uk
Telephone: 0845 241 0383
Text users please use TYPE TALK: 18001 0845 241 0383
http://www.shapingourlives.org.uk/

SERVICE USER RESEARCH ENTERPRISE (SURE)
SURE is a collaborative research team comprising ten people most of whom are or have been mental health service users. SURE aims to do research from the service user's perspective and has developed new methodologies in order to be true to this.

SURE
PO34
Health Service and Population Research Department
Institute of Psychiatry
King's College London
De Crespigny Park
London
SE5 8AF

Telephone: 020 7848 5066/0430
Fax: 020 7277 1462
Contact: Diana Rose (d.rose@iop.kcl.ac.uk) or Andrew White
(andrew.white@iop.kcl.ac.uk)
www.iop.kcl.ac.uk/departments/?locator=300

SURESEARCH
Adrian Fisher, User Network Coordinator
Centre of Excellence in Interdisciplinary Mental Health (CEIMH)
University of Birmingham
Edgbaston
Birmingham
B15 2TT

Email: a.fisher@bham.ac.uk
Telephone: 0121 414 8170
www.suresearch.org.uk

Suresearch is a network of service users in research and education. It welcomes as members users and survivors of mental health services and their allies who have experience and/or an interest in mental health research and education.

SURF
Research and Development Office
Avon and Wiltshire Mental Health Partnership NHS Trust
Hillview Lodge
Combe Park
Bath
BA1 3NG

Email: research@awp.nhs.uk
Telephone: 01225 825423

The Service User Research Forum (SURF) is a group convened by the Avon and Wiltshire Mental Health Partnership NHS Trust, to support research involving the Trust. SURF is a Trust group, chaired by a service user. The forum provides a resource for service users and researchers to increase service user involvement in research and to share research findings. The group operates on a membership basis, and meets throughout the year.

SERVICE USER RESEARCH GROUP, ENGLAND (SURGE)

SURGE
Institute of Psychiatry, King's College London
PO Box 77
De Crespigny Park
London
SE5 8AF

Email: surge@iop.kcl.ac.uk
Telephone: 020 7848 0699
www.mhrn.info/index/ppi/service-user-involvement.html

SURGE is the Service User Research Group for England and is the service user arm of the UK Mental Health Research Network (MHRN). SURGE is a national network set up to support mental health service users and people from universities and NHS trusts, as they work together on mental health research.

UFM NETWORK (USER-FOCUSED MONITORING)

The UFM Network was set up in 2002 to provide a safe and supportive space for coordinators and UFM group members to share their work and learn from each other. It was originally based at the Sainsbury Centre for Mental Health, and many of its original publications can still be obtained from them. It meets quarterly and can be contacted through its website: www.ufm@bristolmind.org.uk. The UFM

Network is made up of projects across England and Wales who have come together to offer mutual support and to establish best practice within User-Focused Monitoring.

RESEARCH GUIDES AND OTHER USEFUL REFERENCES

Buckland, S, Hayes, H, Ostrer, C, Royle, J, Steel, R, Tarpey, M, Walton, J & Yeeles, P (2007) *Public Information Pack (PIP): How to get actively involved in NHS, public health and social care research*. INVOLVE. http://www.invo.org.uk/pdfs/PIP1whatisitallabout.pdf (Accessed 17 December 2008).

Copperman, J, Ferns, P, Tew, J, Keating, F, Wallcraft, J, Sweeney, A, Alsop, P, Castillo, H, Hatzidimitriadou, E, Harris, A, Glynn, T, Wells, S et al. (2003) Where you stand affects your point of view. Emancipatory approaches to mental health research. Notes from SPN Study Day, 12 June 2003. SPN Paper 4. London: Social Centre for http://www.spn.org.uk/fileadmin/SPN_uploads/Documents/Papers/SPN_Papers/SPN_Paper_4.pdf (Accessed 17 December 2008).

Denscombe, M (2007) *The Good Research Guide: For small-scale social research projects* (3rd edn). Buckingham: Open University Press.

Direct Impact Research Group (2005) Research jargon buster. *Mental Health and Learning Disabilities Research and Practice, 2*(2), 151–5.

Direct Impact Service User and Carer Research Group (2004) *Involving Service Users and Carers in Audit, Evaluation and Research and Other Projects to Improve and Develop Services*. South West Yorkshire Mental Health NHS Trust.

Faulkner, A (2004) *The Ethics of Survivor Research: Guidelines for the ethical conduct of research carried out by mental health service users and survivors*. Bristol: Policy Press, in association with the Joseph Rowntree Foundation. (Also available online: http://www.jrf.org.uk/bookshop/eBooks/1861346662.pdf)

Faulkner, A & Nicholls, V (1999) *The DIY Guide to Survivor Research*. London: Mental Health Foundation.

Nicholls, V (2001) *Doing Research Ourselves*. London: Mental Health Foundation.

Nicholls, V, Wright, S, Waters, R & Wells, S (2003) *Surviving User-Led Research: Reflections on supporting user-led research projects*. London: Mental Health Foundation.

Rose, D (2001) *Users' Voices: The perspectives of mental health service users on community and hospital care*. London: Sainsbury Centre for Mental Health.

Rose, D, Ford, R, Lindley, P, Gawith, L & the KCW Mental Health Monitoring Users' Group (1998) *In Our Experience: User-focused monitoring of mental health services in Kensington & Chelsea and Westminster Health Authority*. London: Sainsbury Centre for Mental Health.

SURGE (Service User Research Group, England) (2005) *Service User Involvement in the UK Mental Health Research Network: Guidance for good practice*. London: UK Mental Health Research Network.

Tew, J, Gould, N, Abankwa, D, Barnes, H, Beresford, P, Carr, S, Copperman, J, Ramon, S, Rose, D, Sweeney, A & Woodward, L (2006) *Values and Methodologies for Social Research in Mental Health*. London: Social Perspectives Network; Bristol: Policy Press. http://www.spn.org.uk/fileadmin/SPN_uploads/Documents/Papers/SPN_Papers/Values_and_methodologies.pdf (Accessed 17 December 2008).

Thorne, L, Purtell, R & Baxter, L (2001) *Knowing How: A guide to getting involved in research*. Exeter: University of Exeter.

Turner, M & Beresford, P (2005) *User-Controlled Research: Its meanings and potential.* Shaping Our Lives and the Centre for Citizen Participation, Brunel University. INVOLVE.

UFM Network (2003) *Doing It For Real: A guide to setting up and undertaking a User Focused Monitoring project.* London: Sainsbury Centre for Mental Health. http://www.scmh.org.uk/pdfs/ufm+doing+it+for+real.pdf (Accessed 17 December 2008).

FROM ACTIVIST TO RESEARCHER AND PART-WAY BACK

JAN WALLCRAFT

INTRODUCTION

I am a mental health researcher and an activist. This chapter is about my journey and how I see the advantages and problems of being both.

As a child, I was unable to make any sense of my world. As a teenager I began to want to change it, and even to believe I could. I felt that if I could see injustice, I had a responsibility to act. I can't remember when I first heard Marx's statement that 'Philosophers have only interpreted the world, in various ways; the point however is to change it' (Marx, 1845), but it became a powerful idea for me. At the same time, I lacked self-confidence and the knowledge and skills to make a difference. I was at the start of a journey with more twists and turns than I could have imagined.

RESEARCH AND ACTIVISM

I will briefly define the key terms I am using:

Research is systematic investigation designed to develop or contribute to generalisable knowledge.

Activism is intentional action to bring about social or political change. This action is in support of, or opposition to, one side of a controversial argument.

Clearly there is a potential for a contradiction – or perhaps conflict – between the two activities. A commitment to activism risks compromising the integrity of research, while becoming immersed in research could waste time better spent on trying to correct obvious injustice. Can activism bring something valuable to research, or should it be left behind at the door to the 'liberal university' (Hammersley, 1995)? Hammersley conceives the liberal university and the role of academics as the guarantors of the autonomy and neutrality needed for the pursuit of intrinsically valuable knowledge as a cultural resource. Without this, he argues, there is nothing to prevent research and knowledge production from 'collapsing into relativism' (Hammersley, 1995: 160) – where no shared value systems or truths can exist – or becoming controlled by economic or ideological interest groups.

Hammersley dismisses the claims of feminists and black researchers regarding the importance of research that takes a female perspective or an anti-racist starting point. I am sure that if more had been written on survivor-led research in 1995, he would have taken the same line on that. He argues that 'the purpose of emancipation' is not a legitimate goal of research (Hammersley, 1995: 117).

Mental health system survivors and their allies take a different view, arguing for emancipatory research led by service users, which uses empowering research processes (Mental Health Foundation, 2003), and produces evidence and theory that will enable service users to make more informed choices, have more control over their lives, and participate more in wider society (Tew, Gould, Abankwa, Barnes, Beresford et al., 2006). I believe that involving service users in research – for instance in deciding priorities for research, how research should be done, and in carrying it out – will in time make a huge difference to the knowledge resources available to support mental health policy decisions.

Mental health service users have traditionally been excluded from creating the knowledge that is used to treat us, and many of us have suffered from the misunderstanding of our needs by people who have been taught to see us as by definition incapable of rational thought.

STAGE ONE: MY LIFE HISTORY – THE ORIGINS OF MY ACTIVISM

Nobody, I would guess, becomes an activist in mental health without some roots in personal life experience. Many mental health researchers, too, have personal connections with the subject.

I have written elsewhere about how I came to be a mental health system survivor (Wallcraft, 1993, 1996). Although I had a difficult start in life, growing up on a grim estate in Coventry, I inherited some strengths from my parents. My working-class origins (on my father's side from Liverpool, and on my mother's from the Welsh valleys) gave me a sense that community could and should be the norm, even though we were isolated as a family, and I was a shy and lonely child. My mother encouraged me to read, and there were books in the house, unlike most of our neighbours' homes. My father had an enquiring mind, and taught me the parable of the Six Blind Men and the Elephant, demonstrating that nobody had a monopoly on truth, even if they could claim direct empirical evidence for their beliefs – a valuable lesson to take in at the age of six!

As a teenager I began to see political and sociological explanations for my unhappiness. Joining campaigns and political groups made me feel I belonged. But after a breakdown at the age of 22, and mind-numbing ECT, I felt the only community to which I belonged was that of the outsiders. There was no survivor movement in the early 1970s, so far as I was aware, and so once free of the hospital, I hid my experience as best I could and learned to cope.

Introduction to survivor activism and research came simultaneously for me in the mid 1980s. At the age of 35 I started a degree at Middlesex Polytechnic (now Middlesex University) called 'Science, Technology and Society'. I researched ECT for my final year degree project, carrying out a mini-survey of people's experiences of treatment, and reading widely on the subject. I met another survivor on my course, who invited me to join the group creating the documentary *We're Not Mad, We're Angry*, which was eventually shown on Channel 4 in 1986. I met some of the leaders of the survivor movement for the first time. Tentatively, I began to reach out to others and to reclaim the bits of myself that I had locked away inside: a painful and frightening process. I discovered I needed all the help I could get. I needed the political consciousness-raising of the London women and mental health network, and my friends from the video-making group, but I also went into psychotherapy and joined self-help groups, developing a circle of friends that I could ring when I felt myself start to go into a depression.

WHAT I HAVE LEARNED

At this stage, survivor activism and research were simultaneously helping me to regain my self-esteem, re-integrate my shattered personality, and learn how to talk to others and support others, as well as seek help for myself. I began to learn some ways of managing depression, anxiety and eating problems. As a researcher, I had my induction into how to do systematic information gathering and analysis, and how to write an academic essay. Gaining my degree was an enormous boost to my confidence.

STAGE TWO: ACTIVISM AS A DAY JOB

I began my career in mental health. After my breakdown I had worked in dozens of agency jobs as an audio-typist, as the agencies did not ask too many questions about my past. But at this point in 1987, I had the amazing good fortune to be taken on at the national Mind office, to set up the Mindlink network. This felt like my first real job. I was scared and nervous, but so excited to be given this chance. I was paid to do something I believed in – bringing people together in a supportive community, to change attitudes about mental health. Involving service users was a culture change for Mind, and I struggled at first to make much impression on well-meaning but patronising attitudes. I noticed that as staff left and were replaced, the task became easier. New people came in knowing they were expected to involve service users. In the second phase of my time at Mind, I was able to help develop the UK Advocacy Network, and to set up training courses for service users in the Mind regions.

I was so grateful to Mind for the experience it gave me. Mind and Mindlink were my new family. After a lifetime of loneliness, I now had many friends across the country, and even, following trips to Japan and the USA, around the world.

I left Mind in 1992, to go freelance, and joined Survivors Speak Out's coordinating group. I was recruited, with other survivors, to work with the government's Mental Health Task Force. We were commissioned to create guidelines for patients' charters, to run training for service user trainers, and hold a series of service user conferences to find out people's top priorities for change.

WHAT I HAVE LEARNED

I learned that survivors can be each other's best friends or each other's worst enemies. I learned skills of public speaking and presentation. I learned that change is slow and gradual, and that an organisation needs to make its commitment to involvement clear from the top down. Talking to so many service users showed me the complexities of people's lives, and gave the lie to simplistic solutions to mental health problems.

STAGE THREE: BECOMING A RESEARCHER (1995–2003)

I bravely enrolled for a PhD in 1995. If I had known more, I might have decided to emigrate to the Antarctic as an easier and more pleasant option! At the same time, I continued with some freelance work, including research on the views of black and Asian service users in Waltham Forest, my first experience of recruiting and supporting service user researchers.

For my doctorate, I carried out in-depth interviews on what happened to people before, during and after their first serious mental health crisis. This was a question based on my own experience, and on many conversations with service users. I was sure that the first psychiatric intervention changed the direction of people's lives – often for the worse, but it could potentially, surely, have been otherwise? I hoped to create some theory from the literature and the interviews to understand better what goes on for people at this point. Systems theory, as applied to mental health by Caplan (1964), provided the structure for my work. Caplan compares people to systems in crisis. The psyche temporarily overwhelmed, all normal solutions having failed, the person desperately searches for help outside of their usual experience. All that society has to offer is the acute ward, which for some was a temporary respite, for others an oppressive nightmare. For many, the worst problem is the failure to offer anything else but the ward. What about help to use a crisis as a learning opportunity, look at what has been going wrong, and perhaps take a new direction in life? I was excited by what I was finding, but often near crisis myself because my lack of academic experience and self-confidence made it hard for me to get the best out of the system.

My greatest discovery during this time was the work of Foucault (1967, 1972). At first, I dismissed him on the grounds that his writing was impenetrable. But I realised I needed a theory that would question the legitimacy of the biomedical model of psychiatry. I wanted to see psychiatry in its historical context, as well as understanding the experience of individuals caught up in it. If I had been using a sociological or psychological perspective, I would probably have been restricted to commenting on aspects of people's social recovery from mental illness. But my bachelor's degree was not in sociology or psychology, but in Science, Technology and Society, where I learned to critique science and technology policy.

Foucault conceptualises the diagnostic system, psychiatric research, the history of the psychiatric institutions, the psychiatric professional bodies, and mental health legislation as part of a complex discourse, which had a historical beginning and a trajectory of development. His concept of discourse enables an analysis of how scientific knowledge is socially and politically constructed. A discourse is not just a debate, it is the creation of a concept or set of concepts, and he describes how sets of concepts such as psychiatric diagnoses become embedded and fixed in a system of laws, institutions and professional practices until they are taken for granted, and it becomes unthinkable that they should not exist.

In terms of the discourse of mental illness, we grow up internalising our powerlessness to define our own bodies and minds without the concepts of madness and sanity. We assume it is natural that a special corps of doctors is trained to recognise and treat madness. Even if we are critical, it is almost impossible to conceive that madness might be largely a creation of language and theory, developed to suit particular historical needs. It might no longer be a useful concept in its current form, but it is almost beyond our power to 'unthink' it, hedged around as it is with many writings, and a panoply of institutions. Szasz talks of the 'myth of mental illness' (Szasz, 1961), but Foucault's critique is so much more subtle and powerful. He encourages us to unpick the taken-for-granted words and ideas that underpin science, and examine their history. It is possible to trace when they arose and see how they became so powerful. Then it is possible to imagine a different trajectory, in which these concepts are non-existent or radically changed. Foucault enabled me to write a much stronger thesis than I would otherwise have been able to write.

After four years working on the PhD, with still no end in sight, I was delighted to get a job as a researcher on the Strategies for Living user-led research project at the Mental Health Foundation. Here I could use the qualitative research skills I was developing. As part of my own self-help, I had trained in aromatherapy and Reiki, and now put this to good use in researching and writing 'Healing Minds', a report on research in complementary and alternative therapies in mental health. My purpose was political: I wanted people to have the information to argue for their choice of treatment. But my first draft received some harsh criticism from expert reviewers. I had to rewrite it and eliminate all unsubstantiated claims and editorial opinion. It was much better for the rewriting and I was proud of the final result.

After I had moved on to work as a researcher on the On Our Own Terms project at the Sainsbury Centre for Mental Health (see Wallcraft, Read & Sweeney, 2003), I completed my doctorate. Seven years of hard labour! I had served my apprenticeship as a researcher, and been officially allowed to make a tiny contribution to the world's knowledge resources, which is what a doctorate is meant to be.

WHAT I HAVE LEARNED

This stage took the most patience, and was the least fun – apart from the good friends I made at the Mental Health Foundation and the Sainsbury Centre. Research is hard work and there are strict rules to be observed. Much of my problem in doing my doctorate was the difficulty of abandoning activism and learning to think and write as a scientist. It was a whole new mindset. Once the research question and the methodology are decided on, one's own views must be set aside for the duration. I learned to immerse myself in everything there was to know about my topic. I learned to ask questions without influencing the answer, and to report faithfully what I heard. I learned, at last, some humility, to counter my arrogant teenage belief that I knew what was needed to change the world. Once the evidence is collected, there is room for some creativity, in shaping and writing the story that emerges. But that is only when all the hard work of collection, transcribing and analysis is done.

The most important thing I gained from the PhD was again thanks to Foucault. I realised that the survivor movement is creating a new discourse. Our writings, organisations, research and concepts (such as self-management for hearing voices and manic depression) when put together offer a challenge to the biomedical discourse of psychiatry. I called it the discourse of self-advocacy, for want of a better term.

STAGE FOUR: BRINGING IT ALL BACK HOME

Since completing the doctorate, I have worked for three years as a fellow for Experts by Experience at NIMHE (the National Institute for Mental Health in England). It is, in a way, a return to activism. I have tried to represent service users' and carers' views to committees in NIMHE, and have supported follow-up work from the On Our Own Terms report, working with survivor groups and networks to discuss creating a national network of networks. I am now freelance after resigning the post of manager of SURGE (the Service User Research Group for England), the user involvement arm of the UK Mental Health Research Network, over strategies for genuine involvement in mainstream research and accountability to service users.

WHAT I HAVE LEARNED

My last few years of committees at the Department of Health have shown me the power of the discourse of psychopathology to dictate the research agenda. There is so much research from the voluntary sector showing what service users want, but this counts for little without evidence that what they want achieves the right outcome. Only large-scale clinical trials are regarded as providing real evidence, but there are no plans to carry out trials on non-medical crisis houses, complementary therapies, user-led self-management, and the value of having a therapist or counsellor of one's own choice. If such research were to happen, we would also need new measures to show outcomes that service users value, such as empowerment, confidence-building, self-esteem, getting off medication, managing one's own mood swings, finding a good job, making friends and having a good life. We need a new knowledge base.

Recently I have worked on a consultation commissioned by the NHS Service Development Organisation (SDO), on what mental health research service users would prioritise. Now the SDO knows what research service users want done, perhaps something will change, especially if there is a strong lobby behind the report.

In the end, I believe, as I did at the outset, that everything is part of a great whole. There is no great divergence between commitment to a cause and commitment to knowledge. If done well and honestly, one can complement and enhance the other in a positive cycle. I think I must be a Taoist.

REFERENCES

Caplan, G (1964) *Principles of Preventive Psychiatry*. London: Tavistock.

Foucault, M (1967) *Madness and Civilisation: A history of insanity in the age of reason* (trans, R Howard). London: Tavistock Press.

Foucault, M (1972) *Archaeology of Knowledge* (trans, AM Sheridan Smith). London: Tavistock Press.

Hammersley, M (1995) *The Politics of Social Research.* London: Sage.

Marx, K (1845) *Theses on Feuerbach, Thesis XI.* Available at www.marxists.org/archive/works/1845/theses/theses.htm

Mental Health Foundation (2003) *Mental Health User/Survivor Research in the UK. Updates,* 5(2). London: Mental Health Foundation.

Szasz, T (1961) *The Myth of Mental Illness: Foundations of a theory of personal conduct.* New York: Hoeber-Harper.

Tew, J, Gould, N, Abankwa, D, Barnes, H, Beresford, P, Carr, S, Copperman, J, Ramon, S, Rose, D, Sweeney, A & Woodward, L (2006) *Values and Methodologies for Social Research in Mental Health.* London: Social Perspectives Network; Bristol: Policy Press.

Wallcraft, J (1993) Bitter lessons. *Nursing Times, 89,* 27–32.

Wallcraft, J (1996) Becoming fully ourselves. In J Read and J Reynolds (eds) *Speaking Our Minds* (pp. 191–6). Basingstoke: Macmillan Press.

Wallcraft, J, Read, J & Sweeney, A (2003) *On Our Own Terms: Users and survivors of mental health services working together for support and change.* London: Sainsbury Centre for Mental Health.

'GETTING BETTER – IN THEORY'

CREATING, THEN USING, A FOUCAULDIAN MENTAL HEALTH SERVICE USER/SURVIVOR THEORETICAL STANDPOINT IN MY OWN JOURNEY OF 'RECOVERY'

DAVID ARMES

In late 1998, I saw an advert in the Guardian for a doctoral studentship, at what is now the University of Bedfordshire, to research the effect of community care policy on one of the disabled people's social movements. My application was successful. This is my story of doing a doctorate and the effect it has had on my mental health.

After I started in 1999, and following discussion with my initial doctoral supervisors Kathryn Ellis and Hartley Dean, I decided that one of the aims of my thesis would be to indicate how a theoretical 'service user/survivor standpoint' could be achieved. This would be a synthesis of existing social theory, which could offer new insights into the views and experiences of mental health service user/survivors.

PART 1: MY THEORETICAL JOURNEY

Q: WHAT IS A THEORETICAL APPROACH?

A: Before beginning to look at the theoretical standpoint I produced, I will just say what I think a theoretical approach to research is, since many people are put off by the complexity associated with the word 'theory'. Well, for me, all it means is one person's, or group of people's, ways of understanding aspects of human experience. Looked at like that, is using a theoretical approach any different from going to your grandmother/father for a different, hopefully more experienced and wiser point of view? The fact that you probably know the advice of your parents, or grandparents, before you even ask, is the same as reading enough about the thought of Max Weber or Pierre Bourdieu to be able to say how trying to think like them will give you the best answer or solution to a problem. University lecturers and supervisors can therefore act like respected friends whom you can approach to ask who would be a good person to give advice about a problem (i.e. which social theorist/philosopher will help you understand and explain the academic question you are writing about). It turned out that I was extremely fortunate with my doctoral supervisors. In particular, my primary supervisor Kathryn Ellis is knowledgeable and concerned about the plight of all people with disabilities.

HOW I CAME TO DEVELOP A SERVICE USER/SURVIVOR THEORETICAL STANDPOINT

Q: WHICH THEORIES SHOULD I SYNTHESISE?

A: Theoretically speaking, I did not know very much, was in awe of 'theoretical greats', and thus relied heavily on whatever advice I could get (which I think was very good). I was not able to defend an interest in Giddens' theory of structuration (Giddens, 1984), but I guess most apprentices for any skilled employment will feel this way at the start, since the best usually want to learn everything they can from the master craftswo/men.

I therefore explored Foucault's works, such as *Madness and Civilisation* (1989/ 1961) because it directly addressed mental health; I later discovered that Foucault had experienced severe mental health problems himself (Horrocks & Jevtic, 1999: 14), as had many other theorists. Furthermore, because I valued my own experiences of mental distress and mental health services for their potential to provide insights that other students might not have, the idea of creating a specific service user/ survivor standpoint, to help me focus on the most important aspects of our shared experiences, seemed logical when it was suggested by Hartley Dean in 2000. This would entail taking what Foucault had written, adding a feminist standpoint perspective, and then seeing if the two could be joined together without contradiction (theoretical synthesis) for service users/survivors to make use of.

There were a number of feminist standpoint theorists to choose from. For instance, Hilary Rose's (1983) theoretical concerns are within the sociology of knowledge discipline; Nancy Hartsock's (1983) and Alison M Jaggar's (1983) theoretical discipline is political philosophy; whilst Sandra Harding's (1986, 1991, 2004a/1993) discipline is the philosophy of natural sciences (see Harding, 2004b: 12). I eventually chose to use the work of Sandra Harding. Diana Rose gave me the idea for a Harding/Foucault synthesis when she provided a brief summary of Harding's work in a couple of pages she wrote concerning her own ideas about the user/survivor standpoint presented at the Survivor Researcher Network (SRN) in 2001 (Rose, 2001). I decided Harding warranted further reading. Harding's refusal to theorise about women's experiences as if there were 'one true story' (1986: 194) convinced me that a synthesis with Foucauldian discourse theory was possible. I will now briefly outline the theoretical service user/survivor standpoint that determined the way I analysed interviews with service users/survivors in my doctoral thesis.

Q: WHAT IS A THEORETICAL 'STANDPOINT'?

A: Feminist researchers have developed 'feminist standpoint' theory as a way of telling better stories about women's lives than the stories told about women's lives by male researchers (Ramazanoglu & Holland, 2002: 63). Put in a mental health context, the idea that service user/survivor researchers can use their experience to explain better the experiences of other service users/survivors has a ring of commonsense about it. So far, so good.

Q: CAN A THEORETICAL STANDPOINT ALWAYS SPEAK FOR ALL SERVICE USERS/SURVIVORS?

A: The main problem is that a service user/survivor who says that he or she can tell a better story about the experiences of other service users/survivors implies that service users/survivors can speak with one voice, when this is patently not the case on many issues. For instance, service users/survivors are individuals with highly diverse psychological issues and needs. Furthermore, service users/survivors have different genders, ethnicities, sexualities, social classes, religions, and physical and mental impairments. This clearly means that a researcher cannot talk about the service user/survivor population as being the same, or even similar, in many respects.

Q: CAN A THEORETICAL STANDPOINT EVER SPEAK FOR ALL SERVICE USERS/SURVIVORS?

A: Harding acknowledges this, in relation to her own work on women's perspectives, by stating there is no 'we' of feminism, and therefore feminists should give up the search for a single theory that can tell the only truth (1986: 244) about the gendered nature of social relations. From my perspective, I would also say that there is no 'we' of the service user/survivor population; that is, except that we have all experienced mental distress and *dominant mental health discourses*. However, when I say that 'we have all experienced dominant mental health discourses', it is also necessary to take a form of discourse theory on board in order to make sense of that statement. The discourse theory used in my thesis was 'Foucauldian'.

Q: WHAT IS FOUCAULDIAN DISCOURSE THEORY?

A: If you accept Foucauldian discourse theory, then you agree that there is no single explanation of social relations within the world. Therefore, according to this discourse theory, traditional Marxists are wrong to claim that all history is the history of class struggle, and that all social relations can be explained by that struggle. Foucauldian discourse theorists/analysts would also disagree that Buddhism, capitalism, Christianity, Islam, Judaism, liberal democracy, patriarchy, or socialism can be used as a lens through which the truth about social relations can be explained in every situation. By giving up on the possibility of talking about theories that are true for all people, Foucauldian discourse theorists/analysts can be described as *relativist*. This is because they do not believe that one set of claims about the truth is necessarily any more an expression of the truth than another (e.g. socialism versus capitalism).

Foucauldian discourse theorists/analysts also believe that anything that can be expressed by talking, pictures and/or writing is expressed through *discourses*. A discourse is simply all the possible ways in which statements on a particular issue can be framed/grouped in a set, which in itself decides what the rules are for a statement to be given legitimacy (i.e. allowed to be heard) on the particular issue. This might mean a member of the public may be drawing on the themes with which they are familiar from the popular mental health discourse, supported by strong elements of the mass media, when they converse with you. For instance, these themes may concern danger, homicide, irrationality, nuisance, drain on welfare, incapacity benefit rates, the nature of evil, and malingering. If you think about these themes every time you think about mental health problems, then you could be said to be drawing on *dominant mental health discourses*. (Of course, a service user/survivor may find this both tiring and offensive, in a similar way to how a person from a black and ethnic minority group might feel about the way certain crimes are often associated with particular ethnic groups and not the individuals who perpetrate them.)

If you accept the existence of discourses, it usually means that you accept that all knowledge is relative, because it is framed in a language and imagery that does not correctly describe reality. In relation to mental health, for example, the discourse allows people to make assumptions, ask questions, and draw conclusions informed by the dominant themes that they associate with conversations about mental health.

Q: DO YOU AGREE WITH RELATIVISTS THAT THERE IS NO SUCH THING AS TRUTH, OR RIGHT AND WRONG?

A: See the conclusions.

THE IMPORTANCE OF POWER

Q: SO, HOW DO FOUCAULDIAN RELATIVISTS DECIDE WHOSE STATEMENTS TO SUPPORT?

A: Foucault thought that power and making claims about the 'truth' always go together (Smart, 1985: 80). Therefore, psychiatry is powerful because it controls the way most of the knowledge about mental health is created, which in turn is used to create and maintain *dominant discourses about mental health*. These define service users/survivors negatively (and thus reduce our life opportunities) in the following either/or dichotomies: you are either, rational or irrational, sane or insane, normal or abnormal, healthy or sick, self-controlled or dangerous, predictable or unpredictable, go-getting or work-shy, independent or dependent, and perhaps even good or bad. Subscribing to these either/or notions and going with the majority is one easy way of deciding whose statements to support, since challenging them is sometimes difficult, particularly when the media usually bring up discussion about them in the aftermath of a heinous crime.

There is hope however. Foucault also argued that power does not exist in isolation – there is always resistance (1990/1976: 95–6). Therefore, service user/survivor researchers who highlight strategies such as complementary therapies, spirituality, exercise, art, and education, which other service users/survivors use to live with their conditions (see Lindow, 1994; Faulkner & Layzell, 2000; Gilbert & Nicholls, 2003), are resisting the power of traditional psychiatry. That is, traditional psychiatry that would primarily judge the value of an activity according to whether there is any symptom reduction, rather than whether a service user/survivor subjectively believes the activity is improving their quality of life. Moreover, the research conducted by service user/survivor researchers can be said to be better knowledge than the research of professionals. This is not because it is unbiased: quite the opposite, because it is bringing to centre stage arguably the most important perspective – that of service users/survivors. An example of service users/survivors claiming production of better knowledge is that service user/survivor interviewers have recently found that other service users/survivors will speak in a different way to them, from how they would speak to non-service users/survivors, about their experiences of ECT (see Rose, Fleischmann & Wykes, 2004).

Q: DO SERVICE USER/SURVIVOR RESEARCHERS ALWAYS PRODUCE BETTER KNOWLEDGE THAN NON-SERVICE USER/SURVIVOR RESEARCHERS ABOUT EVERY QUESTION?

A: If you want to know about the general effects of a new medication on particular symptoms, maybe using data from standardised postal questionnaires, you might reasonably go to a medical statistician who need not necessarily be a service user/survivor. Frequently it is statistical research, however, that has the aura of infallibility, and that provides the knowledge that is used to support the *dominant discourses about mental health*, which limit the opportunities, respect, and expectations that we experience. It is therefore very important to remember the two things I stated earlier that are the central focus within the boundaries of a theoretical service user/survivor standpoint:

i) All service users/survivors have experienced *severe forms of mental distress*
ii) All service users/survivors are forced to experience their real lives in relation to the ways they are portrayed by *dominant mental health discourses.*

Q: WHAT GOOD CAN THIS SERVICE USER/SURVIVOR THEORETICAL STANDPOINT DO IN THE REAL WORLD?

A: Foucault's discourse theory allows us to identify, and draw a boundary around, the particular discourses that shape all our lives; a Foucauldian service user/survivor standpoint can then be applied to understand, challenge and hopefully change those discourses (and our lives).

Q: WHICH OPPRESSIVE DISCOURSES CAN THIS USER/SURVIVOR STANDPOINT CHALLENGE?

A: The power of a challenge to dominant mental health discourses, however, would be greatly enhanced if service user/survivor theoretical standpoints were used to challenge a particular mental health discourse that influences many others. Foucault (1989/1961: 64) states that when Western peoples began to create the asylum system during the Enlightenment in the eighteenth century, they stopped living 'cheek by jowl' with 'mad' people. Enlightenment ideas began a process where the value attached to the mental capacity to 'reason' rose far above any other mental capacities, with 'madwo/men' becoming the embodiment of 'reason's' polar opposite – 'unreason'. What is more, Foucault identifies within the Enlightenment the view of the uttering of 'unreason' as 'nothing', or meaningless (1989/1961: 116), because there is no 'reason' within it. A Foucauldian might argue that this is the underlying and fundamental discursive justification for negatively discriminatory behaviour and the use of oppressive discourse which can be described as 'mentalism'.

Q: HOW CAN SERVICE USERS/SURVIVORS RECLAIM OUR CAPACITY TO REASON?

A: The above means that one of the first tasks of a service user/survivor standpoint must be to challenge the 'reason/unreason' dichotomy. Starting from a service user/survivor perspective, it could be argued that service users/survivors can reclaim the term 'reason' in a number of ways, if all that it means is that 'conclusions are drawn from premises' (Oxford University Press, 1990: 999), and 'rationality' refers to beliefs that are 'coherent, not contradictory, and compatible with experience' (Abercrombie, Hill & Turner, 1994: 346). Service users/survivors are well acquainted with the reason of depression, paranoia, obsession, and even psychosis. Certainly, anyone who is suicidally depressed will be familiar with the chain of reason that leads to the loss of all hope. Perhaps it is the use of reason in depression that makes cognitive behavioural therapy (CBT) effective (see Layard, 2006: 1030). What is more, experiencing 'the oneness of the universe' whilst psychotic may lead to the wholly reasonable lifetime view that there is a spiritual power at work in the universe. Not only that, there is now evidence that people with a schizophrenia diagnosis may be better at theoretical reasoning than other 'healthy' people in some circumstances (Owen, Cutting & David, 2007).

Employing a service user/survivor standpoint can help to redefine the term 'madness'. One of my thesis respondents implied that 'losing control' and 'madness' are the same thing. Using this logic, the following cannot necessarily be described as 'madness': depression, anxiety, obsession, paranoia or voice-hearing interpreted in different ways such as telepathy, the supernatural, and/or as the psychological expression of the 'internalised generalised other' within the mind which is thought to be affected by societal norms, rules and values (Kirby, 2007). Indeed, this means that people who lose control ('a moment of madness'), who have never used specialist mental health services, can be equated with people who experience an episode of psychosis – and don't most people think they could lose control under some circumstances?

Q: DO 'NORMAL' PEOPLE THINK ABOUT MENTAL HEALTH PROBLEMS USING ONLY DOMINANT DISCOURSES?

A: I would say that it does not assist service users/survivors in overcoming whatever problems they have if they attempt to make real the oppressive dominant discourses in their own minds by assuming that they will be met with negative reactions by everyone they meet, and thus become isolated. Indeed, my experience is that many professionals, and people in the wider community, are willing to make their own decisions about the people they meet. They may believe that examples of courage, altruism, honesty, integrity, and prior knowledge, as well as, for some people, facial expression, tone of voice, steady eye-contact, and confidence are better evidence about an individual's character than the dominant 'psycho-killer' discourses reported in the media. (Incidentally, Walsh, Buchanan, and Fahy (2002) note that annually only 0.03 per cent of people with a schizophrenia diagnosis are convicted of a violent crime.) A service user/survivor standpoint therefore has to say something about how to ascertain objective reality, as well as discursive 'reality', if it is to be of any serious use to other service users/survivors.

The concluding part of this paper covers how my theoretical journey and service user/survivor standpoint ideas have helped me to cope with my own mental health problems and carry on.

PART TWO: RECENT LIFE EXPERIENCES AND A MORE 'SENSIBLE' APPROACH TO SCIENCE

Q: WHAT HAPPENED DURING AND AFTER MY MOST RECENT BREAKDOWN?

A: The crisis team that visited me, following a psychotic episode in 2007, was adamant that they wanted me to say what I honestly thought to be true, and through this process I was able to see that many of my thoughts were based on what might have been, rather than real reality. The process was hard, and when they left I felt that I had nothing to lose by just being myself. My reason told me that if I allowed my mental life to be based on assumptions, faulty mental models, second-hand knowledge, media reports, and even individual, peer-reviewed scientific journal articles, then I would again be doomed. My only solution would be to find a way of getting nearer to the real truth and speaking it.

Q: WHAT DO I STILL BELIEVE IS VALID IN THE SERVICE USER/SURVIVOR STANDPOINT I HAVE WORKED ON?

A: I still think that the only things that unite all service users/survivors are experiences of severe mental distress, and experiences of the power of dominant mental health discourses on our real lives. I also still think that Foucault was right to challenge the pre-eminent status of the capacity to reason in modern science. Therefore, I still think relativist Foucauldian theory has something valuable to add to the search for truth. The problem was that it was always obvious to me that there are such things as true and false, and moral right and wrong. Therefore the relativism weaved tightly within Foucauldian thinking makes me think this philosophical tradition is severely compromised.

Q: OK, HOW DO I KNOW HOW TO GET AT THE REAL OBJECTIVE TRUTH?

A: I looked back on what I had written about the need for user/survivor knowledge, about, say, spirituality or reason in depression to be treated as just as worthy of attention as the symptoms which interest professionals. This informed my view that the only way to judge between true and false is through the subjective use of all of our senses – physical (touch, taste, sight, hearing, and smell) and instinctual, intuitive, or other emotional and/or spiritual senses (in this respect I contend I am a more 'sensible' scientist than those who say they rely on reason alone). Service users/survivors have reported using all of these in their strategies for living and coping with severe mental distress (see Lindow, 1994; Faulkner & Layzell, 2000; Gilbert & Nicholls, 2003). Moreover, just as we require holistic support (mind, body, and spirit) – something some professionals also acknowledge (see Richards, 2002: 165–78) – I thought a service user/survivor standpoint should stand by any researchers who might want to pursue what could be described as 'holistic science'.

Without a commitment to communicate subjective truth and holistic scientific methodologies, I believe it is less likely that anything objectively true, or truer than existing understanding, will be achieved.

Q: HOW HAS THIS JOURNEY HELPED ME?

A: Number one, it has given me my self-confidence back. This has happened through getting used to mental exercises in subjective truth-telling throughout years of study. Then, through the realisation that I had the courage and the right to speak my mind on anything, although sometimes I have found it may be better to let other people, who have more experience on a given subject, make their points before I make mine – that is, if I still have something constructive to say.

Secondly, I managed to understand my OCD-like (Obsessive Compulsive Disorder) symptoms by listening to my thoughts and emotions, and realising that I was trapped like a Pavlovian dog into set responses to particular situations (which might be similar to thinking discursively). This was because I was not challenging my own mind to approach each situation differently with potentially all, not just some, of my knowledge and experience available for the task. I did not think I could think differently, and I thought my thoughts were 'who I was' (my identity), when in actual fact I found that all I had to do was ask myself whether my thoughts were telling the truth about me to me. I concluded that it is much better to choose an identity, if one is needed, based on what I aim to be, since the human being is always a 'work in progress'. After that, I began to trust my own judgement/memory in small ways, like not checking whether I had locked the door three times before leaving the house. The OCD began to go away.

Thirdly, instead of seeing the 'inner voice/thoughts' (which emerged at the same time as the OCD was retreating) as oppressive, I saw them variously as divine messages, inner thoughts of conscience, and/or telepathic communications, which required interpretation. When I realised that I was in a kind of mental boot camp, where my own mind was demanding that I give respect to myself and others in my daily life, I began to treat the inner voice as an idiosyncratic helper with a strange sense of humour, and mental pain the result of not getting things right.

Fourthly, small altruistic gifts and voluntary work, without any expectation of return, were a self-esteem key to recognising that I have as much right to live and prosper as anyone else. Being prepared to stand up for the perspectives of other service users/survivors through my research also made me realise that I have the courage to live my own life, too.

Q: WHAT BENEFITS CAN DOMINANT MENTAL HEALTH DISCOURSES POSSIBLY OFFER OUR SOCIETY?

A: My view is that elements of the mass media stigmatise mental health problems in order to frighten the majority of people to give up 'wild life' and 'grow up' at the earliest opportunity. The chaos and misery of many mental health service users' lives are thus used as a 'morality play' example of what will probably happen if you do not want adult responsibilities such as career (#1), partnership (#2), and/or parenthood (equal #2). Gordon Brown frequently appeals to 'hard-working families': they are very much included in our society. Not included are those with 'mild' mental health problems who are 'work shy', whilst those with 'severe' mental health problems are, to my mind, the scapegoats for some people's feelings of selfishness, aggression, and weakness. Think about it: when do politicians ever appeal to 'hard-working families with mental health problems and/or alcohol abuse problems' (i.e. families as they are)?

Becoming a 'mentally healthy', responsible, democratic, hard-working, tolerant and relationship-orientated adult is not easy – even if you want it and/or think it is a better way to live. But is there any other way of being mentally healthy in UK society? That is undoubtedly a task for service user/survivor researchers. Personally, I want to be part of society (since I do not want to live on a desert island). In that sense, I acknowledge that almost all people are socialist with a small 's'. This, moreover, makes me better able to appreciate and respect the self-reliant rites of passage ingrained in our culture, in which we are told we are free to explore and make our own minds up about the way we want to live when young, but are expected to make rational choices (in a UK context) during that exploration and come to adulthood eventually. That said, I am still critical, and refuse to become totally conservative with a small 'c' just for the sake of appearances: to me, that would be mentally unhealthy as well. In any case, my awareness that I can realistically imagine taking on the basic responsibilities expected of adults (forming loving relationships [usually ending in a partnership], and providing a living for a partner and any dependents), means that I have no choice but personally to challenge the small 'c' conservative discourses around mental health.

Q: MY ADVICE FOR LIVING WITH LESS MENTAL STRESS?

A: The short existentialist answer is to accept that stress cannot be avoided, and so I began with small steps to help me cope, and then kept on going forward. I have no choice, because I have faith that all lives are worth living.

I think the main thing is just taking the trouble to be interested in other people, and be especially interested in what I myself want out of life. Part of this understanding is the recognition that there is an order in which all responsibilities need to be attended to; there is a relationship between responsibilities, in so far as the primary responsibility is to make sure that you are yourself alive, healthy, and aware of your own independent contribution to your own life and those of others.

In this last respect, I also agree that giving support, and nurturing relationships of care with others, is a basic human need (see Sevenhuijsen, 2000). Many religions believe that the expressed word is holy and should be honest: I know that speaking and writing my subjective truth is absolutely essential for my own mental health. When I realised that, I finally experienced the wonder of making informed and responsible decisions.

In terms of strengthening my mind to cope with the stresses and responsibilities of life, I have found out for myself that nutritious food, giving up all non-medical drugs, regular exercise, a social life, a spiritual life, consistent study and enquiry, an appreciation of nature and art, and a willingness to take risks to build and maintain all kinds of relationships have helped build up the capacities and strength of my mind.

I have only refused to take medication for two periods of three days in the last fifteen years. I do not believe that my psychiatric team is persecuting me (my experience of achieving a doctorate makes me believe that the good characters of doctors are tested), although I do believe they aim to help me fit in with UK society as it is (to think you can live outside society is, in my opinion, deluded). This has sometimes made me feel that my psychiatric team have tried to make me into a different person – that has been scary – but if being a different person means being more aware of the people around me and my effect on them then I am happy with that. (In actual fact what has happened is that I have built on the strengths of my existing character and found that I also have access to hidden strengths which I never thought I had – like the courage to write this chapter). I know that, whatever I choose to do or be in the future, I have no need to fear myself, because I am able to make an honest assessment of myself, and I don't personally accept the 'mad/bad' label. In this respect, I had to learn to be assertive with the frightened people who cannot/do not want to see beyond the label and associated dominant discourses.

The last thing I have to say is that all of the advice for living with stress I have just mentioned has come to me partly as a result of my studies and the realisation that, for me, and perhaps you, it is essential to be able to express and test my own sensual experience. Moreover, sensual data, which may appear and sometimes are delusional, had to be either verified or eliminated via discussion with close family and friends, or professionals (who have all been generally great). This has been difficult for all concerned, but necessary – firstly, because none of us exists in isolation; and, secondly, because if areas of social and sensual experience cannot be discussed, then assumptions rule, which cannot be good for anyone's mental health. Certainly, if I cannot trust my own senses and do not feel able to discuss sensual data, then my sanity is clearly lost. I have found the only way to begin to get it back is to reclaim my right to talk about my own perceptions. My theoretical journey in higher education has helped me do this and, in doing so, has, helped me understand the others in my life too. As well, the others in my life have all eventually understood that, from their own experiences of life and achieving adulthood, I really did have to work my own sanity out for myself, and with their support, and like them, will continue to do so every day.

ACKNOWLEDGEMENTS

Acknowledgements are owed primarily to Kathryn Ellis (my doctoral supervisor who continues to give generous support in areas such as commenting on drafts of this chapter). Hartley Dean, Marian Barnes and David Berridge were secondary supervisors for my PhD and/or advised me to read around the possibility of synthesising feminist standpoint theory with Foucault. I also thank Diana Rose for giving me the specific idea of a Harding/Foucault synthesis at the SRN in 2001, and for commenting on a draft in 2008. Gurch Randhawa is also thanked for commenting on a draft of this article in 2007. Thanks are also due to Peter Beresford, Diana Rose and Angie Sweeney, from the SRN, for their editorial support.

REFERENCES

Abercrombie, N, Hill, S & Turner, B (1994) *Dictionary of Sociology* (3rd edn). London: Penguin.

Faulkner, A & Layzell, S (2000) *Strategies for Living: A report on user-led research into people's strategies for living with mental distress.* London: Mental Health Foundation.

Foucault, M (1989) (Original work published 1961) *Madness and Civilisation: A history of insanity in the age of reason.* London: Routledge.

Foucault, M (1990) (Original work published 1976) *The History of Sexuality 1: The will to knowledge.* London: Penguin.

Giddens, A (1984) *The Constitution of Society.* Cambridge: Polity Press.

Gilbert, P & Nicholls, V (2003) *Inspiring Hope: Recognising the importance of spirituality in a whole person approach to mental health.* Leeds: NIMHE.

Harding, S (1986) *The Science Question in Feminism.* New York: Cornell University Press.

Harding, S (1991) *Whose Science? Whose Knowledge? Thinking from women's lives.* New York: Cornell University Press.

Harding, S (2004a) (Original work published 1993) Rethinking standpoint epistemology: What is 'strong objectivity'? In S Harding (ed) *The Feminist Standpoint Theory Reader: Intellectual and political controversies* (pp. 127–40). London: Routledge.

Harding, S (ed) (2004b) *The Feminist Standpoint Theory Reader: Intellectual and political controversies.* London: Routledge.

Hartsock, N (1983) The feminist standpoint: Developing the ground for a specifically feminist historical materialism. In S Harding & M Hintikka (eds) *Discovering Reality: Feminist perspectives on epistemology, metaphysics, methodology and philosophy of science* (pp. 35–53). Dordrecht: Reidel.

Horrocks, C & Jevtic, Z (1999) *Introducing Foucault*. Cambridge: Icon Books.

Jaggar, AM (1983) *Feminist Politics and Human Nature*. Brighton: Harvester.

Kirby, J (2007) 'I need an explanation for my experience ...' Othering social processes, self-identified difference, and the 'problematic' experience of voice-hearing. Paper given at the British Sociological Association Medical Sociology Group 39th Annual Conference, 6–8 September, Britannia Adelphi Hotel, Liverpool.

Layard, R (2006) The case for psychological treatment centres. *BMJ, 332*, 1030–2.

Lindow, V (1994) *Self-Help Alternatives to Mental Health Services*. London: Mind.

Owen, GS, Cutting, J & David, AS (2007) Are people with schizophrenia more logical than healthy volunteers? *British Journal of Psychiatry, 191*, 453–4.

Oxford University Press (1990) *The Concise Oxford Dictionary*. Oxford: Oxford University Press.

Ramazanoglu, C & Holland, J (2002) *Feminist Methodology: Challenges and choices*. London: Sage.

Richards, M (2002) *A Straightforward Guide to Understanding Mental Illness*. London: Straightforward Publishing.

Rose, D (2001) Some reflections on epistemology in relation to user-led research. Paper discussed at the Survivor Researcher Network. London: Mental Health Foundation.

Rose, D, Fleischmann, P and Wykes, T (2004) Consumers' perspectives on ECT: a qualitative analysis. *Journal of Mental Health, 13*(3), 285–94.

Rose, H (1983) Hand, brain, and heart: a feminist epistemology for the natural sciences. *Signs: Journal of Women in Culture and Society, 9*(1), 73–90.

Sevenhuijsen, S (2000) Caring in the Third Way: The relationship between obligation, responsibility, and care in Third Way discourse. *Critical Social Policy, 20*(5), 5–37.

Smart, B (1985) *Michel Foucault*. Milton Keynes: Open University Press.

Walsh, E, Buchanan, A & Fahy, T (2002) Violence and schizophrenia: Examining the evidence. *British Journal of Psychiatry, 180*, 490–5.

PROJECT ACCOUNTS

JUDY BECKETT, MATT SANDS, STUART VALENTINE,
PHILIP HILL AND SUE GODDARD

A SURVIVOR-LED EVALUATION OF A SURVIVOR-LED CRISIS SERVICE

JUDY BECKETT

It would have been unimaginable for me, way back in 1989, sitting on my bed in a mental health ward, that I would one day be involved in carrying out research and dipping into my direct personal experience of mental health services as a valuable resource.

I first became involved in service user research in 2003, when I was invited to be involved in the evaluation of the survivor-led crisis service in Leeds. I joined a small team of service users working with Alison Faulkner as survivor consultant. This team became a place where I felt accepted, as though I belonged, and where my experiences of mental distress were valued. I found it interesting and rewarding interviewing other service users about their experience of this service. I had not personally used this crisis service, although others on the team had, but I felt it was an exciting development for Leeds.

Dial House (the survivor-led crisis service) in Leeds was offering support to people during time of crisis in a homely environment. The management committee was made up of a majority of current or former mental health service users. It had a faithful service user group who used the crisis house regularly and valued it. The service, however, struggled to attract new service users. Our plan was to evaluate how Dial House was functioning, and to look at the work of the helpline 'Connect', which was based there. Dial House was meeting with new challenges in the face of changing services in the city, and our evaluation was to feed into the further development of the service.

We were trained in interviewing skills, working in pairs to develop these. We received training in confidentiality, developing interview questions, and recording interviews. We used our experience of mental distress and crisis to develop our interview schedule, to decide how the interviews should be conducted, and particularly how to manage any potential distress in the interview situation. Drawing on our own experiences of taking part in research as participants, we considered which things we had experienced as helpful and unhelpful. We took time to consider the most respectful way of conducting the interviews. Managing confidentiality was of real importance to me, as was the need to be clear with people about what would happen to their information. At this time, confidentiality was an area where I had felt particularly betrayed by mental health services, and I considered it to be an area that perpetuated much of the powerlessness experienced by people who use mental health services. I believe the space given for reflection on our own experiences was vital, to allow us to bring this to interviews in a way that did not hinder the process.

Interviewing in pairs ensured that we had opportunity to debrief afterwards, and made sure that we covered all the topic areas. We reflected on our interviews, and received feedback on our work as part of our ongoing training. The project was unhurried and meticulous. We spent weeks reflecting on the information we had collected, how to best present it and discussing the report as it was written. I wrote some sections of the report and, having entered mental health services at seventeen, this was one of my tentative steps back towards writing and using my brain again. The support of the team was invaluable, here, too. I was simultaneously doing a counselling course at Leeds Metropolitan University. Through this research project, my confidence increased: I felt more secure about the value and importance of my life experience, realising that to bring this experience to my work had the potential to enhance it rather than contaminate it as I had feared.

The reality was that this project was one of the first steps on the road back towards employment for me. I went on to gain employment at the University of Leeds as a research assistant. The experience of working as a team was one I prized and still do. I gained the confidence to view the fifteen years of contact with mental health services as a useful and important part of my life experience, rather than feeling as though it was something I should conceal and view as wasted or 'lost' years. For me, this does not minimise the pain I experienced through those years, but it allows me at least to integrate it as part of my lived experience and gain some benefit.

EMPOWERMENT UNDER PERMIT: CANTERBURY AND DISTRICT MENTAL HEALTH FORUM SERVICE USER EVALUATION (SUE) PROJECT

MATT SANDS
(on behalf of the service user evaluation team)

BACKGROUND

In 2000, NHS modernisation was spun as shifting the balance of power: patients and the public were to have a say in how services are designed, developed and delivered. In East Kent, the Joint Commissioning Board (JCB) commissioned research from Kings College London on how to address 'power imbalance'. The answer, in the unpublished research report, was for the service user groups (already represented in service planning meetings) to take a regular role of doing local service evaluations for the service planners. In theory, this would create a service user 'power base', as we would come to have the key role of identifying what needed to change. A pilot 'empowerment' project was set up, with five local service user or carer groups across Kent, each evaluating an aspect of local services.

The project that the Canterbury and District Mental Health Forum chose was to examine 'To what extent are John O'Brien's Five Accomplishments of Normalisation[1] realised within living environments provided for people with mental health problems?'. Normalisation is a philosophy that originated in the United States, where the aim is to enable people to participate in mainstream life and in local communities. Briefly, these five accomplishments are:

- *Competence:* enabled to develop skills, with opportunities to use them
- *Choice:* enabled to make choices
- *Respect:* treated with respect; as a person of worth
- *Community presence:* able to be present in places that define community life
- *Community participation:* involved in community activities

Social services contracts require these to be realised for service users by mental health services they commission.

METHODOLOGY AND FIELDWORK

Our team was trained in the audit cycle technique, and developed understanding of the normalisation concept. We then arranged a stakeholder conference, inviting representatives of local residential service providers to join us in deciding how the accomplishments could be assessed in their houses. From those discussions, 22 standards were identified on which to base our questions. Thus, the service providers took on co-ownership of the standards that we used to measure how well they accomplish the principles to which they sign up. To gather information, our team devised two semi-structured interview schedules: one for home managers and one for residents, plus an observational checklist.

After a pilot visit to a care home, our survey team visited seven sites: three residential care homes, two supported housing projects, one inpatient sub-acute ward, and one mid-to-long term rehabilitation unit. All but one of those working on the Canterbury and District Mental Health Forum project were service users. The evaluation team for the fieldwork (home visits) comprised three mental health

1. O'Brien, J & Tyne, A (1981) *The Principle of Normalisation: A foundation for effective services.* London: The Campaign for People with Mental Handicaps.

service users. For interviewing house managers, one service user would ask the questions and all three would note the answers down on our forms. Then, after the interview, we three would hold a consensus meeting to agree, from our notes, one report of these answers.

We hoped that allowing the managers to see the reports of their interview, to verify that we presented their replies fairly, would overcome problems of their staff feeling challenged. One house manager, receiving our draft interview report, expected us to insert his statement of virtue for the home, which he had not made at the interview. For a time he threatened to withdraw from the project if this was refused.

In each house, we tried to interview more than 50 per cent of residents in one-to-one interviews. We learnt that the fulfilment of normalisation varied. It was not fully recognised that signing up to the accomplishments meant that homes should be concerned with providing more than shelter. Residents' quiet despair, in a 'warehousing' regime of one home was illustrated when a woman resident said to me:

> 'I understand one of your team used to live here?'
> 'Yes,' I replied, indicating him. 'He used to live here. He's in a council flat now.'
> 'Goodness!' she exclaimed, 'How on earth did he get out?'

EMPOWERMENT?

One aim of the project was to assess the ability of service users to influence change. However, it seems the old adage 'he who pays the piper calls the tune' still applies in mental health service commissioning, as our own ability to determine the nature of our work was brought into question. In social services' quarterly 'networking meetings' for the projects, held at their county council headquarters, a few professionals dominated discussions, curtailing whatever did not fit their own views.

Agreements were reached and recorded with those who commissioned the work. When officials chose to overturn these, they denied that the earlier agreement was ever made. Before the projects started, an official announced that the budget would be ten per cent lower than agreed. When we showed minutes recording agreed funding levels, the social services officer responsible waved the paper away saying 'Well, that's just wrong!'

An academic with an 'oversight' role on the project advised that the regional executive never commissioned pilot research without it leading to more. When a service user asked, later, when we would learn of any follow-up from the pilot, the social services officer's reply was 'Forget "pilot". This isn't a pilot!' At the next meeting he spoke again of our work being 'pilot' projects and denied that he had ever said otherwise!

One of the worst things you find in services, as a mental health service user, is that professionals often will not accept the validity of your own experience. Well, we found this very same thing happening in our 'empowerment' scheme!

SELLING OURSELVES?

Having found that our user forum could plan and carry out sophisticated research, our committee wished to advertise our ability. At the time, a majority on the Canterbury and District Mental Health Forum management committee were service users, although more outspoken members who were not service users often overruled them. The vice-chair (a non-service user) drafted a leaflet, the opening paragraph of which stated that we 'offer quality mental health research carried out by those who receive the services'. However, in the next line this implied advantage was cancelled out by stating that this would be 'expertly supervised' by a management committee 'providing the necessary monitoring'. A (non-user) staff colleague saw the contradiction: she said that this meant, in effect, 'We have some *loonies* to do evaluations for you, but don't worry: *normal* people will keep an eye on them!'

AN EVALUATION OF A MENTAL HEALTH SERVICE IN NORTH EAST SCOTLAND

STUART VALENTINE

I was part of a team of eight service users who, with the support of a research mentor and administrative worker, conducted an evaluation of a mental health service in North East Scotland. This involved the service users becoming 'community researchers' to ascertain the views and experiences of all service users, their carers, the staff, the funding agencies and other mental health services in the area.

It was a challenging piece of work with everyone working to a tight schedule. We were ultimately successful in producing a report and a video, which we launched at a special event in August 2005.

My initial apprehension at being involved in this research quickly gave way to excitement and having a sense of purpose in seeing it through to its conclusion. I found I could work as part of a team and discovered skills I was not entirely sure I possessed. The main point for me though was discovering that a serious undertaking, which this was, could be enjoyable and even fun!

My colleagues and I found ourselves delving deeper into funding issues and the politics of mental health services. Our relationships with staff and other professionals in the field also came to the fore. The voice and, more importantly, the involvement of service users in all aspects of mental health is promoted and encouraged now, and we were able, with quality help and guidance, to achieve a positive outcome.

I learned a lot myself and we all learned a lot from each other. I and other members of the group are hoping to use the skills and experiences gained from this project and apply them in other areas.

It may appear daunting to be involved in a piece of research but if you can overcome initial doubts, you will probably find it very worthwhile!

MY EXPERIENCE OF DOING ACADEMIC RESEARCH TO ATTAIN A RESEARCH DEGREE

PHILIP HILL

I have been a mental health survivor since 1987, having had two periods as a mental health service user in the late 1980s. I have been unable to shake off my medical label, because I am still dependent on medication.

I was given the opportunity to register as a PhD/doctoral student from October 1997 until February 2003 at the University of Birmingham's Institute of Applied Studies. A doctorate or PhD is one of the highest degrees you can get from a university and is awarded for original research written up in the form of an academic document called a thesis, which is usually between 60–100,000 words in length.

WHAT MY RESEARCH WAS ABOUT

I was accepted as a student because my research proposal or plan of my research was considered original and realistic. In this plan, I set out why and how I wanted to 'identify the main characteristics of paid work that could enable fellow mental health service users to find, retain, and thrive in employment'.

WHAT I WAS TRYING TO FIND OUT

Part of my approach was to study the relationship between an individual's mental health and well-being, and nine characteristics of their work environment in their most recent or present job. These job characteristics were very complex, but some of them were factors like task variety, degree of autonomy at work, level of pay, opportunity to socially interact, and so on.

The research method I used to find out this information included a survey using a self-completion questionnaire. Another part of the process was to interview service users using a semi-structured interview schedule, which drew on a list of important topics brought up with the mental health service user in his or her self-completion questionnaire. I carried out 20 interviews of this type, and I used the topics to explore each person's experience of mental health/illness and employment.

My aim was to find out which types of support, supervision, and social and physical environments enabled mental health service users to retain work. I also wanted to know what kind of strategies enabled interviewees to find work. As well, I interviewed ten employers who had had direct experience of working with people who had had mental health problems at work, using a pre-set list of topics.

I wanted to enable interviewees to be able to tell their stories, and this determined the topics I chose. Interviews therefore began with their early experiences of employment. It was important to be able to understand from their early experiences what did not work in jobs, just as it was important to try to understand what for some interviewees may have worked or not in later jobs or in sheltered workshop settings. For those who were not currently working, it was also important to understand the relationship between their work and their mental health, and whether work contributed to mental health problems. It was also important to understand the barriers to employment encountered by mental health service users, and any lack of support or flexibility from employers.

HOW I ANALYSED THE INFORMATION

When analysing the information from the interviews, I split my findings into two chapters of my research thesis. Firstly, I identified themes from all the individual interviews, dividing them into negative and positive themes or issues. Secondly, I analysed the transcripts individually to look for key themes. I took key themes to be those that occurred in many transcripts, such as mental health service users being driven to suicidal thoughts by work. I used an approach to analysis that sought to enable interviewees to be treated as experts in their own experience, and which recognised that they could be generators of theories, as well as one that enabled the researcher to test out theories. Interviewees who were still happy with their existing jobs were considered by the interviewer and by themselves to have positive experiences. Other interviewees considered their experiences of work to be negative. The interview was also intended to help individuals make sense of their experiences of work and mental health/illness. When an individual interview transcript is analysed in this kind of intensive way, to understand how individuals to interpret their own experience, it is called a narrative approach.

I also analysed the questionnaires from the survey to measure the relationships between how mental health service users perceived the quality of their present or last work environment, with their perception of the quality of their own mental health.

THE CHALLENGES THAT FACED ME AS A MENTAL HEALTH SURVIVOR WHEN DOING SURVIVOR RESEARCH

Whilst carrying out and transcribing my interviews with fellow mental health survivors, an unexpected interview topic emerged. Some survivors had mentioned that when attempting to manage their mental health through difficult periods, they had encountered suicidal feelings. Reflection on these interviews and interview transcripts was difficult for me as researcher, because I was revisiting emotional issues that had caused my first nervous breakdown. However, with the help of a friend called Fiona, I was able to get through this tricky period.

Analysing many pages of interview transcripts and splitting the interviews into segments that corresponded with different themes was challenging. However, as the themes began to emerge from my analysis, it felt as though the whole research project was beginning to come together, like completing a giant jigsaw puzzle. This experience of research analysis was one of the most exhilarating of my academic life. The chapter of findings based on my analysis seemed virtually to write itself because everything came together so well.

However, when I presented my 80,000-word thesis for examination, the view of my examiners was not favourable, although I felt that I did well at the viva where I was verbally examined about what I had written. Unfortunately, I ran out of time and money to do all the rewriting that was required for me to gain my PhD. I therefore did a partial rewrite and was awarded a Master of Philosophy. Despite this, the whole experience of failure that day made it one of the worst days of my academic life.

POSITIVE ASPECTS OF MY EXPERIENCE

The main benefit of the research was that my writing and editing skills improved dramatically. The experience of working with fellow mental health survivors enabled me to contextualise my own experience as a mental health survivor. Working as a researcher made me much better at working towards deadlines and prioritising my work accordingly. My social skills also improved enormously because I had to interact with a range of people including academic staff, fellow students and fellow survivors as well as employers. So there were real gains and achievements for me.

NEGATIVE ASPECTS OF MY EXPERIENCE

I had to manage on little more than £5,000 per year from a research bursary, as a result of which I had to work six days a week for about four years to make ends meet. Consequently I was unable to focus on the research as much as I would have liked. This is a common problem for research students.

Despite failure to reach my goal of a doctorate, I was awarded a lower research degree, as I have said, called a Master of Philosophy after major amendments to my thesis, which took twelve months to complete. I was bitterly disappointed with this result and still have occasional nightmares about it now.

Firstly, if you can, try to ensure that your research is adequately funded so that you can focus and concentrate on it in a professional manner. Secondly, be organised about the way you manage your work to ensure you meet all your deadlines. Finally, never give up – even if you have to take time out to deal with personal or health-related issues during a research project.

RESEARCH AND EVALUATION IN EAST BERKSHIRE

SUE GODDARD
(with input from members of Slough User-Led Consultation (SULC) and Windsor, Ascot and Maidenhead Consultation (WAMCon))

Slough User-Led Consultation (SULC) and Windsor, Ascot and Maidenhead Consultation (WAMCon) are two groups of service users who have been undertaking research and evaluation in East Berkshire since 2002. A researcher at East Berkshire Mind set up the research groups, with the intention of giving users a chance to have their say and put ideas back into local mental health services.

Initial members were recruited in a number of ways, including contacting potential researchers through day services such as the local therapeutic day unit and drop-in centre. The feelings of the newly recruited members at that time were that they were keen to carry out research, to develop their skills, and to draw on their personal experience of using mental health services. At last they had a chance to put something back and help develop a better future for people with mental health issues. One member said of that time: 'My confidence was very low in the NHS and mental health services. The group is very positive and structured and when research started it was a way forward – a way to "put back" into the system for future clients.'

Everyone is different: it would not be the 'real' world if we weren't. Each and every one of us has different opinions and ideas. All of us have reached a certain point in our lives and have different experiences. This in itself brings knowledge to our group: we can all learn from this and from each other, understanding others, and communicating to each other within the group.

We are all still learning: each day there is always something new for us to learn. As members of the group, we visit different mental health services to collect users' views; we also attend seminars and workshops. We are supported by East Berkshire Mind and also work alongside a local employment service to provide mental health awareness training throughout Berkshire.

So far we have undertaken a number of research and evaluation projects that include:

- *All Talk:* an in-depth qualitative study exploring the role of talking in mental health
- A number of evaluations and consultations using a range of quantitative and qualitative research methods. The aim of these projects has been to inform local decision making, usually by the local implementation team, around planning and improving local mental health services. These projects have sought out local service users' views about the following types of services and issues: advocacy, counselling, crisis response, local restructuring, and how to move forward towards identifying the needs of service users from black and minority ethnic communities
- Looking at the incidence of diabetes amongst mental health service users
- Evaluating a local World Mental Health Day event, and at the same time identifying public attitudes about mental health and mental health service users

From all the projects mentioned above, we have chosen the diabetes and mental health project to explain in more depth how we work. A questionnaire was designed and a roster of shifts was drawn up. On the day, members asked the general public a set of questions about whether they had diabetes, whether they had mental health problems, and their experience and knowledge about both. We interviewed people at a Diabetes Week event that took place at a local mental health day centre but that was open to the general public. The information was then analysed. The end result showed us that having diabetes often appears to be linked with having a mental health problem.

From these projects we have developed our own skills and have become a strong group. We are still 'training' and always will be: there is always something to learn! From past projects, the group's members have become more positive and confident. At our meetings there is always feedback from colleagues and discussion, which in turn helps us to assist one another. The future for SULC and WAMCon will be that we will get stronger and stronger, growing more in confidence and developing our skills.

Our upcoming projects include: developing an evaluation tool for local inpatient services across Berkshire; evaluating this year's World Mental Health Day events in Slough and Maidenhead; and identifying in detail the needs of black and minority ethnic service users in Slough.

Our two research teams have proven their strength and value to other mental health service users. The future now looks more positive.

TELLING OUR TRUTHS,
BRINGING ABOUT CHANGE

BEING A SURVIVOR RESEARCHER

TINA COLDHAM, JASNA RUSSO
(AND OTHERS)

When we started a chapter about being a survivor researcher, we thought the best way to do it was to let people write this chapter themselves. We wanted to open a space in the book for a personal perspective, because we knew how much it motivates our work. We invited survivor researchers to write what it was that drove them or mattered to them about being a survivor researcher. When we look at the outcome, it seems a space where personal meets political, as one of the editors noticed.

We sent an invitation for a piece of writing of up to a maximum of 600 words to all the contributors of this book, as well as through various survivor research networks. Our question was:

What does it personally mean to you to work as a survivor researcher/service user researcher?

Or, alternatively:

What is your motivation to work as a survivor researcher/user researcher?

After an initial silence, which made us realise that the questions were not easy to answer, we were overwhelmed with responses, which came from all over the UK as well as two from Australia. We felt privileged reading them.

Each piece is its own story, and reveals a real person behind the research. There are experiences and views that we share, but we did not want to reduce or analyse the richness of why we do research. We gave up the idea of trying to structure contributions, and decided to arrange them in alphabetical order by first name. This is because we find all the pieces equally important, and because we don't want to deprive the reader of the right to make his or her own journey through this chapter. We thank all the contributors for taking up our invitation and writing this chapter together.

TURNING THE TABLES

ALISON FAULKNER

I started my research life in a university psychology department, followed shortly by working for Mind (one of England's leading mental health charities) on a project investigating Section 136 of the 1983 Mental Health Act. Under Section 136, the police can detain people if they are deemed to be 'mentally disordered' in a public place, and taken to a 'place of safety' (usually a hospital or police station). My job was to interview police officers, psychiatrists and the people detained in this way (where possible), and it was indeed a fascinating job. However, I had huge reservations about attempting to interview people detained by the police once they were in hospital. The few I managed to see on the ward were often distressed and angry; I both felt inadequate for the task, and that I was acting inappropriately by attempting to interview them at all. It was a memorable learning experience regarding the meaning of ethics and ethical practice. Some years later, in hospital myself, I was to remember this experience when a professional of some kind invited herself into my cubicle to interview me for her research. I know not what it was, this research, but I found myself unable to engage with her questions *and* unable to turn her away, so vulnerable did I feel at that time.

What it means to me to work as a service user/survivor researcher is to try to turn these experiences into new ways of working that endeavour to equalise the relationship between researcher and researched, to empower people to say 'no' if they want to, or to take more control over the research if they want to. I have worked with many people over the last few years since the start of the Mental Health Foundation's Strategies for Living programme in 1997, and I have continually been amazed by people's capacity to change and grow in the carrying out of research. It is not just about developing skills that research offers us as service users, it is the opportunity it gives us to reflect and to think about our personal experience in a different way alongside others. I am fortunate in that I achieved a professional life through doing research alongside using mental health services. Sometimes I feel as if I fall between the two stools: being too professional to be a 'real' service user and insufficiently academic to be a 'real' researcher, but often I can feel that I am both things and that it is good.

MICKEY MOUSE SCANS?

ANGELA SWEENEY

When I was twelve, my mother had her second breakdown. Although we did not realise it at the time, this was to shape both our lives for many years to come.

Back in 1973, my mother had been exposed to psychiatry's most brutal face. Her memories of locked wards, unwanted ECT and, on disclosing childhood sexual abuse, being told never to say such things again, had left her frightened of hospitals, their treatments and their staff. Second time around, it seemed little had changed. My mother needed support and understanding. Services offered ECT and fought to admit her. Our family had an unthinking, unquestioning belief in her right and ability to make her own life choices, including which treatments to try. And so we all fought back. Working through hallucinations and chlorpromazine my mother was able to gain a degree in English and American Literature from the University of Kent.

This experience of fighting against psychiatry was in some way mirrored by my own experiences. At thirteen, I was referred to a psychiatrist because of significant mental distress. The psychiatrist's suggestions were not what I wanted, and my family successfully argued for my support to be shifted to a youth counsellor. It seemed that rather than exploring with me what was needed, the psychiatrist had 'objectively' assessed the situation and given his verdict. This powerful verdict then had to be battled against.

All this had a great impact on me as a deeply political, working-class teenager. Like many, I questioned authority rather than accepting the status quo. The power held by psychiatrists seemed yet further evidence of the injustices prevalent in our society that divide the powerful from the voiceless.

Discovering sociology at sixteen was a joy. All the frustration and disaffection I felt could be explored through reading and debate. The subject gave me an accepted way of expressing the things I felt. I also became interested in local user group activities through my mother. Her links were a way of vocalising the anger she felt at her treatment by the mental health system. The user group channelled this into mutual support and a collective desire to improve services.

I went on to study social sciences at university as a mature student. During the second year, we conducted small research projects. I eventually decided to look at users' experiences of psychiatric hospitals. I also experienced another bout of depression. For months I hid in my room. I lost all concentration, yet somehow I could immerse myself in the research project, even though I could not face anything else. Alongside my passion for sociology, I was uncovering a love of research and discovery.

So why do I do survivor research? It seems natural that all these experiences have led me to this point: from early experiences of fighting for my mother's right to choose, to seeing the power of the local service user movement, to the pleasures of a disaffected teenager discovering sociology and research. I believe in the need to generate knowledge from the perspective of the least powerful groups in society. Within mental health research, this means discovery and exploration with and for the people who use and refuse psychiatric services. This idea is currently very popular and I have collaborated with clinical academics who share this view. However, a recent conversation with a clinical colleague reminded me of the power those who produce knowledge have. I was explaining that my mother had gained her degree through severe psychosis. He laughed, saying, 'It must have been a Mickey Mouse degree'. According to his research, all people who have experienced psychosis are permanently brain-damaged and he 'has the scans to prove it'.

Comments like these cause me great frustration. But at my strongest, they motivate me to continue working as a survivor researcher.

BENEFIT OF THE DOUBT

ANNE-LAURE DONSKOY

I became a service user researcher by chance, first involved in the local User-Focused Monitoring project as a UFM user worker, then in collaborative research between the local mental health trust and university as a user researcher. I have not looked back. Now I am actually coordinator of that UFM project while conducting my own research. This, after some fifteen years spent 'elsewhere', in the parallel and often messy world of the user movement.

It has been, and still is, a long journey of discovery, of soul-searching moments, of steep learning curves, of great expectations and hope. What underpins this is a drive, a will to see real improvement for service users in terms of treatment options, of people actively participating in their care, and in terms of social inclusion. I think that for me it has become more than a journey of discovery or a healing process; it is also now a political engagement, an act of citizen participation indeed (and as a citizen from a different country, I am even more aware of the engagement that comes with it). I can use my experience and my new research knowledge, share those with others with a similar outlook, and aim to make a difference. It is ambitious but it has to be.

I am acutely aware of the fact, and am often reminded of it, that as service user researchers, we are definitely a new breed. I often have to fight, probably a bit harder than most, to get recognition, not only of the work I am trying to do, but also of the perspective I am coming from, that of grounded experience – my own or that of the service user community. In a research world where quantitative research and large-scale surveys prevail, it is difficult trying to promote the importance of often small, or smaller scale, often more qualitative research work and findings, and striving to feed those back 'quickly' into local services.

I feel that I am often seen as some kind of harmless creature, someone who does not represent a threat in the very competitive world of research. Others just do not seem to know what to make of me. Some give me the 'benefit of the doubt', as it were; others reject me outright. Is this because my background does not make me 'credible' as a researcher? Is this because I did not go down the more traditional route of university research training? I wonder. It is interesting to note that since I have gone back to university (it came as a surprise to some that I already had post-graduate degrees), precisely to do a Research Masters, some people are considering me differently and pay more attention to my work or to me. I am becoming visible, which is a very odd feeling. It is great when it is about acknowledging the work and the journey; it is not so appealing when it is about status and politics. The world of research can be messy too, but I feel that as user researchers, we have a pretty unique contribution to make, and that is why I am hopeful.

CHALLENGING BELIEFS

BRIGID MORRIS

I have been involved in training and supporting local mental health service users to undertake their own research and evaluation for about seven years now. It is a process that has always made sense to me at both a personal and professional level. Prior to this work, my career had involved working as a support worker and assistant psychologist within mental health and learning disability services, and then being out of work for a couple of years owing to a depressive breakdown.

There are two key factors that have motivated me to support teams of service user researchers. The first is that I feel user-led research is an excellent way in which to bring to light the views of everyday service users. Service user researchers highly value the opinions and experiences of their fellow service users. They believe that service users have a right, and an ability, to speak up for themselves and to influence the types of opportunities and treatments that are provided to them by others. As well as being ideally placed to know which topic areas to research and which questions to focus on, service user researchers appear to go the extra mile in thinking through the best ways in which to collect information respectfully from other service users. I continue to be impressed by the considerable amount of time, energy and care that is spent by service user researchers in thinking through how to make a postal questionnaire or interview situation as comprehensible, meaningful and comfortable as possible to research participants. As well as providing a positive experience for those participating in research, I believe that this time and care often leads to higher response rates and more valid research.

The second factor that has kept me motivated is working side by side with the individuals who comprise the research teams. Undertaking research appears to be a highly meaningful activity to most of these people; indeed, service user researchers are often very passionate about and committed to their work. This is perhaps not surprising, as such projects provide people with an opportunity to learn new skills, to work closely with other like-minded people within a team, to engage in a high-status activity, to be challenged mentally, to engage with professionals at a different and perhaps more equal level, and to work practically towards improving mental health services either locally or nationally. I have continuously been moved and impressed by the passion and commitment that service user researchers bring to their work and by the ways in which individuals have developed with regards to their confidence and self-actualisation. Research work is varied and challenging. Adequately funded and supported user-led research projects frequently appear to provide a supportive and flexible place within which people with mental health problems can potentially challenge their own beliefs, and perhaps also the beliefs of others about them, and about what they can and cannot achieve.

It has frequently felt an enormous privilege to work with groups of service user researchers. I have been forced to question again and again the purpose of research and the ways in which it can be carried out. Whilst projects are often hard work, time intensive and fraught with politics at many levels, the process is usually exciting and creative. I have learnt much about myself, about other people, about group dynamics and about how to undertake thorough and sensitive research. I am still learning.

WE DON'T START OFF WITH THE AGENDA TIED UP

CATH ROPER

I have occupied a 'consumer academic' role at the University of Melbourne (Australia) in the school of nursing for the past five years. It is a half-time position. In fact, I have a BA in literature and a teaching degree, but no higher education and no research background. The title of my position is meant to describe the capacity to be involved in research, teaching and other projects.

I do not think what follows is just parochialism (though there may be an element of it still in Australia). When it comes to research in mental health per se, there are tensions, which I share, around a number of issues. These include the insufficiency of resources, as well as the more complex question of why consumers should get involved in research – in those distant, theoretical things – when research does not address the need for urgent changes, when people are still unable to access services, and when they do access them, they do damage, or do not meet their needs.

But the other side to this, and the reason I want to do survivor research, is that as we all know, if money is spent on projects we have identified as important, and they have been conducted in ways that conform to our ways of working, then they are more likely to be useful to us, rather than less likely.

In Victoria, the area we have been least able to influence is research. Only some of us are interested in having conversations about what a survivor research agenda might look like. Only very few of us would want to expend energy in driving a research agenda forward. Mine is the only role in the state that could potentially facilitate an interest in setting a survivor research agenda on salaried time.

The piece of research I am currently involved in is looking at outcome measurement and whether it satisfies the objectives of service users. While we originally thought that people might be interested in recommending the development of a scale that reflected their own values and domains identified in previous studies (for example, discrimination, rights, and recovery), we found, instead, that the consumers to whom we talked were more interested in measuring things like iatrogenesis (injury or harm acquired through service use) and framing that as a clinical outcome. They were also interested in accountability, including the need for governments and services to act upon commentaries and findings relating to consumers' experience of services, and in looking at the structures needed to ensure this.

This is why I am motivated to initiate survivor research projects. Our way of working is to allow the commentary we hear absolutely to influence the direction of research or any given enterprise. We do not start off with the agenda tied up. We do not ignore findings that contradict our studies: we use them to inform the next steps. We do not get involved in research that does not benefit our community. We make sure we are in constant touch with a critical reference group for our work, which means those people that the research is *for* – service users. While it is absolutely necessary that survivor perspectives are included in all stages of research, for the time being, I want to devote my energies to the development of a survivor research agenda, and to the conduct of survivor-led research.

BEING A SURVIVOR RESEARCHER
HELPS ME SURVIVE

DAVID WEBB

My 'recovery' from persistent suicidal feelings came about through spiritual self-enquiry after all the psycho-medications and talking therapies had failed and sometimes made things worse. Following this spirit of enquiry, it now seems fairly natural (though blessed with much good luck) that before long I found myself doing a doctorate looking into the first-person perspective on suicidality. Doing a doctorate has been its own extraordinary journey and adventure.

Of course I hope that my research might help us understand suicidality better, so that we might help those struggling with these feelings and, even better, help prevent suicidal feelings arising in the first place. Of course I hope that my work will help bring more of the first-person – consumer, user, survivor, whatever – perspective into our understanding of mental health crises. Of course I hope that my work might encourage more and more survivors to consider research as one of the ways we can challenge the madness of modern psychiatry. Of course I hope that my research is heard by more than my three examiners and not silenced by the exclusive, ideological, commercial and 'evidence-based' prejudices that currently dictate the mental health agenda. Of course I have hopes that my research may be of value to others.

But the real reason, the real motivation, for being a researcher is a selfish one. My well-being today, including keeping suicidality at bay, depends on maintaining a ruthless, passionate, spiritual dedication to telling the truth as best as I possibly can. Most importantly, this is being honest *with myself*. Next, it is being honest with those near and dear to me. And then, it is to be honest in my work – currently as a researcher. Research – 'disciplined enquiry' – is a wonderful and privileged opportunity to pursue the spirit of ruthless enquiry, on which my personal sense of well-being depends. Research suits me. Research satisfies me. Research helps keep me sane in my madness. Research helps keep me alive.

This is what really motivates my research. But another, almost equal, motivation is my many suicidal soulmates. I can easily recall drawing the blinds on the motel room never expecting to leave that room alive, and, when I do, I think of the many who are doing likewise today ... and tomorrow ... and again the next day ... . I am appalled at our current understanding of suicidality, poisoned by ridiculous notions of defective brains, and I weep for my comrades, some of whom will die, some of whom will survive but be forever scarred by their agony. And I weep for the world I live in, that has so little to offer those facing such a noble struggle.

My research is giving voice, as best I can, to these tears. And this helps me survive.

NOT JUST SOMEONE WHO TAKES

DEBBIE MAYES

To me, being a service user researcher means being on the inside, getting the opportunity to influence what goes on in research, and trying to redress the balance. In this way, I hope to ensure that things might begin with the service user rather than just using them as subject matter. On a personal level, I feel I have got my pride back, that I am seen as someone who has something to contribute rather than just someone who takes. My status is very important to me, as I believe it is to everyone. I don't want to be seen as some poor thing that gets examined through the microscope of social research, I want to be contributing in a real way and making a difference and having something that I can talk about with professionals on an equal basis. This is something that is about my mental health, not in the sense of being a victim, but in an empowering way, and it feels good!

HAVING A DOUBLE IDENTITY

DIANA ROSE

My academic career and my psychiatric career started at the same point in time – when I took the finals of my first degree in a psychiatric hospital. My psychiatrist was my invigilator. This was very weird, as he also kept turning up at my bedroom window at night with teacups full of whisky in his hands.

After that experience, I had fifteen years of academic life during which I hid my contact with psychiatric services. This definitely was not easy, as at the time I was self-injuring quite a bit. The treatment I received in Accident & Emergency (A&E) was appalling. I was called 'manipulative' and 'attention-seeking', and sometimes they stitched me up without an anaesthetic 'to teach me a lesson'. At the time, I believed they were right and I was wrong

Despite this, I did continue an academic career for nearly fifteen years. At that point it became impossible, as I started to bring my problems to work and engage in behaviour that my employers could not tolerate. I was medically retired at the age of 35.

Then two things happened. I became a 'community mental patient', living on benefits, attending a day hospital and on very heavy medication. But I also became involved in the user movement in its early days in the UK. I vividly remember my first meeting where there was a woman standing up talking about the injustice of A&E Departments for people who self-injure. The scales really fell from my eyes.

After about five years I became fed up with being a community mental patient and decided to apply to do a doctorate. This was not easy: the college was very suspicious, as they knew about my psychiatric history. Still, they accepted me. I took a part-time, miserable administrative job to fund my studies, but was grateful for any work at all. Once again, I was back in academe, although it never occurred to me that I would actually get another job there.

I did not give up my contact with the user movement. Our group did a survey of patients' experiences on the decanted acute wards, and we often ended up presenting our work on the same platform as a psychiatrist called Matt Muijen. He then became director of the Sainsbury Centre for Mental Health and, in the final year of my doctoral studies, offered me a part-time, one-year contract to work there. Now my psychiatric history and involvement in the user movement was an advantage, and so my 'double identity' began.

I stayed at the Sainsbury Centre for seven years and then, in 2001, got a job in a new user-focused unit at the Institute of Psychiatry in London. I am now co-director of the Service User Research Enterprise (SURE), and I consider myself to be exceptionally lucky. My two identities have been brought together and I can apply my research skills in a way that I hope is useful to service users and the user movement. At the same time, I will never forget what the movement has done for me.

WORKING IN A TWILIGHT ZONE

HEATHER JOHNSON STRAUGHAN

If I had not had mental illness, it would never have occurred to me either to work or to research in the field. Being such a selfish and unaware soul until that point, I had not even considered mental health until I became ill and no longer had it. But when that happened, it was life changing.

I initially started a PhD to test out my idea of a recovery training, now seen to be effective, and to gain the highly acclaimed 'doctoral' status, so as to achieve equal footing with those who have for too long remained on their pedestals of power, whilst others – we service users – have for too long stayed on our knees. Naturally, I lived this hypothesis all the while: I mean, what choice did I have but to hope to recover?

As those years of researching have progressed, my motivations for remaining in the field of research, from a user standpoint, are more the desire to influence the final outcome – that this work becomes of practical help to others; that this practical help might offer a few more positive choices for others to make things better for themselves. Help that I was not offered by those whom I consider it their job to have provided it. It was for transformation, not transient change, that I undertook research: no fad or fashion. It is my fear that user research might just be a flash in the pan. But I had a deep-seated belief that what I was doing, my perspective of having lived mental ill health and recovery, was more valid than what textbook researchers without this vital insider knowledge might bring to the subject. When I think of a service user researcher, the idea of a trans-cultural tour guide comes to mind as the ideal person to bridge both the experience and the research methods, and translate one to the other for better understanding. Mental health is subjective and always will be: researching the field will need a shared understanding of participant and researcher in order to translate into real, personal, individual benefit, not the achievement of some criterion of objectivity.

As my research continued, so too did the need to ensure that others received the benefits of it. I felt I had the obligation to ensure that my work would not end on the shelf, but in the hands of those who would use it for themselves. Regaining empowerment myself meant supporting others to regain theirs. Recovery for me meant not living within the confines of somebody else's definition of the job, and ensuring that others were allowed to do likewise.

I like the idea of service users taking back what really should have been their domain in the first place, that is, their own lives and mental health. I would like to see more service users step up to take a greater part in active research devoted to transforming services. I feel I am working in some twilight zone, in some undefined virgin territory that we might carve out for the benefit of service users through researching and shaping services through service users' views. If they, the professionals, had had all the answers, why would they have come to us to ask our opinions in the first place? When asked, it would make sense for them to listen to us too.

TALKING BACK TO POWER

JASNA RUSSO

In my opinion, clinical research repeats what ordinary psychiatric treatment does, only on a different level. Like individual psychiatrists, clinical researchers ask the wrong questions that lead them to wrong, irrelevant or damaging conclusions. They are often incapable of reaching the realities of their subjects. They try scientifically to observe, measure and interpret either their patients or their research subjects, but they fail to understand them.

Being a survivor researcher opens up the possibility of combating what I could not combat in the course of my psychiatric treatment. I was not asked for my opinion on my own problems, nor my definition of what support is and what it is not. The psychiatrist strongly recommended that I leave my studies, because I was to accept that I was ill forever and would never achieve a university degree. I needed to leave that context completely behind. I needed to stop being a patient in order to be me again, in order to be, and in order to stop losing. Working as a researcher ideally means taking observation, measurement and interpretation into my own hands. It means doing all the things that treatment denied me. I do not think that I research better than those who have not been subjected to psychiatric treatment, but I certainly do it in a different way.

Until now, I have had the pleasure of working only in collaborative projects. This usually has meant wanting to be more than a 'user researcher' decorating the project or being expected only to provide participants. My role in design, analysis and writing the report in collaborations is never guaranteed or waiting there for me. I always try to influence the whole process the best I can and this can become very exhausting.

Unlike research, there was no way for me to influence the treatment I received, no matter how I tried. Survivor research opens a space for me to influence the science behind such treatments, and I find that easier. I find it easier because things shift away from me and my individual 'case history'. But the memory of it continues to influence and motivate my research work.

I once wrote a letter to my psychiatrist about how I felt and what kind of support I needed from her. Among other things I complained of medication and said, 'I need my personal chaos in order to get out of it'. She underlined this sentence and said that this worried her the most. Instead of replying to my requests, she gave me back an analysis of my letter.

I see psychiatric treatment as an attempt to deny, suppress and control what it is not capable of reaching and responding to. And when you cannot reach something, I think you should try to come closer to it. This is what survivor research means to me.

I research because of my belief in a different science, in one that is not scared of its topics and its subjects. I believe in one that does not step back from people's lives, and does not construct closed, simple categories to reduce their realities. As a survivor researcher, I do not need to protect and distance myself from 'subjects'. I do not need to prove that I am not one of them. I do not need a big name and career. I just want to get as close as I can and keep telling truth in all its complexity.

ALCHEMY: A MIRACULOUS TRANSFORMATION, OR THE MEANS OF ACHIEVING THIS

KEITH HALSALL

When I had my breakdown, it was a very traumatic time for everyone around me. I ended up going into a forensic hospital, as a result of expressing myself violently. While it was necessary to go to a secure hospital, I endured a lot of treatment that was unhelpful. I also suffered intensely.

After I left the inpatient system and went back to living in the outer community, I undertook a long period of recovery, which was led by myself. The state services forced on me were largely unhelpful, and so I sought healing from those who could and did help me. I did long-term, spiritually based psychotherapy, used nature as a healer, learned Real Reiki for myself and others, improved my diet, undertook martial arts training, derived immense pleasure from dancing, and did other therapeutic groups and activities.

The rehabilitation or rebuilding has taken eight years and is ongoing. However, over the last three years I have reached the point where I am now strong enough to go back in and work in mental health services. It is something that I have anticipated doing right from those dark days when first arriving in the institution in a state of mental collapse and shock. When I left hospital I was offered work as a forensic user worker, but it was the last thing I needed to do at that time, such were the depth of my wounds. It has been essential to do this recovery work on myself prior to going back in.

I am very fortunate to be able to begin to transform so many very difficult experiences by using them to understand the position of others and help them, both staff and service users. It is very satisfying to do this. Last year I led a Department of Health funded research project at a secure unit in London. The aim of the research was to give the users there a voice, and find out what they would like to see being researched, in order to improve their lives. The people there had an opportunity to speak their minds, they suggested ways to improve services, they were rewarded for their time financially and with social events, and I am disseminating the findings as effectively as I can.

Doing this work has been part of my healing journey. It has been very challenging at times, but I have gained a lot from it. As with other things in life, there is enormous confusion and disinformation surrounding forensic mental health – I like to think I can dispel some of that.

BANGING AGAINST THE BRICK WALL

MARY NETTLE

I studied market research at college many years ago, and worked for a few years in a market research agency researching the buying habits of those purchasing electrical goods and financial services. I ended my career with a well-known manufacturer of breakfast cereals and pet foods. In pet foods research, it is interesting to know who is the consumer: the animal or its owner? The appearance and smell have to appeal to the owner but not be rejected by the animal. I can see a link with mental health research, can't you?

My life changed when I entered the mental health system with a bang in 1978. For a long time I was a passive recipient of services, until by chance I discovered these people called service users and a nebulous body called the user movement. After some time my talents were recognised by some of my fellow service users, and I tentatively began, with another service user, my first research project where personal experience of being a patient (in an old asylum) was essential to our credibility as researchers.[1] It was a ground-breaking piece of research, as we spent two weeks staying in the asylum and most of that time was spent with patients on the long-stay wards. We were paid for our work on quality standards but it was never published. We were proud of our work, but as we were paid for it we did not have ownership of it.

Finding research work after that proved difficult. Service users are still looked upon as subjects or objects of research rather than potential researchers. The argument for using survivor researchers such as myself is that service users are more likely to describe how they feel about things to someone who reveals that they have used mental health services themselves. The research world feels that by doing this, objectivity is compromised. The riposte is that no one can be truly objective and that researchers are deluding themselves if they think they can be. Survivor researchers are at least upfront about where they are coming from when they conduct research. So being a survivor researcher means confronting stigma and discrimination dressed up as scientific methods and good science. As someone dismissively said recently, survivor research is a mere sociological exercise.

I wonder why talking to people using their language and recording the results is considered valuable in the commercial world of marketing research that I used to inhabit, but is not considered good evidence in the academic and medical world.

If focus groups are good enough for the government as a valid way of finding out what people think and feel, then the people who research users of public services

---

1. I talk about this experience in Nettle, M (1996) Listening in the asylum. In J Read & J Reynolds (eds) *Speaking Our Minds: An anthology* (pp. 202–6). Basingstoke: Macmillan/Open University.

should ask themselves why funding for their research is so hard to find. Maybe it is because they are not using the right people, survivor researchers, to help them ask the right questions for which people want to know answers.

It is still considered unusual for service users to be commissioned to do pieces of work. I am fortunate to be part of INVOLVE (see www.invo.org.uk), which is funded by the Department of Health in England to support the involvement of the public in all aspects of health, public health and social care research. Despite this encouragement, it is still the case that ten years after my first piece of research it is the exception rather than the rule to commission service users to undertake research projects. Goodwill does not translate often enough into the true involvement of service users in the research process.

I enjoy what I do immensely: it is challenging, and sometimes you get a headache banging against a brick wall, but all that banging has made a difference and there are chinks in the wall. All in all, it is more satisfying than researching pet food!

SHOCKING MEMORIES

PETE FLEISCHMANN

It was while sitting in a rather imposing committee room in central London that I first really understood just what a potent force for change user/survivor research can be. The committee was discussing new guidelines about the use of electroconvulsive therapy (ECT). I was there as one of a number of user/survivor representatives. Users'/survivors' powerful and emotional testimonies about ECT experiences were being traded with the dry statistics of clinical research. The committee was prepared to listen to survivors' claims of long-term memory damage due to ECT. However, it was plain that it was the meta-analysis of ECT trials that carried the most weight. Owing to a number of factors, traditional psychiatric research tends to gloss over ECT's potential for long-term memory damage. However accurate, articulate and moving survivors' personal accounts were, this sort of committee would normally dismiss them as anecdotes.

Happily that day we had a secret weapon, an innocuous-looking document, photocopied and ring-bound, entitled 'Consumers' perspectives on electro convulsive therapy'.[2] This user-led literature review contained analysis of user testimonies and research studies. Not only was the review focused on the perspectives of users, it was also systematic, rigorous and produced under the auspices of a venerable and respected

---

2. Rose, D, Fleischmann, P, Wykes, T & Bindman, J (2002) Review of consumers' perspectives on electro convulsive therapy. Final report. London: Service User Research Enterprise, Institute of Psychiatry. http://www.ect.org/resources/consumerperspectives.pdf (Accessed 17 December 2008).

177

academic institution. The review showed that, across all literature sources, long-term memory damage was reported by at least a third of people. All these ingredients made the review hard to ignore and difficult to dismiss. The review supported many of the accounts of unwanted ECT effects made over the years by recipients of ECT. To my amazement, the committee was taking us seriously – really seriously. This was because we had the evidence to back up what we were saying. When the committee issued its guidance, it recommended that the use of ECT be restricted and astoundingly it acknowledged ECT's potential to cause long-term memory damage. The Royal College of Psychiatrists actually tried to appeal against the guidance, as they thought it went too far. Wow, I thought, this research stuff can be really powerful!

Among service users, the fact that ECT can potentially cause long-term memory damage is a truism; it is common sense. But in the wider world, and especially in the sphere of traditional psychiatric research, this knowledge is liable to be dismissed. What made 'Consumers' perspectives on electro convulsive therapy' different was that two members of the research team (Diana Rose and I) and the majority of our reference group had direct ECT experience. This meant that we had a different perspective from most ECT researchers, and the research we produced reflected this.

Spiralling back in time to watch my younger self, anxiously waiting in the grim gloom of the hospital day room to be led into the ECT suite, I feel angry. If I knew what I know now, I doubt very much whether I would have agreed to have ECT. I was told the usual platitudes: it saves lives; side effects are rare. Back in those days, this disinformation went unchallenged. There was no internet, no advocacy, and certainly no user-led ECT research.

Like many others I wish for a very different mental health service. To achieve this, we need activism and we need passionate, courageous people to speak out about what is wrong with our current system. In addition, we need to find ways of investigating and representing the richness and diversity of user knowledge so that it cannot be ignored or dismissed. My motivation for being involved in user research is that I believe it is an essential part of the development of a decent, humane and helpful mental health service.

SURVIVOR RESEARCHER: AN HOLISTIC ROLE

PETER BERESFORD

I identify as a survivor researcher. But I must make something clear. I do not see myself only as a researcher. I also see myself as an activist, a writer, a campaigner and, I hope, an educator. I say this because I think that it is important to see being a survivor researcher as part of a constellation of things that I – and that we – need to do together in order to bring about change. And it is bringing about change in line with what we as survivors want, to safeguard and extend our human and civil rights, which for me is the most important thing.

I also cannot see myself as only a researcher in another sense. For me, the term has to be coupled with survivor or service user because this status is a core part of my identity, and crucially influences how I come to research. Someone – a career researcher – once said to me, 'I see you more as a researcher who is a service user than a service user who is a researcher'. I don't know how she felt able to draw this distinction. I certainly cannot: for me, I am a service user first and researcher second.

There are two other key motivations for me as a survivor researcher. Research is often an individualistic, hierarchical business. People work in hierarchical teams, from research assistant to professor. The career ladder, individual achievement, and even writing on your own as a 'sole author', are all valued in academic and research life. But in survivor research, we have chances to do things in more equal and collaborative ways with other people. This book – and this chapter – are expressions of this, and that is important for me.

My final reason for working as a survivor researcher centres on the chances that it offers to tell truths from our own perspectives. Every mental health service user/survivor knows that many people find it hard truly to believe what they say, truly to trust in their rationality. It is an unpleasant and disconcerting, but not uncommon feeling to sense this. Survivor research gives us a chance to tell our truths through research, which, bit by bit, is gaining its own credibility and legitimacy.

This means that our 'take' on things, our perspectives, insights, experiences, understanding and knowledge, will be less readily dismissed in the future. They will have to be taken more seriously. They will have to be seen as having a collective as well as individual worth and merit. Even if our experience and knowledge continue to be dismissed, and we have to continue in our struggle to see them respected by others, such telling of our truths is an undeniably empowering act for all of us, and one I – and I am sure many other survivor researchers – feel proud to be associated with.

NOT AN ACADEMIC IN AN IVORY TOWER

PHILIP HILL

My motivation to conduct research was to acquire academic qualifications so that I could embark on a career as an academic. When I was young, I fantasised about one day becoming a university professor coming out with a theory as ground-breaking and original as Einstein's General Theory of Relativity or Keynes' insights regarding economics. When I experienced my first nervous breakdown three weeks after my first degree, I realised that a diagnosis of paranoid schizophrenia meant I had something in common with one of the sons of Einstein, not Einstein himself!

My motivation to pursue postgraduate study was my feeling that everyone who knew my diagnosis had treated me as a fool. One care officer even doubted that I had a degree, and had to apologise when other staff informed her of my past. I even began to doubt that I had any intelligent thoughts left as I weathered the storm of the initial side effects of medication six to twelve months after being diagnosed. But rather than my brain being destroyed by the illness and the medication, I realised that my intellect was not destroyed, it was merely in a deep-freeze.

After getting a masters degree in economic development and policy, I realised I did have something intelligent to say, at least on economic policy. Next, I decided to aim for the stars by registering as a doctoral student. Doctoral students study for a research degree called a PhD. This qualification is one of the highest a university can give, and is awarded to students who carry out original research. This has to be presented in the form of an academic document called a thesis, and is then examined at what is called a viva. This is a verbal or spoken examination where you have to discuss and explain what you have written.

I felt that I gave a very good performance at my viva during which the examiners checked my understanding of what I had written. My thesis was adjudged substandard, however, and after another 12 months of work I received a Master of Philosophy in social policy. This is a good research degree but not a doctorate, which means I cannot call myself Dr Hill. For me, this was a real loss and disappointment. It does mean, though, that I now feel I have something intelligent to say about economics and economic development, and can quote my own original research about what enables mental health service users to find, retain and thrive in a paid job.

I may never write a great theory about anything, and I am unlikely to be a professor. However, my experience as a disabled person and my ability to contextualise my experience by talking to other disabled people as a researcher will, I hope, make me a better social worker.

I am remodeling myself not as an academic but as someone who can help mental health service users explore and understand similar journeys to mine. I want to be a mentor to those mental health survivors who feel they can engage with fellow survivors, not only to improve and inform professional practice, but as a means of enabling themselves to understand their own experience in relation to other disabled people.

MISSIONARY ZEAL

RUTH SAYERS

I joined the ranks of user researchers as someone who has long been haunted by the need to change the world. I come from a large family of evangelical activists – vicars and missionaries. For me, there seems little point in research, training or maybe even thinking, unless it can lead to changes, whether in perspective, behaviour or philosophy.

In 2000, when I moved from a rural area to enter a world of activity amongst people who use mental health services in the city, the concept of a service user representative (SUR) was new to me. There seemed to be SURs everywhere – on committees and working groups, perhaps wherever change might occur. Whether such change was for good or for ill, SURs were there, present as witnesses, and possibly also as agents of change.

However I slowly came to wonder how much change all this representation did bring about. There was certainly little visionary change towards my paradise of mental health services built around the needs of people in distress.

I began to look for other ways to contribute to change, and found an opportunity to use skills I already had as a lecturer in sociology and research. I happened upon an application form for research grants from the Mental Health Foundation's (MHF) Strategies for Living project, and applied to explore the experiences of people who had lost their work following mental health problems. The topic arose from my own experience of withdrawing from, or being ejected from, jobs and courses when I became stressed and ill. But I was also motivated by what I saw as a shocking waste of resources, training and talent, as thousands of skilled people were barred from making a contribution to society.

I was awarded a grant and vital support from the user research team at MHF. I invited other service users to join me in the research. A lot of people expressed interest; nine joined the team. But I was taken aback when others/SURs said they were dissatisfied with the topic I had developed. It was elitist, they argued. Some service users had never been employed, so I was excluding them: I should research a broader topic that everyone could relate to, and which included everyone. It seemed that if I set myself up as a user researcher (even without pay), other service users had huge expectations of me.

As our (research) questionnaires were returned, I began to see that one of my roles, and my motivations, was to act as advocate – an amplifier – so that people could get their voices heard. The words of many respondents were passionate, eloquent and moving: they deserved a hearing. Yet many were writing about that experience of never being listened to, or asked anything about their losses. As a researcher, contracted to produce a report, I had the opportunity to capture, record and disseminate the words of these articulate experts on my topic.

As we began to talk about our findings, I realised another motivation to be a researcher: to have something tangible/published that was bigger and more important than just me and my voice, something that could catalyse change. Our topic was 'hot': there were numerous opportunities to insert our evidence into debate, training, policy making, and further research. We contributed to practical, accessible resources that could improve the outlook for local service users. Dropping these voices into the pond of debate had caused ripples that developed a life of their own.

What more could be needed to satisfy my missionary zeal …?

THE SICK AND THE WELL?

SARAH CARR

It occurred to me that there was no difference between men … so profound as the difference between the sick and the well.
(F Scott Fitzgerald, *The Great Gatsby*)

This quotation by F Scott Fitzgerald seems to encapsulate something I feel deeply about being a survivor researcher. I realise that sickness and wellness are relative, and that some people who experience mental distress refuse a sickness label. But the point is that we experience distress, are treated as sick, and only we can know what it is like. We have unique insights and standpoints that non-survivor researchers cannot have. In 1900, a German clinician remarked of psychiatry, 'We know a lot and can do little'. I would say to him, 'But do you really know what your patients think, feel and need? You could do more if you asked them. You could do even more if you let them speak for themselves.'

As people who experience mental distress, perhaps we are all researchers into our condition and its treatments. I have been taking medication for over twelve years and have come to recognise that each time a person is treated with a drug, it is an individual experiment. As individuals, we will have our own responses to both 'symptoms' and treatment. Some of these may not be accounted for in the clinical research, and clinicians are not always in the best position to offer us advice on recognising and managing them. It is vital, then, for service users and survivors to share our experiences through research and discussion. Perhaps this can be likened to the difference between a visitor to a foreign country reading a tourist guidebook, and actually speaking with people who have lived there. And so we can write our own guidebooks.

As someone who has taken paroxetine, I took interest in the controversy over the drug. As a survivor researcher, I was especially interested by the fact that the clinical research had ignored the service user's voice, but those service users had come together to be heard. It was not until a critical mass of people who were experiencing disabling and dangerous withdrawal symptoms and side effects came together to share knowledge and take action that the pharmaceutical company was forced to acknowledge the problem. To me, the whole situation exposed the perilous shortcomings of biomedical research that dismisses or suppresses the direct experiences of the people taking the medication. It also showed the power of the collective to bring about change.

I did not start out identifying as a survivor researcher, but through my work I have met with many remarkable survivors who have enlightened and inspired me. I have been very fortunate in this respect. One of the things I feel strongly about psychiatry, and indeed academe, is that they strive to keep us from each other. As 'patients', we inhabit a system that prevents us from sharing our experiences on our own terms, and as academics we are forced into competitive situations not conducive to sharing experience and knowledge. I have been inspired by the way in which pioneering survivor researchers have supported each other and organised to resist this, by their emancipatory approach to research and by, quite simply, their courage to speak out. I would like to thank the pioneers for raising my consciousness, and for giving me the chance to develop a professional identity where I can value my personal experiences, emotions and political beliefs.

ON BOARD THE GOOD SHIP SURVIVOR RESEARCH

TINA COLDHAM

I liken the idea of research as a voyage of discovery. You may think you know where you are going, but be prepared to be surprised. Maybe you do not know where the research will lead you, and so it is a voyage of uncertainty, which can be fascinating, interesting, as well as challenging.

I also like to think that as someone who did not achieve great academic heights as a young person, I can knock on the door of academics, be welcomed inside, and work alongside them as an equal – and maybe even become one. I want to work on research that matters to us, research work that will, I hope, make a difference to users and survivors. Why do you need to know if bread falls butter side down, and, if it does, why that is? You cannot eat it afterwards!

Research for me is a process where there is an end product that can make a difference. I am not naive enough to believe that this is always the case, but as someone with continuing mental health issues, I can put enough effort into only so many things, and so they therefore need to count for something. Research must be real, and in mental health services, it must change things for the better.

So many times, I see and hear that services miss the point completely from a user/survivor perspective. If we can work to open the eyes of others to our needs, then research has a definite place in a busy work schedule for me. My collective and eclectic efforts all have the one main aim of making a positive difference.

I salute my survivor researcher colleagues. They are on a long and sometimes difficult voyage, where the waters can be muddied and unwelcoming. But we plough a furrow through the deep ocean. Risking drowning, but ultimately seeking new lands. Lands where people are treated as equals, treated with respect and dignity, treated so they can repair their lives and move on.

CONTRIBUTORS

DAVID ARMES

I was recently told by a West Yorkshireman that I am an honorary Northerner since I was born in Derby. Being labelled as liminal (being on the threshold of something) has been a characteristic of my life so far. My greatest liminal challenge has been to square the circle between being diagnosed 'schizophrenic' with being included in UK society. I hope the achievement of a PhD and my work as a researcher challenges the public and clinicians/professionals to see mental health service users in a new light.

JUDY BECKETT

Judy has spent most of her life in Leeds and used mental health services for a total of 15 years. She has been working at the University of Leeds since 2004 as a researcher in The Mental Health Services Research Office. Judy has an MA in counselling and continues to take a keen interest in involvement in all areas of mental health. Judy's other work includes training and consultancy as well as supporting other service users and survivors to become involved in doing research and evaluation.

PETER BERESFORD

Peter Beresford OBE is Professor of Social Policy and Director of the Centre for Citizen Participation at Brunel University. He is a long-term user of mental health services and Chair of Shaping Our Lives, the independent national user-controlled organisation and network. He is also a member of the Advisory Board of the National Institute for Health Research and INVOLVE and a Trustee of the Social Care Institute for Excellence. He has a long-standing interest in issues of involvement and empowerment.

TINA COLDHAM

Tina has been a user of mental health services for over 17 years, and still is a practising depressive. Her interest in research stems from simply wanting better mental health services from a user perspective. She has been involved in project managing research in local services, user input to academic research, and working as part of a team in national research projects.

ROSIE DAVIES

Rosie Davies, BSocSci, MSc, was Research Coordinator/Chief Investigator for a three-year user-led project based at Bristol Mind. The study explored access to and engagement with services for people with severe mental health problems who are labelled 'hard to engage'. She has also delivered Cognitive Behavioural Therapy to groups of women with depression and anxiety, and worked as a Research Assistant at Bristol University. When diagnosed with bipolar disorder Rosie developed an interest in self-management and got involved in user-led research in mental health as a volunteer. Research areas included acute inpatient care and the impact of loss of occupation following mental health problems.

KARAN ESSIEN

Karan Essien is a mental health service user who conducted a user-led research project for the Mental Health Foundation's Strategies for Living project. She currently lives in Yorkshire. She recently gave a lecture on user perspectives in mental health and does voluntary work reviewing NHS research proposals.

ALISON FAULKNER

Alison Faulkner works as a freelance researcher, trainer and consultant in the mental health field. She has over 20 years' experience in social research, and has worked for Rethink, the Mental Health Foundation, the National Centre for Social Research, Mind and the Sainsbury Centre. Alison is herself a mental health service user/survivor, and has written and presented extensively on services from a user perspective and service user involvement in research. She drafted the guidance on service user involvement for the MHRN Service User Research Group, England, and researched and wrote 'The Ethics of Survivor Research' (2004). As a user of services, Alison has experienced acute inpatient care, crisis services, psychotherapy and medication.

PETE FLEISCHMANN

Pete has experience of using mental health services. He was development worker and then coordinator of Brent Mental Health User Group (BUG) from 1991 to 1996. Until 2004 he worked as an independent consultant. Contracts have included working with the Service User Research Enterprise (SURE) at the Institute of Psychiatry, developing user involvement at Revolving Doors Agency and working in Eastern Europe to build the capacity of non-governmental organisations. Pete was appointed Principal Advisor in Participation at the Social Care Institute for Excellence (SCIE) in 2004 where he works four days per week.

SUE GODDARD

At the time of writing her contribution, Sue Goddard was a member of SULC (Slough User-Led Consultation). SULC comprised a group of people with experience of using mental health services, who were involved in designing, carrying out, writing up and presenting research, evaluation and consultation work. The aim of their work was to gather the views of local service users and feed them into the development of services in the Slough area. The work of SULC involved a report called *All Talk* in 2003 which explored the important role of talking in mental health from the perspective of those who use services. Other work involved seeking views about counselling services, inpatient care, world mental health day events and the experience of those from black and minority ethnic communities.

PHILIP HILL

Philip Hill is a qualified academic researcher and a professional social worker. He gained his MPhil in Social Policy by finding out what enables mental health service users to find and keep a job. Philip comes from an economic background and gained an honours degree in Economics and Economic History before his first breakdown in July 1987. Since his last illness in 1989 he has been dependent on medication. Despite teething problems, Philip, in the words of his manager, is 'an effectual social worker who manages his mental health very well'. 'I have only recently found happiness and fulfilment in my job,' Philip said about his experience as a social worker working with adults with learning disabilities. Philip is happily married to Geraldine who typed up his recently published autobiography entitled 'Living Out of the Book: A journey from a diagnosis of a learning disability through periods of mental illness to a career as a professional social worker' published by Chipmunka Publishing.

BRIGID MORRIS

Brigid has supported people with experience of mental distress to undertake their own research and evaluation since 1998. She learnt her trade whilst working for the ground-breaking User Focused Monitoring and Strategies for Living projects at the Sainsbury Centre for Mental Health and the Mental Health Foundation respectively. Since then she has worked freelance and part time for a wide range of organisations supporting people to gain the skills and confidence to speak out for themselves, usually via the research process. Brigid is currently Project Manager for Open Up, a user-controlled anti-discrimination project and undertakes research-related consultancy work.

MARY NETTLE

I became a user of mental health services in 1978 and turned this negative into a positive in 1992 by becoming a mental health user consultant. I am self-employed promoting patient and public involvement in mental health research and services. Voluntary work includes being Chair of the European Network of (ex-)Users and Survivors of Psychiatry and much more …

CAREY OSTRER

Carey travelled around the world, worked in human rights organisations, was a Shop Steward, and won a scholarship to Ruskin College before becoming overwhelmed with depression in the economically depressed times of the early 1990s. The stigma and insecurity of long-term unemployment became intensified by the stigma of becoming mad! She owes her life and present degree of sanity to two psychoanalytical therapists. Finding voluntary work was also key to her recovery. Carey later became involved with clinical research when she was asked to advise on service user involvement. She found that the people who are the subjects of research rarely have input into the research agenda, design or analysis, which often leads to inappropriate questions. Carey also found the academic establishment to be a pompous, elitist, and quite strange group of people used to determining their own work. Although Carey still has a strong interest in mental health research, it is not her sole interest. Her passion also lies in the environment, and she is currently Environmental Officer for Islington.

DIANA ROSE

Diana Rose is a social scientist and has also been a user of mental health services all her adult life. After a very difficult time in a lecturing job, followed by five years as a 'community mental patient', she brought her two identities together to do user-led research. This was strongly influenced by her involvement in the UK user/survivor movement. The first project was undertaken in an NGO where she developed a way of evaluating services from the service user perspective. In 2001, she moved to the Institute of Psychiatry, King's College London, to work in the Service User Research Enterprise (SURE). She now co-directs SURE and has been appointed Senior Lecturer in User-Led Research.

JASNA RUSSO

Jasna Russo is a survivor researcher living in Berlin, Germany. She has a degree in clinical psychology and comes from former Yugoslavia where she had experienced forced psychiatric treatment. She is a Board member of the European Network of (ex-)Users and Survivors of Psychiatry. Jasna has worked on both collaborative and survivor-controlled research projects. Her research reports include *Taking a Stand:*

Homelessness and psychiatry from survivors' perspective (together with T. Fink, Berlin, 2003); *From One's Own Perspective: Users' experiences of person-centred care* (together with F Scheibe and AK Lorenz, Berlin, 2007).

MATT SANDS

Matt Sands is a service user working since 2000 as Patients' Council Worker, conducting a collective advocacy project, offering St Martin's Hospital inpatients a chance to meet and share comments about the service, and make proposals for improving hospital life for all patients. Over the years Matt has represented service users' views on many committees, and worked on service user projects, including the SUE project looking at the needs of users living in residential care. He received the Kent Health and Social Services annual Nigel Gregory Award in 2008, for outstanding contribution to service user involvement.

HEATHER JOHNSON STRAUGHAN

Dr Straughan is Research Fellow at the Centre for Mental Health Recovery, University of Hertfordshire and Chair of West Herts MDF/The Bipolar Prganisation. Her PhD explored 'In-Sight', a user-led recovery group training for people with bipolar disorder. Heather is a founding trustee and was first chair of ViewPoint, Hertfordshire's user charity. Her work has appeared in the *Journal of Public Mental Heath, Mental Health Today, The Observer on Sunday* and in the NICE bipolar guidelines through a personal testimony. Heather was interviewed by the BBC for online accompaniment to Stephen Fry's documentaries on bipolar disorder. The 'In-Sight' training was published by OLM-Pavilion in 2008.

Heather completed her PhD work in 2006 and gained her title of 'Doctor' in 2008. The two-year gap is explained by her appeal of her first viva examiners due to bias against user research and non-positivist methodologies, which was upheld. A second viva was then successfully arranged. Heather would like to thank Dr Debbie Tallis who supported her throughout the appeal process. (h.straughan@btinternet.com)

ANGELA SWEENEY

Angela Sweeney is an independent mental health user/survivor researcher. She has conducted research and/or lectured at the Institute of Psychiatry, the University of East London and London Metropolitan University, and a variety of mental health charities. Angela has presented her work in North America, Canada and England, and reviews research proposals for organisations such as the National Institute for Health Research (NIHR). She is currently completing a PhD at the Service User Research Enterprise (SURE, Institute of Psychiatry, London) in which she has used mixed methods to generate and test a user-defined outcome measure of continuity of care.

DEBBIE TALLIS

I obtained a PhD entitled 'The process, context and consequences of attributing a personality disorder diagnosis to people' after being detained in hospital for a significant period of time. Although this time was a negative experience, it gave me the passion to enter research and work with other user researchers in order to make changes in mental health services. I have drawn on my experiences of being a mental health user/survivor to become a researcher. However, I have now changed my career to enter the legal profession to help mental health service users in a different way. (dtallis@ntlworld.com)

JAN WALLCRAFT

Dr Jan Wallcraft is a freelance researcher whose work is informed by experience as a mental health service user and activist. Her most recent post was as Manager of the Service User Research Group for England (SURGE), part of the Mental Health Research Network (MHRN). SURGE's role was to support and encourage involvement of mental health service users in mental health research. Jan has held many other user involvement posts in statutory and non-profit organisations and has been a lead researcher in several national consultations of service users, including 'Strategies for Living', and 'On Our Own Terms'.

INDEX

BEING HUMAN

REFLECTIONS ON MENTAL
DISTRESS IN SOCIETY

EDITED BY ALASTAIR MORGAN

ISBN 978 1 906254 06 3
Retail Price £20.00 (£19.00 direct)
Published September 2008

An array of critical voices from across various disciplines in the humanities – including philosophy, psychiatry, psychology, history and literature – are brought to bear upon the subject of mental distress as an experience that appears within particular social and cultural environments. The book attempts to shed a new and different light on the intersections between mental health, mental distress and society, without offering any programmatic methodology or declaration of intent.

Being Human provides a powerful statement of the importance of thinking through the humanities for any non-reductive understanding of the meaning of mental distress, and gives compelling insights on a range of problems, including the understanding and representation of mental distress, the history of symptoms and critiques of psychiatry, and what a critical practice within mental health care means. At the heart of this collection lies a concern with the experience of mental distress as central to any understanding of what it means to be human.

Alastair Morgan is a lecturer at the University of Nottingham, UK. He has worked in the mental health field for a number of years, and is also a trained philosopher with a particular interest in Critical Theory.

CONTENTS

STRAIGHT TALKING INTRODUCTIONS TO MENTAL HEALTH PROBLEMS
series edited by Richard Bentall
To be published throughout 2009

A STRAIGHT TALKING INTRODUCTION TO

The Causes of Mental Health Problems *John Read* Due June 2009

Psychiatric Diagnosis *Richard Bentall*

Psychiatric Drugs *Joanna Moncrieff* Due June 2009

Children's Mental Health Problems *Sami Timimi* Due June 2009

Psychological Treatments for Mental Health Problems *David Pilgrim* Due June 2009

Caring for Someone with Mental Health Problems *Jen Kilyon & Theresa Smith* Due June 2009

Being a User of Psychiatric Services *Peter Beresford*

Rather than accept that solutions to mental health problems are owned by the medical professions, these books look at alternatives and provide information so that the users of psychiatric services and their families and carers can make more decisions about their own lives. Becoming more active in mental health issues requires knowledge — this series of books is a starting point for anyone who wants to know more about mental health problems.

These books also introduce ways of working collaboratively with doctors, psychiatrists and counsellors, and offer a better chance of building a constructive life with hope for the future.

For users of psychiatric services, carers, support workers volunteers and all in the helping professions

---

To order direct from the publishers
online www.pccs-books.co.uk

fax: +44 (0) 1989 763 901 or telephone your order: +44 (0) 1989 763 900
PCCS Books Ltd, 2 Cropper Row, Alton Rd, Ross-on-Wye, HR9 5LA, UK